PRECARIOUS CROSSINGS

PRECARIOUS CROSSINGS

IMMIGRATION, NEOLIBERALISM, AND THE ATLANTIC

ALEXANDRA PERISIC

THE OHIO STATE UNIVERSITY PRESS

COLUMBUS

Library of Congress Cataloging-in-Publication Data is available online at catalog.loc.gov.

Cover design by John Barnett
Text design by Juliet Williams
Type set in Adobe Minion Pro

∞ The paper used in this publication meets the minimum requirements of the American National Standard for Information Sciences—Permanence of Paper for Printed Library Materials. ANSI Z39.48-1992.

CONTENTS

ACKNOWLEDGMENTS

I envisioned *Precarious Crossings* as a dialogue between authors, languages, and disciplines. This conversation became conceivable only because my friends and colleagues shared their expertise in their specific fields, pushing me to refine my arguments. Over the past five years, University of Miami has been my home, and without the support I received there, I would not have been able to finish this book. My mentor Gema Pérez-Sánchez was always incredibly generous with her time and advice. Joel Nickels was one of my first intellectual interlocutors at UM, and his comments resonate throughout chapter 1. Lillian Manzor helped me conceptualize the anti-detective novel in chapter 3, while Ralph Heyndels helped refine the theoretical framework of chapter 4. George Yúdice and Yolanda Martínez-San Miguel offered judicious advice on the book's proposal and the publishing process. Logan Connors, a colleague who has also become a close friend, held down the fort, leaving me time to write.

I can only hope that over the past five years, my graduate students have learned from me as much as I have from them. I continue to be inspired by the conversations I have in and outside of the classroom with Salim Ayoub, Zayer Baazaoui, Fély Catan, Helen Hernández Hormilla, Elizabeth Langley, Lilianne Lugo Herrera, Hicham Mazouz, Nadia Naami, Nicholas Sheets, Jordan Rogers, and many others. Thank you also to Sarah-Louise Raillard, who helped with the translations; as a nonnative speaker of English, I desperately needed her translating prowess.

The Faculty Fellowship at The Center for the Humanities was an invaluable experience. My gratitude goes to Mihoko Suzuki, Mary Lindemann, and all the other fellows who were a part of our intellectual community: Kathryn Freeman, John Kirby, Karen Mathews, Martin Nesvig, Jessica Rosenberg, Robyn Walsh, Ashli White, Alok Amatya, Allison Harris, and Drewry Wofford. Without the Provost Research Award, I would not have been able to complete the book in due time. I would also like to thank the College of Arts and Sciences at the University of Miami for supporting the book's publication.

So many other mentors, scholars, and colleagues shaped my ideas and writing. Madeleine Dobie expanded my knowledge of Francophone literature and postcolonial studies, continually exemplifying academic rigor. Souleymane Bachir Diagne was always available to share his infinite wisdom and precious life advice. Graciela Montaldo ensured that I feel confident venturing into Latin American Studies, while Kaiama Glover guided my readings of Francophone women writers. Michael Dash and Renée Larrier provided vital advice at a crucial moment. During a very difficult year, Joanna Stalnaker offered much needed support. Hakim Abderrezak's work was a theoretical and methodological inspiration, and I am incredibly grateful for his insightful suggestions.

My time in New York would not have been the same without the input, support, and friendship of Nijah Cunningham, Casiana Ionita, Sarah Lazur, Mehammed Mack, Elizabeth Marcus, Noémie Ndiaye, Leanne Tyler, Erin Twohig, Paul Wimmer, and many others. The late Philip Watts was a reassuring presence and a wonderful interlocutor. I owe special gratitude to Pascale Hubert-Leibler whose pedagogical advice I remember every time I enter the classroom.

My friends and comrades from Occupy Wall Street, Strike Debt, and the Miami Committee on State Violence have tremendously influenced not only the way I think but also the way I live. Christopher "Winter" Casuccio continues to remind me that theory must return to practice. Jason Wozniak, who helped me theorize debt, is also the incarnation of unconditional hospitality. David Backer has transformed the way I understand and practice pedagogy. Joe North is living proof that brilliance and humbleness can coexist. He has also been the most comprehensive, generous, and supportive reader of my work. So many others need to be thanked: Laura Hanna, Ann Larson, Astra Taylor, and Thomas Gokey for being a force to be reckoned with; Andrew Ross and George Caffentzis for proving that public intellectuals still exist; Max Cohen, Ohyoon Kim, Zane Mackin, Chelsea Szendi Schieder, and Conor Tomás Reed for being my coconspirators on so many occasions; Rebecca Wood and Tim Ryan for making Miami feel like home; Tanya Zakrison for feeding me on innumerable occasions and taking me in when I needed a place to live. During my last summer of writing, my parents were hugely helpful; my mother read my work multiple times and my father took care of my canine friend while I traveled. N'Zinga, the friend in question, with her rebellious spirit and unconditional love, made sure that I went on multiple daily walks whenever I was around.

Thank you also to my editor Kristen Elias Rowley, who was supportive of the project from the moment she received the proposal, and to Rebecca Bostock for all her help during the editorial process.

Parts of chapters 2 and 3 were initially published in *Research in African Literatures* and the *Cambridge Journal of Postcolonial Literary Inquiry,* respectively, while an excerpt from chapter 1 appeared in *Francosphères.* I would like to thank the journals and Indiana University Press for allowing me to reproduce this material.

Finally, infinite gratitude goes to Jacques Laroche for his unlimited patience, generosity, and kindness. Everything I know about building a life together (and cooking), I've learnt from him.

INTRODUCTION

Globalizing the Atlantic

In "Trans-Atlantic Trade and Its Discontents," published in the *New York Times* in 2013, Karl-Theodor zu Guttenberg and Pierpaolo Barbieri praise the achievements of the nearly twenty-year-old North American Free Trade Agreement, as they urge a similar agreement between the US and the EU. Given that the title of the article refers to Joseph Stiglitz's now canonical book, *Globalization and Its Discontents,* which in turn borrows its title from Sigmund Freud's *Civilization and Its Discontents,* tacit continuity is established between civilization, globalization, and the trans-Atlantic—convergences further framed by the notion of discontent.[1] Discontent is not, as the reader might assume, related to the widespread consequences of two decades of free trade, but to the fact that EU countries are still reluctant to fully open up their markets.

The measure of NAFTA's unquestionable success is Mexico, "now a manufacturing powerhouse," claim the two authors—a former German defense minister and an Ernest May Fellow at the Harvard Kennedy School of Government. Conveniently absent from this story are the labor conditions in Mexican *maquiladoras,* the destruction of communal agricultural land known as the *ejido,* and rising social inequalities within the country.[2] NAFTA's accomplishments could spread into Europe, the argument continues, if not for the EU's—and in particular France's—resistance to a free-trade agreement with the United States. France, in fact, has threatened to block the negotiations if the EU does not preserve its "cultural exception," which protects audiovisual arts. This is supposedly another example of politics standing in the way of the market. The authors hope that this hurdle will be overcome, allowing for "a US-EU trade deal eventually to serve as a platform for the inclusion of regions with which both parties have negotiations or agreements, in Latin America and a wider Atlantic basin." This outcome, the article concludes, "is worth fighting—and waiting—for." The moment worth fighting for is, thus, the complete neoliberalization of the wider Atlantic, which could subsequently serve as a model for regional free trade. This scenario is blocked—somewhat ironically—by France, who along with other former colonial powers is responsible for the initial spread of capitalism across the Atlantic.

The Atlantic, including all the countries touched by the triangular trade and marked by a history of population displacement and cultural mixing inaugurated through colonialism and slavery, has always been a crucial site for the development of capitalism. Without the free labor generated through slavery, the plantation economy, and the production of sugar and coffee, capitalism would not have developed as it has.[3] If the Atlantic trade instated capitalism, NAFTA represents one of the milestones of its neoliberal stage. The history of capitalism and the history of the Atlantic are thus intertwined. And, as we can see from "Trans-Atlantic Trade and Its Discontents," so are their futures. The future of global neoliberalization, it seems, depends on yet another Atlantic agreement, one in which only countries of the Global North are participating. The authors, in fact, take it for granted that two Northern powers should decide upon the future of the wider Atlantic. Would global neoliberalization generate equal enthusiasm if the story were told from the perspective of the Global South?

In *Precarious Crossings,* through a comparative study of contemporary trans-Atlantic immigrant narratives in French, Spanish, and English, I offer a literary account of a multilingual Atlantic under neoliberalism. Contemporary authors from the Caribbean, Sub-Saharan Africa, and Latin America have reconceptualized the Atlantic from a triangular into a multipolar space, introducing new destinations for contemporary immigrants and establishing new Atlantic connections. In traveling beyond the postcolonial route that connects the formerly colonized and the former colonizer, they also shift focus from cultural difference and national belonging to precarity—a condition characterized by a lack of economic and social stability and protection—as a shared characteristic under global neoliberalization. The vision of the present that emerges from these works is very different from the one offered by the *New York Times* article, as discontent is related to the global spread of neoliberalism, rather than its incomplete implementation. Contemporary Atlantic narratives underline the contradictions inherent in neoliberalism as an ideology and strain against the demands of a neoliberal subject. They further participate in Atlantic literary and cultural dialogues, pushing against literary conventions of various genre, as they explore the complexities of a globalized Atlantic.

Moving between multiple national frameworks, these narratives underscore the ethical and political stakes of comparative thinking. Given its global extent, only a multiracial and multilingual approach can challenge neoliberalism. Different forms of multiculturalism within specific national frameworks are insufficient, as they do not account adequately for the transnational dimensions of neoliberal production and subjectivation. Nor are monolingual and monoracial transnational approaches adequate, because neoliberal governance mobilizes racialized and gendered modes of marginalization to prevent solidarity between groups, forcing them to compete for state (and international) protection that is only ever extended in limited and conditional ways. Challenging this logic, contemporary trans-Atlantic narratives consider how precarity operates in differential yet complementary ways across race, gender, sexuality, and national belonging to sustain global neoliberalization.

They thus invite a cross-cultural analysis of neoliberal precarity, which would not lead to cultural conflation. This challenge exists on multiple levels. Within the novels, as they travel between various locations, characters attempt (and often fail) to build various forms of interethnic and interracial solidarity. At the formal level, the focus on a multilingual Atlantic allows authors to experiment with different literary genres including detective fiction, the travelogue, and the epic. At the level of *Precarious Crossings*, I propose a comparative Atlantic framework, which identifies aesthetic and political similarities across different national contexts while remaining attentive to local differences as well as racialized and gendered modes of marginalization. I would like to begin with a personal story that might clarify the ethical and political stakes, as I conceive them, of a comparative, multilingual approach to global neoliberalization.

I come from the Balkans, from the area now commonly known as ex-Yugoslavia (though I still refer to myself as Yugoslav). I lived in France when I was younger, and I pursued most of my studies in the United States, graduating with a PhD in Francophone studies and a comparative focus on Latin America. I often have to justify my "strange and unusual" choice: why would someone from the Balkans be interested in the Francophone Caribbean? My students are often surprised and perplexed. They would be more comfortable with a professor from the Caribbean, because then they could rely on their cultural authenticity; someone from the United States would also be acceptable, since Americans have an imperial duty to study the rest of the world. Those of us from the Global South have two options: work on our own regions and serve as contemporary versions of a native informant, or study Western literature and culture, due to its assumed universality. This is of course not a rule, and there are plenty of exceptions aside from myself, but it is nonetheless, as many readers will recognize, often the case. It is significantly less common for individuals from the Global South to show interest and have knowledge of other countries of the Global South. Even though our contexts share similarities because we occupy a similar position in the current organization of capital because most of us have gone through structural adjustment programs and are familiar with neoliberalism, austerity, deregulation, and privatization. In this book, I support these lateral interests and lateral connections. As much as I support the choice that someone from the Balkans be interested in the Francophone Caribbean, I advocate for a dialogue between Latin American, African, and Caribbean writers. These interchanges have important ethical and political implications.

Beginning in the 1990s, Yugoslavia went through a brutal civil war and a violent economic restructuring guided by forced privatizations, austerity measures, market liberalization, and heightened unemployment. When I was visiting what was no longer Yugoslavia, sometime in the mid-2000s, I had an interesting conversation with a friend who was appalled that the "transition" government would raise taxes on local materials and lower taxes on imports, eventually destroying local production in favor of foreign products. She was perplexed by this decision and asked me whether I could believe it. I, in fact, could. Because I was very familiar with structural adjustment programs and neoliberal policies in other countries of the Global South. I knew what Mexico, Jamaica, Senegal, and so many other countries had gone through, and it was analogous. Had we in the Balkans had the opportunity to learn about these countries, maybe we could have predicted our future. However, the pervading assumption is that because of cultural differences, we do not have much in common (even though historically, this is not true). The works in my corpus move against this assumption, as they identify precarity to be an increasingly trans-Atlantic condition. Following these narratives, I strive to build a multilingual Atlantic framework. *Precarious Crossings* exists at the intersection of Francophone, Anglophone, Latin American, postcolonial, and economic studies. I ask the reader for some patience as I weave between these different fields to tell the story of a globalized, literary Atlantic.

GLOBALIZATION, AN OUTDATED TERM?

Most scholarly writings on globalization attempt to answer, in one form or another, the following three questions: Is globalization happening at all (or are nation-states still the main loci of power)? Is globalization something new or has it been happening for centuries? Does the deterritorialization we see today differ only in degree or also in form from deterritorializations that accompanied previous stages of capitalism? Following Immanuel Wallerstein's world systems approach, I consider that the economic interconnectedness and interdependence of the world is not a recent development, and that the emergence of the modern world economy (characterized by market trade, a single division of labor but multiple cultures) has existed in various forms since the sixteenth century.[4] Yet, the latest phase of globalization has been sustained by a specific political and economic ideology: *neoliberalism*. I contend that the term globalization needs to be qualified as we are currently in the era of neoliberal globalization or, as I prefer to call it, global neoliberalization. I favor the second option because it underscores that neoliberalization is a process, one that does not go unchallenged and that remains incomplete.

International financial institutions like the International Monetary Fund (IMF) and the World Bank exemplify the combination of dispersal and centralization that characterizes global neoliberalization. Since the 1970s, the politics of structural adjustment programs, austerity measures, privatization, and precarity have created a common social context across various Atlantic rim nations, so that we can establish new points of comparison that support a multilingual study of the Atlantic world. In *A Brief History of Neoliberalism*, David Harvey defines neoliberalism as "a theory of political economic practices that proposes that human well-being can best be advanced by liberating individual entrepreneurial freedoms and skills within an institutional framework characterized by strong private property rights, free markets, and free trade. The role of the state is to create and preserve an institutional framework appropriate to such practices."[5] Neoliberal creed could be further expressed through one word: *flexibility*. Proponents of neoliberalism insist that competition as well as the deregulation and flexibilization of labor are necessary for a healthy economy. Labor unions have thus become the biggest obstacle to progress, and short-term contracts the only solution. The system maintains worker control through performance reviews, peer evaluations, individual "merit"-based salaries, and looming unemployment.

As an economic model, neoliberalism prioritizes "financial motives, financial markets, financial actors and financial institutions in the operation of domestic and international economies."[6] This is not necessarily a new phenomenon, given that capitalism has always oscillated between periods of material and financial expansion.[7] However, since the 1990s, financial speculation in secondary markets—like the derivatives market—has significantly increased. Annie McClanahan, following Harvey, argues that globalization and financialization operate conjointly: whereas the former is a "spatial fix" that extends the space of commodity production and circulation, the latter functions as a "temporal fix," allowing "capital to treat an anticipated realization of value as if it has already happened."[8] Constantly assessing its investments, the finance industry, Étienne Balibar notes, has "the ability to decide which industries to enhance and which to suppress (together with their installations, accumulated experience, and employees)."[9] But how did neoliberalism become the dominant ideology?

The era of Keynesianism or "embedded liberalism," which supported government investment and higher wages as means of lowering unemployment and increasing consumer demand, faced "stagflation"—a combination of high inflation and rising unemployment—in the 1970s. The explanations for the crisis vary dramatically, including the high cost of the Vietnam War, the unpegging of the dollar from the gold standard, and rising oil prices. According to David Harvey, this was the perfect moment for the wealthy class, whose assets diminished in postwar decades, to dismantle Keynesianism. In fact, neoliberal economists insisted that high taxes—particularly on the wealthy—and economic regulation had caused the crisis.

The rise to power of several political figures, according to Harvey, facilitated the spread of neoliberalism: in China, Deng Xiaoping undertook the liberalization of the communist economy in 1978.[10] On a different continent, as he became chairman of the US Federal Reserve in 1979, Paul Volcker implemented a new monetary policy, known as the "Volcker Shock." Volcker raised interest rates in order to place inflation under control and end the crisis. Massive recession and unemployment rates of over ten percent ensued, weakening the power of organized labor.[11] Soon thereafter, in 1980, Ronald Reagan was elected president of the United States. As a proponent of "trickle-down" economics, Reagan argued that lowering taxes for the wealthy would incentivize them to invest in society and generate economic growth. The benefits would ultimately trickle-down to everyone. Reagan cut the top marginal tax rate from 70% to 50% at first, and then to 28% in 1986. He further reduced the maximum tax rate on capital gains to 20%, the lowest since the Great Depression (he then raised it to 28% in 1986).[12] Around the same time, on the other side of the Atlantic, Margaret Thatcher became prime minister of Britain, emulating Reagan's policies.

Even before the arrival of Reagan and Thatcher, neoliberal experiments were conducted in Latin America. The democratically elected socialist president Salvador Allende came to power in Chile in 1970, only to be deposed by General Pinochet in the violent coup of 1973. With the backing of "the Chicago boys," a group of US economists headed by Milton Friedman, Pinochet undertook large-scale privatizations, cut tariffs and government programs, and deregulated the labor market, turning Chile into one the first tests of neoliberal governance.[13]

Throughout the 1970s, in Latin America, and in Mexico in particular, national debt became one of the primary tools of neoliberalization. After the OPEC oil embargo of 1973, oil-producing Arab States began to recycle their petrodollars through Wall Street investment banks. Due to stagflation within the US, the banks found it more lucrative to issue high-interest loans to developing countries affected by the global financial crisis than to invest at home. Unfortunately, as the loans were in dollars, in the aftermath of the Volcker Shock and the jump in interest rates, countries like Mexico faced crisis. In fact, in 1982, Mexico announced it was no longer able to pay its sovereign debt, setting in motion the "Third World debt crisis." A default would have been detrimental to the US investment banks that held the debt; an intervention was necessary: "Internationally, the core neoliberal states gave the IMF and the World Bank full authority in 1982 to negotiate debt relief, which meant in effect to protect the world's main financial institutions from the threat of default."[14] The IMF and the World Bank renegotiated Mexico's debt, in exchange for a series of rapidly implemented neoliberal reforms, including privatization of state-owned companies, a dismantling of labor unions, and cuts to public programs and subsidies related to food, healthcare, transportation, and education. Mexico also committed to keeping inflation low, thus guaranteeing that the value of its debt would not diminish. What could have posed a problem for Wall Street turned into a great opportunity: debt, it turns out, is a great tool of global neoliberalization.

A similar set of reforms was implemented throughout the 1980s and '90s across Latin America, Africa, and the Caribbean. Harvey explains that "by 1994 some eighteen countries (including Mexico, Brazil, Argentina, Venezuela, and Uruguay) had agreed to deals that forgave them some $60 billion in debt."[15] In order to repay their outstanding national debts, governments have had to procure foreign currencies; as a result, in many countries subsistence crops have been abandoned in favor of export programs, cash crops, and monocultures, creating dependency on transnational corporations that control the market.[16] Jason Hickel asserts that global neoliberalization created "a widespread race-to-the-bottom," where in order to attract foreign investment, countries of the Global South compete to offer the cheapest labor and resources, and the highest tax exemptions.[17] Whereas these measures are conducted in the name of development, "the number of Africans living in basic poverty has more than doubled since 1980."[18]

Contemporary globalization and neoliberalism are thus for me inseparable. This economic shift has relied on technological innovation and the development of communication networks.[19] These networks have a strong cultural and economic dimension involving the transmission of advertising and television programs, as well as transfers of capital and computerization of labor.[20] The two cannot be separated, cultural globalization cannot be analyzed independently from economic globalization.[21] As Paul Jay argues: "No contemporary approach to economic flows of power under the forces of globalization can do without a clear historical understanding of how cultures and commodities are embedded within each other."[22]

Speaking about global neoliberalization from a literary standpoint is an important task because as a governing regime, neoliberalism relies on the formation of a neoliberal subject. The characters in my corpus explore the contradictions and failings of this subject, as they point to linguistic, aesthetic, and interpersonal experiences that exceed the neoliberal logic. Wendy Brown, in *Undoing the Demos: Neoliberalism's Stealth Revolution*, maintains that in the neoliberal era, the primary and sole purpose of the government is to enhance economic growth. All other concerns (except for national security) are secondary.[23] Values such as equality, liberty, and inclusion have become subordinate to capital enhancement, and social justice and social equality are pursued only to the extent that they support and encourage economic growth.[24] They are valued so long as they attract consumers and investors, but no longer in their own right. Thus, neoliberalism cannot simply be characterized as a system that creates wealth disparities through privatization, deregulation, and austerity. It is also insufficient to claim that neoliberalism converts every human desire or endeavor into a profitable business (though it does all of the above). Even more importantly, neoliberalism is "an order of normative reason that, when it becomes ascendant, takes shape as a governing rationality extending a specific formulation of economic values, practices, and metrics to every dimension of human life."[25] The model of the market extends to all spheres of human activity. In addition to looking to maximize her profits, the neoliberal subject has become human capital. She does not generate profit solely through her activity; she is the activity that generates profit. The neoliberal subject is thus continuously looking to "strengthen its competitive positioning and appreciate its value,"[26] within structures "that produce insecurity and . . . *a reserve army of employees rendered docile by these social processes that make their situations precarious*."[27] Precarity upholds neoliberalism.

NEOLIBERAL PRECARITIES

Literary criticism has still not fully engaged an aesthetics and ethics of contemporary precarity. Within the context of contemporary immigrant narratives, precarity permits us to move beyond the framework of nation, integration, and assimilation. A theoretical focus based on precarity challenges the assumption that immigration is just a domestic issue, positing instead that domestic concerns are related to the reconfiguration of the global economy. Within this framework, immigration can be theorized from an earlier point in the process, from the vantage point of global forces that are pushing people to emigrate. This is, furthermore, an opportunity to move beyond multiculturalism as the main solution for social conflict: "Precarity cuts across identity categories as well as multicultural maps, thus forming the basis for an alliance focused on opposition to state violence and its capacity to produce, exploit, and distribute precarity for the purposes of profit and territorial defense."[28]

Following Fred Moten and Stefano Harney, I believe that the desire to help marginalized groups—a position that ultimately furthers the interests of the helper—is not sufficient to sustain coalitions fighting against neoliberal precarity. On the other hand, the recognition that the system is killing everyone, though some people "much more softly" than others, can serve as grounds for solidarity.[29] Precarity can be at the basis of such a coalition, one that challenges every instance of the devaluation of life while engaging in a serious analysis of why and how certain lives are more devalued than others are. I thus do not mobilize precarity in order to ignore or supersede differences. Rather, I consider it as a characteristic differentially assigned according to race, gender, class, *and* as a site of possible solidarity. As such, it can become a "promising site for coalitional exchange."[30]

Economic reforms brought by global neoliberalization, particularly the fetishization of flexibility as a precondition for economic growth, have deepened precarity.[31] Guy Standing, in his revealing book *The Precariat: The New Dangerous Class*, explains that neoliberal flexibility includes multiple components: adapting remuneration to the demands of the market (mainly by lowering wages), easily hiring and firing workers, moving employees between positions, changing company structures, and finally, adjusting workers' skills. As more risks are displaced from the state and employers onto workers, insecurity, anxiety, and fear become the norm.

Members of the precariat are, however, not always easy to identify. In fact, one of the precariat's primary characteristics (and the reason why, according to Standing, it still doesn't form a distinct class), is its heterogeneity. Precarious workers include refugees and migrants, care workers, service workers as well as the new "creative freelancer." These disparate groups share a few characteristics, nonetheless. First, the precariat is not part of the working class because it no longer has "long-term, stable, fixed-hour jobs with established routes of advancement, subject to unionisation and collective agreements."[32] Unlike the proletariat, the precariat "has minimal trust relationships with capital or the state."[33] Furthermore, while some workers may still be advancing in their respective fields, the precariat suffers from a "lack of a secure work-based identity."[34] Most importantly, precarious workers have no prospects for a career, as they are employed in jobs "without traditions of social memory, a feeling they belong to an occupational community steeped in stable practices, codes of ethics and norms of behavior, reciprocity and fraternity."[35]

Precarization extends beyond work; it "embraces the whole of existence, the body, modes of subjectivation," Isabell Lorey notes.[36] No longer relying (exclusively) on direct domination, neoliberalism is "governing through insecurity."[37] The withdrawal of social protection, increased uncertainty, and the impending realization of the unforeseeable, generate fear, and ultimately obedience. Precarity creates fearful, anxious bodies, relentlessly competing against one another to escape their life of contingency. As a political condition, precarity intersects with ontological precariousness. Everyone experiences precariousness, as all human beings are prone to suffering, violence, and death. However, the unequal distribution of precariousness across categories of gender, race, nationality, class, and sexuality creates precarity. According to Judith Butler: "The more or less existential conception of 'precariousness' is thus linked with a more specifically political notion of 'precarity.' And it is the differential allocation of precarity that, in my view, forms the point of departure for both a rethinking of bodily ontology and for progressive or left politics in ways that continue to exceed and traverse the categories of identity."[38] All life is precarious and in need of protection. However, political, economic, and social institutions assign this protection differentially, based on nationality, class, race, gender, sexuality, and ability. Precarity thus designates "that politically induced condition in which certain populations suffer from failing social and economic networks of support and become differentially exposed to injury, violence, and death."[39] While exposed to arbitrary state violence, these populations also have no choice but to seek protection from those very states.

The rise of police states and surveillance mechanisms in the aftermath of 9/11, claims Butler, was precisely an attempt to deny precariousness, asserting sovereignty in the face of others.[40] This sovereignty can be avowed only at the expense of others, whose lives become less grievable. That some lives are less grievable than others became discernible during the recent refugee crisis and terrorist attacks. The image of Alan Kurdi, a three-year-old Syrian boy who drowned off the coast of Turkey in 2015 as his family was trying to reach Greece, is now engraved in the public imagination, mostly a result of social media campaigns. This was a moment of pause during a crisis that began long before Alan's death and has continued in its aftermath. This tragedy also underscored the power of media in allocating, and by extension withdrawing, grievability.

In the aftermath of multiple terrorist attacks, similar questions proliferated on social media. The November 2015 attacks in Paris and Beirut were only a day apart. As the hashtag #IamParis went viral on social media, many wondered about the whereabouts of #IamBeirut. The mainstream media was similarly silent in the aftermath of the July 2016 bombings in Baghdad: no hashtags, no dismay, no grieving. Social media posts proliferated, asking why we mourn Paris, Brussels, and New York but not Beirut and Baghdad.[41] I recount these events, because they summon us to extend our comparative frameworks, in order to understand the unequal, global distribution of precarity and grievability. Comparative literature can contribute to the development of a necessary, twofold argument: a critique of precarity as privileging the grieving of some, and a reclaiming of precariousness as an acknowledgement that "radical forms of self-sufficiency and unbridled sovereignty are, by definition, disrupted by the larger global processes of which they are a part, that no final control can be secured, and that final control is not, cannot be, an ultimate value."[42] To be human is to be vulnerable to others; to assume one's precariousness is to acknowledge that our life depends on complete strangers. A political and ethical commitment can stem from this vulnerability.

While proceeding under the conceptual framework of precarity, we need to be mindful of some of its limitations. Used across disciplines, the term risks losing its specificity and thus becoming, as Rob Horning has warned, "a trendy thing to say to forestall rather than develop analyses."[43] Like globalization, transnationalism, and resistance, precarity often encompasses a whole variety of very different realities and practices. If, in the current economic and political system, everyone is precarious, then disparate experiences can quickly become equated. In the United States, the debate between the #BlackLivesMatter movement and its #AllLivesMatter counter underlined the importance of analytic precision. Members of the Black Lives Matter movement have rightly pointed to the racist dimension of substituting "Black" with "All."[44] The emphasis on "Black" in Black Lives Matter underscores the fact that not all lives matter equally, and that subsequently, we should focus on those lives that cannot survive so that others can live peacefully. "All" replaces a serious analysis of structural racism with an empty humanism. The danger with precarity is similar to that of "All" in #AllLivesMatter. I thus fully agree with Tavia Nyong'o that "if 'precarious life' is to offer a means towards new solidarities based on shared vulnerabilities, then those who proceed under its sign must remain scrupulously attentive to the constitutive and uneven distribution of that vulnerability, and must not simply fall back upon a well-meaning but empty humanism."[45] If we are to use precarity as a conceptual framework, we must also account for the growing inequalities within the precariat itself. By conceptualizing how race, gender, class, and nationality make some lives more prone to social and economic violence, contemporary immigrant narratives can help us precisely to avoid the potential homogenization of precarity.

Precarity, it should be noted, is also not necessarily a new phenomenon. Capitalism has in fact always kept the working class in precarious conditions. Given that the system is "built on the profit that can be extracted from forcing people to sell their labor power to survive, a certain amount of survival panic is always built in."[46] This was certainly the case for seventeenth- and eighteenth-century European peasants[47] and nineteenth-century industrial workers; utmost precarity was also experienced by slaves in the Americas and colonized labor in Africa and Asia. Within the French colonial empire, precarity was institutionalized through legal documents such as the *code noir* and the *code de l'indigénat,* which defined the conditions of slavery and the status of the colonized. The main novelty thus, it could be argued, is the extension of precarity to the middle-class creative worker in the United States and Western Europe. Furthermore, by insisting that precarity is new and a product of neoliberalism, we risk idealizing Fordism and corporatist capitalism of the 1950s and '60s. Bhaskar Sunkara has thus argued that instead of insisting on a new phase of capitalism, we should talk about a return to pre-Fordist capitalist modes of production; instead of inventing new terms, we should consult history books.[48] In fact, with the dismantling of the welfare state and the Fordist mode of production (even though these mostly benefited workers in the Global North), we are in many ways returning to pre-Fordist modes of production with, however, important differences. First, most of the Global South has entered an era of sovereignty (at least officially). Unlike colonial rule, neocolonialism is more indirect, as it operates through international institutions, structural adjustment programs, and debt—mechanisms that have intensified immigration to the Global North. Standing and Seymour both acknowledge that the incorporation of a large number of immigrant workers distinguishes the contemporary precariat. Furthermore, the advent of new technologies has changed modes of communication (though access to technologies is still quite limited on a global scale) and of resistance. The precariat, as Richard Seymour maintains, can serve as a "populist interpellation," a subjectivation that could lead to a politically productive antagonism.[49]

In *Precarious Crossings,* I limit my focus to representations of the precarious lives of immigrants. This approach enables me to consider precarity transnationally, while containing the concept. Immigrant narratives extend the analysis of precarity from the country of origin to the country of destination. Often subject to multiple levels of precarity, immigrants lack social protection as the cheap labor force in both the Global South and the Global North. If undocumented, they are also deprived of political protection, a vulnerability compounded by rising racism and xenophobia on a global scale. Trans-Atlantic immigrant narratives no longer focus solely on integration, assimilation, and cultural difference within a single national setting. Rather, they depict precarious subjects whose lives are affected by the global debt, labor, and environmental crisis. Through their daily lives and struggles, these protagonists conceive of social relations outside of the logic of precarity as they approach the question of ethics in a precarious world. Migrating to new and uncommon Atlantic destinations, these narratives are reshaping the immigrant literary tradition.

SHOULD I STAY OR SHOULD I GO? IMMIGRATION IN THE AGE OF GLOBAL NEOLIBERALIZATION

Francophone works of fiction have historically approached the topic of immigration through shifting lenses.[50] In the 1980s and '90s, questions of assimilation and integration complemented the colonial era concern with travel and education,[51] as the "beur" novel allowed second-generation Maghrebi immigrants to explore the cultural and linguistic divide with the generation of their parents. Caught between a country of origin that they do not fully understand and a French society that rejects them, they found themselves at an impasse. In order to negotiate this "double unbelonging" and create a third way, they often resorted to fiction.[52] While critical discourse has initially privileged authors of North African origin and the question of Maghrebi immigration, in the late 1990s and early 2000s, critical focus extended to first-generation Sub-Saharan African authors living in Paris.[53]

In the twenty-first century, traditional immigration patterns have significantly shifted, inviting a multilingual approach to contemporary narratives. Christopher Miller notes that "one sign of change in recent years . . . has been a new global turn taken by certain African writers. . . . Numerous authors have taken at least a few steps beyond the borders of the Hexagon, sending their characters on forays to other states of the European Union."[54] Within the context of the Mediterranean, Hakim Abderrezak has similarly identified "atypical migrational trends," new reasons for leaving and modes of traveling that constitute "ex-centric migrations."[55] I analyze "ex-centric" migrations within the framework of the globalized Atlantic. The latest wave of trans-Atlantic immigrant fiction, published in the twenty-first century, introduces new frameworks for thinking about immigration. Unlike many immigrant narratives of the 1980s and '90s, contemporary works no longer revert to the *bildungsroman* as their preferred form. Instead, they redefine traditional literary genre, including the novel, the travelogue, and detective fiction, as they provide a global outlook. Often written in the third person, these works no longer position France as the only destination for French-speaking migrants, exploring instead new transnational entanglements brought on by global neoliberalization. As these narratives turn their attention toward non-Francophone countries, they invite a comparative Atlantic context. We can fully address the question of global precarious subjects only from a multilingual standpoint.[56]

In fact, a set of Latin American and Caribbean immigrant narratives, written in English and Spanish, have followed a similar development. Instead of focusing on immigrant life in the United States and Europe, they depict interregional migrations and represent aspects of immigration that thus far remain undertheorized, like conditions for departure and return. They furthermore do not separate economic immigration from other forms of migration and travel, including business and tourism. These narratives question the division between cosmopolitan and immigrant subjects, and outline ways in which these different global flows intersect; the protagonists often struggle with precarious conditions in multiple countries, underlining global neoliberal policies rather than national immigration politics.[57]

Contemporary trans-Atlantic immigrant fictions require a theoretical framework that extends beyond an analysis of the representation and self-representation of immigrants within a national setting. Global dynamics that cause migration inflect questions of identity, cultural negotiation, assimilation, and integration. Contemporary "economic" immigration often involves several stages: immigration from rural to urban centers and to wealthier and more stable regional neighbors very often precede immigration to the "developed world." Without taking into account the cultural and economic entanglement of the Global North and the Global South, and the ideology of global neoliberalization, the analysis of these movements remains incomplete. I engage authors who think about the imbrication of the emigration and immigration processes. Fatou Diome's *Le ventre de l'Atlantique* [*The Belly of the Atlantic*] (2003) relates Senegalese emigration to national debt. Many of these contemporary authors represent first-generation migrants, focusing on reasons for leaving as well as the crossing itself. Individual and collective identity has not disappeared as a problem, but it is no longer the sole focus of the work. A completely new set of economic issues, stemming from global neoliberalization, plays a prominent role.

Another important issue in this context is the claim by some scholars that the increased critical interest in immigrant narratives has led to a debate regarding their instrumentalization. Within the Francophone context, authors have raised concerns about an ethnographic reading of their novels, arguing that works by "Franco-French" authors are valued for their literary qualities whereas Francophone works serve as illustrations of sociological theories. They have objected to the assumption that their fictions directly translate the experience of certain ethnic or national groups, questioning the use of literature as sociological evidence.[58] I hope that this book will contribute to the debate, demonstrating the impossibility of a clear separation between a thematic and a formal analysis, and the importance of reading immigrant narratives not merely as illustrations of global neoliberalization but also as sites of a poetics of contestation.

Analyzing economic and political processes like neoliberalization, immigration, and precarity through works of literature is a worthwhile endeavor, and not because literary works illustrate what social scientists have hypothesized. Literary works do not simply reproduce the world we live in, they theorize and recreate it; they represent experiences, raise questions, and look at issues from angles that other disciplines may not. I thus do not consider them as evidence for preexisting theories, but as theories in their own right, which enter into dialogue and often challenge discourses from other disciplines, building interdisciplinary conversations. At the same time, these are aesthetic objects, posing aesthetic questions about representation, genre, and language. They challenge us, literary scholars, to generate new concepts and approaches in order to address their global outlook, and they invite the field of comparative literature to move in new directions. These two aspects summon intersecting interpretations: through their aesthetic choices, contemporary Atlantic fictions theorize immigration and precarity. Concurrently, their focus on specific economic and political issues informs their aesthetic choices. I believe these works to be of great interest to literary scholars and students while we reflect on the current state of the discipline and its future possibilities. They also can be of interest to other scholars and nonscholars alike, not as evidence of their own theories, but because they add new perspectives to existing dialogues. Fatou Diome's novels establish connections between neocolonialism, immigration, and debt that are not addressed in current theoretical discourses on debt. Other works analyzed offer us equally innovative insights into the experiences of global neoliberalization, precarity, and immigration. This is not merely a matter of describing the world-as-is. Literary works also imagine the world as-it-could-be, encouraging transnational connections, solidarities, and modes of relating that are deeper and fuller than what the neoliberal model has to offer.

One could object that the authors in my corpus are now "speaking for" precarious subjects, with whom they do not always share a class background. Throughout this book, I underline a variety of literary strategies that authors mobilize to avoid such a representative status. Most of the works contain a multiplicity of characters with different class, national, and racial backgrounds that experience—like the authors themselves—varying degrees of precarity. In other words, these novels do not convey an authentic experience of *the* precarious immigrant. Rather, through portrayals of a diversity of characters they point to ways in which precarity is experienced differentially and reflect on the (im)possibilities of solidarity between different groups. Within the realm of fiction, they connect characters from across the globe as they explore building across lines of demarcation. All the while, they reflect on genre, character building, and the narrative voice. Their focus is thus less on "explaining" precarious subjects and more on staging ethical encounters that exceed the logic of precarity. Immigrant characters in my corpus identify the reasons for rising precarity; they also engage in acts of daily resistance and point to modes of social engagement that move beyond it. They travel to multiple Atlantic destinations, think comparatively, and identify new possibilities for "coalitional exchanges." Many of these exchanges ultimately fail. Contemporary Atlantic narratives investigate both the possibilities and the difficulties of cross-cultural solidarity, underscoring the advantages and the limits of precarity as a mode of cross-cultural exchange. Works of fiction, they are also in dialogue with literary and cultural traditions of the wider Atlantic. Through their ex-centric migrations, they are remapping the Atlantic, steering us toward the hardest question that this book confronts: how do global neoliberalization, precarity, immigration, and the Atlantic conceptually intersect? How can we approach the aesthetic, ethical, and political complexities of a multilingual, multiracial Atlantic?

TOWARD A MULTILINGUAL ATLANTIC

Contemporary novelists like Maryse Condé and Caryl Phillips represent a multiracial and multinational set of characters who strive and struggle to build across differences based on a shared experience of neoliberal precarity. Phillips notes his indebtedness to Black Atlantic authors, yet also the need to expand the Black Atlantic framework to allow for new connections based on the experience of mutual precarity. In an interview entitled "Other Voices," Phillips explains that his first experience of solidarity was based on class, rather than race. In the North of England, white immigrant teachers "with weird names" were the only ones to support him throughout his schooling, prompting his exploration of the intersections between race and class.[59] He similarly laments, in *Color Me English*, his inability to stand in solidarity with a Muslim student, bullied by their fellow classmates. Phillips's anecdotes serve as the starting point of this book: what aesthetic and ethical frameworks would allow for these solidarities to materialize?

The idea of the Atlantic as a diasporic site in which European and African populations and cultures have come together, producing new social and cultural forms, is associated, in particular, with Paul Gilroy's seminal work, *The Black Atlantic: Modernity and Double-Consciousness* (1993). Gilroy understands the Atlantic "as one, single complex unit of analysis," due to the "economic and historical matrix in which plantation slavery—'capitalism with its clothes off'—was one special moment."[60] He criticizes cultural studies for adopting a nationalist focus and embracing the idea that "cultures always flow into patterns congruent with the borders of essentially homogenous nation states."[61] Nationalist frameworks are not, in Gilroy's view, "an adequate means to understand the forms of resistance and accommodation intrinsic to modern black political culture."[62] As an alternative, he proposes that modern black culture strives "to transcend both the structures of the nation state and the constraints of ethnicity and national particularity."[63] While Gilroy's critical reflection has undoubtedly marked the fields of cultural studies and literary criticism, it is now also commonly acknowledged that his work remains limited to Anglophone authors who are primarily from the US and UK.

In response, Francophone, Hispanophone, and Lusophone studies turned toward the Atlantic.[64] Whereas Christopher Miller demonstrates the interdependence of the three poles of the Francophone triangle in literature and cinema, Bill Marshall expands the French Atlantic to include spaces like Montevideo and Quebec City.[65] Similarly, *Cultures of the Lusophone Black Atlantic*, examines the historical and cultural enmeshment of Portugal, Brazil, and Africa. While these critical developments "push back the boundaries of (trans)atlantic studies," as Thea Pitman and Andy Stafford remark, "they are still limited by an essentially monolingual/monocultural and, at times, monoracial, interest in the field."[66]

Yet, Gilroy already claimed that Black Atlantic cultural productions "repeatedly articulate a desire to escape the restrictive bonds of ethnicity, national identification, and sometimes even 'race' itself."[67] His theoretical framework thus already invited a multilingual, multiracial counterpart. Thinking about the Atlantic in these terms is, however, a daunting task; risks of historical and cultural imprecision and inadequate attention to racialized modes of oppression and marginalization loom everywhere. However, confronting these difficulties is necessary. Following Alison Games, I believe that we need "to restore the ocean to Atlantic history . . . not simply north-south hemispheric connections between Africa and Europe or within the Americas, but transatlantic connections."[68] This is a particularly salient task now, given that global neoliberalization has reinforced existing trans-Atlantic connections and created new ones.

In the work of contemporary trans-Atlantic authors, the globalized Atlantic surfaces as "a *vision,* an ideal or aspiration of solidarity and interconnection."[69] The writers in my corpus explore visions of nonneoliberal and nonprecarious forms of life; they offer us lines of flight, ways of reimagining social relations outside of the logic of global neoliberalization. And they do so from a multinational perspective. The Black Atlantic remains a central node of the globalized Atlantic. We cannot analyze contemporary precarity without acknowledging as a point of departure the precarity of enslaved bodies and the role of the triangular trade in the construction of the Atlantic world. Christina Sharpe speaks of "the continuous and changing present of slavery's as yet unresolved unfolding,"[70] which globally takes the form of "the disastrous time and effects of continued marked migrations, Mediterranean and Caribbean disasters, trans-American and -African migration, structural adjustment imposed by the International Monetary Fund that continues imperialisms/colonialisms and more."[71] The works in my corpus explore the neoliberal afterlives of slavery but they also address neoliberal governance in the context of *maquiladoras,* the US–Mexico border, Puerto Rican immigration, and the global war on terror. A globalized Atlantic is not merely a result of the accumulation of different modes of marginalization or oppression, nor a simple extension of the Black Atlantic. Rather, it is a "rethinking of cartographies of encounter," as Simon Gikandi phrases it, in "a form of epistemic disturbance or interruption."[72] These new cartographies of encounter outline positions from which to recognize (and sometime misidentify) complementary modes of precarity. Recognition cannot be reduction to the same; this is an aesthetic and ethical issue with which contemporary authors contend.

The terminology of the globalized Atlantic transects the concept of the Global South. The Global North/South division has entered critical vocabulary, replacing the now outdated First/Third World opposition. It traces, approximately, the geographically uneven distribution of capital, resources, and power between the Northern and the Southern hemisphere. While the

North is composed of privileged and affluent nations, the South is reserved for economically marginalized ones. In our current day and age, this dichotomy does not constitute an exact representation since the neoliberal elite encompasses dwellers of both the North and the South, and certain populations (especially of color) in the Global North face the same level of marginalization and poverty as those in the Global South. However, taking a cue from Chandra Mohanty, I find that "as a political designation that attempts to distinguish between the 'haves' and the 'have-nots,' the Global South has 'a certain political value.'"[73] It is particularly useful as a figurative division, where, following Arif Dirlik, "North" designates the areas with an uneven accumulation of global capital, and the "South" refers to the marginalized populations across the world.[74] Conceptually merging the Atlantic and the Global South, Kerry Bystrom and Joseph R. Slaughter demarcate the Global South Atlantic as a space marked by "cultural, social, and intellectual transactions and interactions among Africa, Latin America, and the Caribbean," which "allows us to think about the social, economic, political, and cultural forces and contingencies that make certain geo-specific configurations possible."[75]

The immigrant narratives of *Precarious Crossings* complicate the division between the North and the South Atlantic, as characters immigrate from the South to the North, the North to the South, and between different regions of the Global South. The memory of slavery and European colonization echo across their lines, preserving the Atlantic geographic, aesthetic, and political framework. However, this is not the only Atlantic history to surface. The globalized Atlantic is also marked by the strong presence of the United States, the fiercest proponent of global neoliberalization. Unlike European colonialism, US imperialism is "associated with the emergence of transnational capitalist corporations which, though they may have a basis in one or other nation state, spread themselves across the map of the world in ways that were unthinkable in the earlier phases of imperialism," as Harvey explains.[76] The globalized Atlantic exists (perhaps?) at the juncture of these intersecting histories: the Atlantic slave trade, colonization, cultural mixing in the Americas and the Caribbean, intraregional migrations, US imperialism, and neoliberalization. The Atlantic vision that I propose is thus certainly not univocal; it moves across, in between, and in excess of these different histories and their presents, "turning the geographies of Africa, Europe, South America, and North America *inside out,* so as to better study the idea of a uniquely circumatlantic flow of peoples, goods, and cultures."[77]

The risk with extending the Atlantic so far and wide is to reproduce an approach that, according to Emily Apter, "in promoting an ethic of liberal inclusiveness or the formal structures of cultural similitude, often has the collateral effect of blunting political critique" and creating a "reflexive endorsement of cultural equivalence and substitutability."[78] Postcolonial studies, to which I am highly indebted, countered the cultural conflations of different parts of the world. One of its disciplinary objectives has been to return specific, local (hi)stories to a Eurocentric tradition of historiography and literary criticism, bringing—against the abstraction and self-referentiality of postmodern writing—an attention to local particularities and cultural difference. Postcolonialism reacted against the violence of Western universality and metanarratives in general (including Marxism), and the idea that a universal model of resistance and change can be imposed on different locations without considering local particularities. The intention has been to promote diversity, multiplicity, and heterogeneity in the face of historical and ongoing homogenization.[79]

I contend that comparison is an imperative political project in the age of neoliberalism because it enables us to reignite multilingual and multiracial conversations across the Global South. A comparative approach is possible given that countries of the Global South occupy a similar (note: not the same) position within the global configuration of power. While as scholars we may believe in the importance of preserving local and cultural differences, the IMF, the World Bank, and Washington, who have been dictating the world's economic policy over the past few decades, are not particularly concerned by it. Structural adjustment programs have imposed similar models on very different geographical locations, creating analogous social, political, and economic contexts. Furthermore, the works I analyze mostly do not take place in the author's country of origin, inviting a comparative approach.

Attention to cultural differences and local histories has been crucial in countering Western universalism. At the same time, afraid of conflating different historical and cultural developments, we have become too reluctant to extend our comparisons too far: but what is the point of understanding historical and cultural differences if we do not know how to think and work across them? Other scholars have raised similar questions before me. In *Postcolonial Representations,* Francoise Lionnet wonders if feminist theory can "articulate common questions for a multicultural practice." She further inquiries into "the preconditions under which the formulations of identity and difference do not risk becoming static categories used to polarize and fragment intellectual and political communities."[80] In *Precarious Crossings,* I pursue this line of inquiry in relation to global neoliberalization. How can we articulate common questions for a transnational aesthetic and ethical practice? I address these questions through comparisons of works of literature emanating from countries that occupy a similar position in this age of global neoliberalization. The trans-Atlantic literary imaginaries that I analyze overlap and intersect. This, of course, does not mean that neoliberalism operates everywhere in the exact same way, nor that its ultimate goal is complete homogenization and erasure of difference. The global spread of neoliberalism has resulted, as David Harvey has shown, in uneven geographical development.[81] Neoliberal governance mobilizes differences, which it strives to incorporate into its vision of the world. While these processes are not everywhere alike, I believe them to be comparable, because the neoliberal vision of the world remains the same.

By conducting a multilingual analysis of contemporary immigrant narratives, I identify instances of what Françoise Lionnet and Shu-mei Shih call "minor transnationalism." Lionnet and Shih argue that minority subjects often "identify themselves in opposition to a dominant discourse rather than vis-à-vis each other and other minority groups."[82] Immigrants in France thus strive to assimilate into a specific vision of "Frenchness" rather than see commonalities with other immigrant groups in a similar situation. This approach, though it claims to center marginal subjects, ultimately relates the minority position back to the center, effacing connections and relations that exist between different marginalized groups. Lionnet and Shih are interested in the "micropractices of transnationality in their multiple, paradoxical, or even irreverent relations with the economic transnationalism of contemporary empires."[83] Seeking new and uncommon Atlantic destinations, immigrant characters in my corpus often enter into contact with other immigrant groups, establishing networks of immigrant cultures. Comparative literary criticism itself can perform acts of minor transnationalism. Whereas many of the authors in my corpus are not in direct dialogue with one another, placing them in conversation, studying their differences and similarities, contributes to creating networks across the Global South.

In my choice of a comparative and multilingual approach, I also take a cue from Franco Moretti who speaks of "inter-related literatures" and invites us to go "against the grain of national historiography . . . in the form of *an experiment*."[84] Following Moretti, I consider that "world literature is not an object, it's a *problem*," which requires us to "define a unit of analysis . . . and then follow its metamorphoses in a variety of environments."[85] Yet, I also disagree with other aspects of his argument, especially his repudiation of close reading, which, according to Moretti, inevitably leads to a selection of a small number of "representative" works and thus a formation of a canon. Instead, he proposes the concept of distant reading "where distance . . . *is a condition of knowledge*: it allows you to focus on units that are much smaller or much larger than the text: devices, themes, tropes—or genres and systems. And if, between the very small and the very large, the text itself disappears, well, it is one of those cases when one can justifiably say, Less is more."[86] Being literary critics, we are confronted with the task of selecting works, whether we perform close or distant reading. In *Death of a Discipline*, Gayatri Chakravorty Spivak writes that "to withdraw in-depth language learning and close reading from Comparative Literature when it moves to the global South is to decide that the only relationship the United States can have with those areas is based on considerations of security, that the critical intimacy of literary learning must remain isolationist in the Euro-US."[87] Furthermore, in the absence of close reading, Moretti arrives at problematic conclusions about the entirety of Third World literature. Consequently, I identify cross-cultural tropes and tendencies while preserving close reading as the primary tool of literary analysis. My corpus is thus not at all comprehensive; many other works could have been included. *Precarious Crossings* is only a beginning, an initial step toward a different way of thinking about trans-Atlantic immigrant narratives.

My comparative approach builds on existing discussions surrounding globalization, world literature, and mono/plurilingualism. The debate around world literature was given a higher profile than ever before in 2007 with the publication in *Le Monde* of a manifesto entitled "Pour une 'littérature-monde' en français" ["Toward a 'World Literature' in French"] followed by a collection of essays under the same name, edited by Michel Le Bris.[88] Endorsed by forty-four writers, the manifesto calls for, at the same time as it proclaims, the end of Francophonie and its replacement with a "littérature-monde" in French. In its hyphenated form, "littérature-monde" is highly influenced by Edouard Glissant's concept of the "Tout-Monde," which he defines as "le monde actuel tel qu'il est dans sa diversité et dans son chaos" [today's world as it is in its diversity and chaos].[89]

The manifesto gestures in two directions. First, it elaborates a critique of the neocolonial aspect of Francophonie, which still posits the metropole at the center of the Francophone world. Signatories object to the fact that writers from former colonies are continuously marginalized under the category "Francophone," their works considered inferior to the "French" canon. This argument inscribes itself into an ongoing French/Francophone debate. In 2006, Amin Maalouf, a Lebanese writer who a year later signed the manifesto, published (also in *Le Monde*) an article entitled "Contre la Littérature Francophone" [Against Francophone literature].[90] Maalouf argues that it is time to dispense with sterile and discriminatory literary categories such as South/North, black/white, periphery/metropole, all of them contained within the Francophone/French opposition. He further contends that this move has already occurred in the Spanish- and English-speaking worlds, where one can no longer distinguish between Hispanophone and Spanish, Anglophone and

English writers.[91] France should learn from other former colonial powers and end these discriminatory practices.

The second direction distances this "new" literature from the tradition of structuralism and poststructuralism. Refuting literature's posited self-referentiality, contemporary transnational works return to the world, the referent, history. This argument can also best be understood in relation to the French literary sphere. For a long time, writers from former colonies have lamented the fact that their works are often classified as inferior because they are read as ethnological texts, social documents, considered not "literary" enough, where literariness is associated with highly self-referential and linguistically experimental texts. The return to the referent as a distinguishing factor of the new world literature can thus be read as an attempt to challenge the supposed nonliterary value of Francophone texts. The signatories contend that their literariness emerges *from* their specific engagement with the world.

But the most surprising aspect of the manifesto is its monolingualism. Jean-Pierre Cavaille notes that a world literature in French is an oxymoron.[92] While declaring the death of Francophonie, the signatories are in fact not at all dispensing with the category but merely reframing it in order to be more inclusive of writers outside of the metropole. While the Anglophone and the Hispanophone contexts are mentioned, it is merely as models to the French-speaking world, since no attempts are made to establish any lateral links with writers writing in other languages. The manifesto advocates for a deconstruction of binaries, yet the categories of the French-, Spanish-, and English-speaking worlds remain unquestioned, and the principal relation is still between the metropole and its former colonies.[93] Whereas critics have noted the contradictions inherent in concepts such as Francophone or Latin American globalization and world literature, and strides have been made toward building more comparative frameworks, significant work remains. *Precarious Crossings* proposes to bring these conversations one step further. Instead of simply using the Francophone, Anglophone, and Hispanophone contexts as models for one another, I strive to place them into a productive dialogue.[94]

In the first half of the book, I examine the intersection between the memory of the Atlantic trade and the experience of Atlantic neoliberalization. In the second half, I extend the Atlantic paradigm beyond the afterlives of slavery to demonstrate, following Yogita Goyal, "how questions of Black Atlantic modernity and circulation intersect with newly ascendant conceptual frames."[95] In *Precarious Crossings,* these ascendant conceptual frames include intra-Caribbean immigration, special economic zones, and the global effects of the never-ending war on terror. Each chapter traces connections between inventive strategies that stretch or subvert literary conventions and new perspectives on global neoliberalization and precarity. The first chapter analyzes the connection between past and present precarities, the second the relation between debt and precarity, and the third the relation between precarity and multinational corporations. To formally address these questions, authors like Maryse Condé and Bessora submit the conventions of the novel to significant experimentation. The aesthetic turn of some contemporary authors toward opacity and its relation to precarity, is the focus of the fourth chapter. The final chapter considers how the shared condition of precarity can serve as a basis for an alliance between immigrants and so-called terrorists, and a new literary language.

In the first chapter, "The Atlantic Revisited," I analyze the textual super-position of the question of contemporary migration, circulation of capital and goods on the one hand; and the Middle Passage, the memory of slavery and the Atlantic trade on the other. I focus in particular on works by Sylvie Kandé (*La quête infinie de l'autre rive: épopée en trois chants*, 2011), Maryse Condé (*Histoire de la femme cannibale*, 2003), and Caryl Phillips (*The Atlantic Sound*, 2000). The three authors insist on the importance of historicizing global neo-liberalization, questioning the idea of a postracial present. Yet, they also pro-pose a dynamic relation between the past and the present, where the latter is not a mere reenactment of the former. The histories of slavery and colonization have left their mark, but global neoliberalism has added new dynamics to the equation. Phillips and Condé underscore the need to constantly rethink and reinvent our comparative frameworks, instead of repeating old models like Negritude or Pan-Africanism, or striving for a return to an idealized past. They underscore the need for a new set of identifications, attentive to the functioning of global neoliberalization. Comparisons in this chapter are both geographic and temporal. Kandé proposes a new temporal link between con-temporary immigrants and historic African explorers, questioning the Middle Passage as the sole historical precedent for contemporary immigrants. As they remap the Atlantic, the authors also strain against the literary conventions of their respective genre: the detective novel, the travelogue, and an epic poem, exploring aesthetic forms that can encapsulate new lateral connections within a globalized Atlantic.

"The Indebted Immigrant" focuses on the creation of precarious, indebted immigrant workers in the global neoliberal economy through a reading of novels by Franco-Senegalese writer Fatou Diome (*Le ventre de l'Atlantique*, 2003; *Celles qui attendent*, 2010). In Diome's work, the entry of new immigrant destinations like Italy and Spain complicates the postcolonial relation between France and Senegal. Traveling and thinking between these different poles, the characters encounter indebtedness as an increasingly trans-Atlantic condition.

Debt, in fact, is one of the mechanisms that maintains precarity. In *Le ventre de l'Atlantique,* Diome considers debt through the character of Moussa, a Senegalese soccer player recruited by a French team, who has to repay his debt to his recruiter. In *Celles qui attendent,* immigration is explored from the viewpoint of those who are left behind, mothers and wives patiently waiting for the return of their sons and husbands. As the original breadwinners leave, women often resort to debt in order to sustain their families. Diome analyzes the superposition of the different dimensions of debt: leaving indebted countries, immigrants often finance their trips through debt, only to be told they "owe" the new country for this opportunity. At home, families expect them to repay a local debt by sending remittances. Neoliberal debt thus operates both at the national and individual levels, as indebted countries beget indebted local and immigrant subjects. In this chapter, immigrant debt connects the Global South to the Global North, becoming a new lens for conceptualizing the globalized Atlantic. The characters in both novels position themselves in relation to a global debt system, which also never fully defines their experiences, as they point to modes of relating that exceed the logic of debt and precarity.

Chapter 3, "How to Get Away with Murder: Multinational Corporations and Atlantic Crimes" examines the work of two contemporary writers: Swiss-Gabonese Bessora (*Petroleum,* 2004) and Chilean Roberto Bolaño (*2666,* 2004). In both novels, multinational corporations are at the center of detective mysteries. Multinationals exemplify the complex relationship between the national and the transnational in the age of global neoliberalization. Operating within, but also beyond and across states, they increasingly challenge national sovereignty, pointing to transnational circuits of corporate power. Often eluding both national and international jurisdiction, multinationals participate in the creation of nonaccountability zones, thus becoming a formative site for disposable subjects. It is thus not surprising that in contemporary novels, they are the site of crimes. Both authors trace global networks of neoliberal violence within a literary form I describe as the neoliberal anti-detective novel. Neoliberal crimes exceed the objectives of the traditional detective novel and the capacities of a traditional investigator. The neoliberal anti-detective novel deals with the complex questions of accountability, responsibility, and guilt in a context where the culprit is the status quo. The various Atlantic nodes are here rhyzomatically connected through crimes that remain unsolved.

In "Opacity and trans-Atlantic Citizenship," I analyze authors who have resorted to an aesthetics and ethics of opacity as a means of representing precarious subjects. The characters in the works of Marie NDiaye (*Rosie Carpe,* 2001), Yuri Herrera (*Señales que precederán al fin del mundo,* 2009), and Yolanda Arroyo Pizarro (*Los documentados,* 2005) are opaque and impenetrable, offering us no possible grounds for identification. The narrative focus in these novels shifts from the characters' interiority to the many geographical spaces that the characters traverse. I conceptualize, in this chapter, the globalized Atlantic through intersecting acts of withholding and refusal. The novels invite an ethical relation between the characters and the reader based on an acknowledgement that the other can never be fully understood. Instead of trying to "explain" their characters, these authors trace the interconnectedness of these opaque lives. I bring opacity in conversation with two other terms: refusal and disidentification. These novels move away from a more traditional model where ethics stems from the identification with a specific character. Here, the reader is invited to disidentify from a world where the privilege of some depends on the precarity of others.

In the final chapter, "Atlantic Undercommons," I focus on *United States of Banana* (2011), a postmodern and allegorical mixed-genre work by Puerto Rican writer Giannina Braschi. In the longest part of the novel, Giannina, Zarathustra, and Hamlet head to Liberty Island to free Segismundo from a dungeon situated under the Statue of Liberty. Segismundo, Puerto Rico's allegory, was imprisoned at birth by his father, the king of the United States of Banana. His crime is his very existence. In their many philosophical and theatrical debates and discussions, Segismundo, Giannina, Hamlet, and Zarathustra discuss Puerto Rico's three political options: wishy, washy, and wishy-washy (independence, statehood, or colony). In the dungeon, they encounter numerous prisoners of war, so-called terrorists, who have been detained indefinitely without a trial. In this chapter, I explore the juxtaposition of these two characters, the immigrant and the terrorist, as well as their potential solidarity based on their mutual precarity. Exchanges between these characters further lead to the creation of a new literary language, which Braschi calls "foreign speaking English." Foreign speaking English is the language of the contemporary precarious subject who engages in a creative destruction of the English from inside the language. *United States of Banana* is a literary insurrection of a multinational set of characters who are experiencing political precarity within the global state of emergency. The novel is a declaration of interdependence (rather than independence): political, philosophical, and linguistic. The state of emergency and indefinite detention without a trial have, unintentionally, created new Atlantic connections and alliances. As all the transnational characters in the novel learn to cooperate across their differences, they collectively create an experimental literary language.

Through an analysis of African, Caribbean, and Latin American writers, I read literature as a site that both represents and responds to neoliberalism and precarity. As their immigration patterns exceed the route that connects the (post)colonial periphery to the (post)colonial center, characters from different sides of the Atlantic confront a common condition—global neoliberalization lived as precarity. New and often unusual Atlantic connections also become an opportunity for contemporary authors to globalize multiple literary genres, including the travelogue, the epic, and the detective novel. Through their aesthetic choices, the authors in my corpus propose different models of comparative thinking that allow us think across identity categories, while being attentive to the ways in which precarity operates differentially across them.

CHAPTER 1

The Atlantic Revisited

In 2011, Franco-Senegalese author Sylvie Kandé published an epic poem that imagines the fate of Mansa Aboubakar II of Mali, who in the early 1300s, with two thousand canoes, embarked on a voyage to America.[1] In her "epic poem in three cantos," Kandé envisions the possible outcomes of this voyage, as well as its historical and philosophical relation to contemporary African immigration to Europe. The poem addresses alternative trajectories and stories contained within the Atlantic, specifically, one where an expedition from the imperial Mali reached the Americas before Columbus. The poem unravels on the Atlantic; the sounds of past and present roaming oars are textually superposed as the ending portrays the present attempts of young Malians to reach "the other shore." Kandé's work is emblematic of a broader interest in contemporary writing to reimagine the Atlantic from new vantage points.

While over the past few decades many Francophone writers created their immigrant fictions from the purview of Paris, this is no longer predominantly the case. Various authors, including Kandé and Guadeloupean Maryse Condé, have recently written about the Atlantic from their homes, not in Paris, but in New York City. The increased presence of the United States contributes to a reframing of the Atlantic from a triangular to a multinodal space. In this chapter, I analyze this displacement of the figure of the Atlantic triangle in three contemporary works: Maryse Condé's *Histoire de la femme cannibale* (2003) [*The Story of the Cannibal Woman*, 2007], Caryl Phillips's *The Atlantic*

Sound (2000), and Sylvie Kandé's *La quête infinie de l'autre rive: épopée en trois chants* (2011) [*The Never-Ending Quest for the Other Shore: Epic Poem in Three Cantos*]. The authors of this chapter reevaluate Atlantic pasts in light of the neoliberal present and reframe the present in light of its past. The African continent is here at the center of past and present flows of people, capital, and goods. Yet these flows also exceed the continent and the framework of the Black Atlantic to forge new South–South connections.

A few years before Kandé, Guadeloupean Maryse Condé wrote *The Story of the Cannibal Woman*, a novel set in South Africa, symbol of a globalized Atlantic. Through Rosélie, a Guadeloupean woman living in Cape Town, Condé reassesses the history of the Atlantic in light of global neoliberalization. Similarly, at the very beginning of the twenty-first century, Caryl Phillips, an Anglophone writer, wrote a book-length essay that addresses the changing configuration of the Atlantic episteme. Condé's and Phillips's lives and careers bear some resemblance. From her native island of Guadeloupe, Condé moved to France and then to Guinea, Ghana, and Senegal, in order to finally settle in the United States (via Guadeloupe). As an infant, Phillips arrived from St. Kitts to England, where he grew up and studied. After teaching at universities in Ghana, Sweden, Singapore, Barbados, and India, he also opted for the United States. While Phillips's earlier novels deal with the postcolonial relationship between England and its black population, his later works—like *The Atlantic Sound*—take on a more global perspective, addressing what he calls "the new world order."

All three works explore the relation between current forms of marginalization and past violences. In an interview, Condé explains: "While my first books depict the paradisiacal nature of the Antilles that people dream of, *La Belle Créole* is in the here and now, as is *Histoire de la femme cannibale*. It's very hard to write about the present. You don't have all the artifices that allow you to seduce the reader. You really need to shine a harsh light on things."[2] Condé shines a harsh light on things through interweaving reflections on the past and the present. Kandé's and Phillips's works similarly imagine different Atlantic pasts to propose alternative framings of the present. In *The Atlantic Sound*, historical Atlantic crossings are overlain with contemporary trips to Ghana, the United States, and even Israel. The here and the now is ultimately at stake for all three authors.

The authors of this chapter underscore the importance of thinking *comparatively*, across space and time. Condé and Phillips highlight the need to historicize global neoliberalization, establishing a link with earlier phases of capitalism, colonialism, and slavery. Condé criticizes South Africa's belief that it has overcome the past, which, supposedly, no longer seeps into the present.

Yet, the present is also not a mere repetition of the past. The three authors represent the African continent in a constant process of transformation at the center of contemporary flows of people and ideas. Twentieth- and twenty-first-century intellectual movements crisscross the African continent, including Negritude, Pan-Africanism, and Afropolitanism. Past violences shape current inequities—they are responsible for Condé's and Phillips's nonbelonging—yet they do not determine the present. To borrow from Yogita Goyal, the three works perform both "an acknowledgement of the transformative impact of the Atlantic paradigm and . . . an invitation to explore new directions and map new geographical, historical, and conceptual itineraries."[3]

Condé's South Africa, with its violence, its difficulty dealing with the past, but also its many multicultural encounters, becomes a metaphor for the contemporary world. Unusual encounters between multinational characters allow for new comparisons, which are not always easy and often fail. Throughout her career, Condé has expressed skepticism toward any unifying ideology that oversimplifies differences within the African diaspora, including Negritude and Pan-Africanism.[4] In *The Story of the Cannibal Woman*, Afropolitanism comes under her literary scrutiny. Yet, her criticisms do not amount to a rejection of comparisons. In "Order, Disorder, Freedom and the West Indian Writer," she objects to the assumption that a Caribbean writer must turn toward either Europe or a mythical African past: "West Indians should be as changing and evolving as the islands themselves. . . . A writer confined to a small and isolated village of the West Indies is free to dream of 'Another Land' and make of it the subject of his/her fiction. Creative imagination goes beyond the limits of reality and soars to areas of its own choice."[5] In *The Story of the Cannibal Woman*, Condé engages in extending the realm of acceptable comparisons. A Caribbean writer has the right to soar and imagine the present of, for instance, South Africa.

In *The Atlantic Sound*, Phillips criticizes Pan-Africanists from the US and "Hebrew Israelites" (a group of African Americans who have settled in Israel) for falling into pregiven forms and holding onto past identifications instead of working to constantly rethink and reinvent them. This is not an outright dismissal of Pan-Africanism, a movement that, as Anne W. Gulick points out, "serves as a vital corrective to definitions of globalization that conceive of movement as occurring exclusively within the binary structures of North and South, metropole and periphery."[6] It is rather an invitation to continue updating, extending, and nuancing our comparative frameworks. James Clifford notes that diaspora is based on "identifications not identities, acts of relationship rather than pregiven forms: this *tradition* is a network of partially connected histories, a persistently displaced and reinvented time/space of crossings."[7] Phillips is similarly looking for identifications instead of identities, which, in the age of global neoliberalization often extend beyond the Black Atlantic. For both authors, the role of art is, precisely, to constantly rethink and reinvent identifications.

In Kandé's poem, the comparison is temporal, between fourteenth-century Malian explorers and contemporary immigrants. The poem circumvents the Middle Passage, as it shifts from what preceded it to what came in its aftermath. Kandé questions the Middle Passage as the predominant framework for thinking about the past and present of the African continent. In the poem, the Atlantic coheres as a unit of aesthetic investigation outside of the history of European colonialism, as contemporary immigrants follow in the footsteps of historic African expeditions.[8]

I dedicate the first chapter to these authors because their critical engagement with the necessity and difficulty of comparative thinking inspire the project as a whole. Gulick contends that "for Condé, comparativism is itself a form of globalization, the creative construction of connections across space and time that *enables* the type of critical practice in which she herself is so heavily invested."[9] The creative construction of connections across space and time is similarly my objective in *Precarious Crossings*.

RECONFIGURING THE TRIANGLE: SOUTH AFRICA AS DESTINATION (NOT HOMELAND)

The rethinking and remapping of the Atlantic triangle have long been a part of the Francophone literary tradition. Whereas the effects of the triangular trade undoubtedly extend beyond abolition, decolonization, and departmentalization, Christopher Miller observes that "the figure of the triangle is not all-encompassing: as a mercantilist plan it could not be fully enforced over time and space, and as a projection of the French nation-state it invited resistance from within, below, and outside."[10] In his *Cahier d'un retour au pays natal* [*Notebook of a Return to the Native Land*], Césaire rewrites the French Atlantic, directly connecting the Caribbean and Africa, without the intermediary of Europe. The gaze shifts from Europe to Africa as a lens for understanding the Caribbean. Edouard Glissant complements Césaire's "retour" with a "détour," a ruse, an initial turning away and traveling beyond. This shift, he argues, is only gainful if it concludes with "a rising acknowledgment of the new land,"[11] a temporal and spatial grounding in contemporary Caribbean reality. *Hérémakhonon* (1976), Maryse Condé's first novel, challenges the myth of the return to Africa as a way to reclaim one's heritage. It further questions the idea of a preexisting solidarity based on a common fate imposed by the trans-Atlantic slave trade. The protagonist, Véronica, is a young Guadeloupean woman who decides to move from France to Africa in order to find her "roots." Miller argues that "the novel articulates a deeper objection to the conflation of time and space. Seeking to recapture the past, to find your own ancestors or those of mankind in general, by traveling in the present—a classic mind-set of Europeans in Africa—is delusional."[12] *Hérémakhonon* has paved the way for Condé's later work. If *Hérémakhonon* still operates within the triangular paradigm, Condé's subsequent novels depict a more multidimensional Atlantic space. *Moi, Tituba, sorcière—: noire de Salem* (1986) [*I, Tituba, Black Witch of Salem*] centers on a young female slave from Barbados, one of the first to be tried in the seventeenth-century witch trials in Salem, Massachusetts *Célanire coucoupé* (2000) [*Who Slashed Celanire's Throat?*] focuses on Célanire, a Guadeloupean oblate (nun who has not taken her vows yet), who at the beginning of the twentieth century travels from Lyon to the Ivory Coast to pursue missionary work. The novel takes place across the Ivory Coast, Guadeloupe, Guiana, and Peru.

The Story of the Cannibal Woman is in many ways a rewriting of *Hérémakhonon*, three decades after the fact. Condé has commented upon this analogy: "I believe that in the end, you always say the same thing. I make an effort to vary the settings and to include a diversity of characters, but it seems to me that if you look at Véronica (from the first book, *Heremakhonon*) and compare her to Rosélie (from *Histoire de la femme cannibale*), they aren't very different. My books always deal with women who have trouble living their lives."[13] The two may not be very different, but they are also not quite the same. Rosélie knows what Véronica needed to learn: return is impossible. She no longer travels to an unnamed African country in search of her ancestors. Instead, she decides to settle in a globalized South Africa.

Rosélie notes the restructuring of a no-longer Francophone Atlantic triangle: "Le triangle s'était inversé. Avant le Cap, le *Christ-Roi* avait abordé à La Pointe où il s'était chargé d'autres bois que des bois d'ébène" (52) ["The triangular trade had been reversed. Before arriving in Cape Town, the Christ-Roi had anchored at La Pointe, where it had replaced its ebony cargo with other species" (38)].[14] South Africa in *The Story of the Cannibal Woman* is not the equivalent of the unnamed African country in *Hérémakhonon*. It does not provide access to a pre-Atlantic trade past; rather, it has become a destination. The reimagining is twofold: Condé is rewriting the myth of the return to Africa as well as the contemporary immigrant narrative. The two are connected, as South Africa becomes a hub for contemporary immigrants.

Rosélie lives in Cape Town with Stephen, an Englishman who works as a literature professor at the local university. The novel unfolds as a crime mys-

tery; one evening, after leaving to buy cigarettes, Stephen is mysteriously murdered. Rosélie first interprets Stephen's death as a consequence of Cape Town's
pervading street violence. Yet, as the plot progresses, we learn that Stephen
had various homosexual affairs and that an ex-lover's boyfriend first black-
mailed and then murdered him. In the aftermath of Stephen's death, Rosélie
attempts to reconstruct her life by working as a healer, primarily helping civil
war refugees who have trouble sleeping. Descriptions of contemporary South
African society are interspersed with Rosélie's memories of her childhood
in Guadeloupe and her life with Stephen. Another narrative emerges within
the novel, the story of Fiéla, a South African woman accused of killing her
husband and stashing his remains in the freezer (these accusations are never
proven). Rosélie begins to conflate her identity with Fiéla's, no longer able to
distinguish who is speaking.

Burdened by the legacies of the apartheid era, South Africa becomes a
transnational site of encounter for characters from around the Atlantic. Episodes taking place in New York reflect on the internal divisions of the category black, further complicating the practice of black transnationalism.
The novel poses as a question, how can we think across Guadeloupe, France,
South Africa, and New York? Cape Town is a globalized, multicultural space
where people from different African, European, and Caribbean countries have
found a home. After meeting a new client from Rwanda, Rosélie comments:
"Encore une histoire d'immigré! Dans ce pays, tout le monde en déballait,
des cocasses, des ridicules, des rocambolesques, plus abracadabrantes les unes
que les autres" (21) ["Yet another immigrant story! In this country everyone's
got one up his sleeve; some are comical, others ridiculous or grotesque, each
one more unlikely than the next" (9)]. Condé's novel contextualizes the African continent not merely as a homogenous source of emigration, but rather
as a heterogeneous space traversed by diverse migratory routes, resulting in
the formation of an African cosmopolitan (Afropolitan) culture. Yet, Condé
also warns against an uncritical adherence to Afropolitanism as a replacement
and supposed progression from Negritude and Pan-Africanism. In the novel,
Afropolitanism is predicated upon specific class belonging. The Story of the
Cannibal Woman, in fact, points to a disjuncture between three co-existing
narratives: an Afropolitan Cape Town, the stories of civil war refugees, and
the history of slavery and apartheid.

AFROPOLITANS AND REFUGEES

Afropolitanism as a concept reached a wide audience when in 2005 Taiye
Selasi published her essay, "Bye-Bye Babar" in The LIP magazine. Selasi draws

a portrait of Afropolitans; young, artistic, and multilingual, they come from Dakar, Abidjan, Lagos and Accra, and live and work in Europe and the United States:

> They (read: we) are Afropolitans—the newest generation of African emigrants, coming soon or collected already at a law firm/chem lab/jazz lounge near you. You'll know us by our funny blend of London fashion, New York jargon, African ethics, and academic successes. Some of us are ethnic mixes, e.g. Ghanaian and Canadian, Nigerian and Swiss; others merely cultural mutts: American accent, European affect, African ethos. Most of us are multilingual: in addition to English and a Romantic or two, we understand some indigenous tongue and speak a few urban vernaculars.[15]

Selasi further traces the genealogy of this new generation who are "not citizens, but Africans of the world." It all began in the 1960s with a brain drain, when a class of highly educated people from various African countries decided to leave the continent and move to the US, Canada, and Britain. The Afropolitans are this generation's offspring. Some were born in Africa and educated abroad; others, born abroad, spend their summers in their parents' country. Even better educated than their parents, they are not afraid to "complicate Africa." They strain against media's portrayals of Africa in order to construct their selves in relation to multiple histories, geographies, and languages: "Ultimately, the Afropolitan must form an identity along at least three dimensions: national, racial, cultural—with subtle tensions in between."[16] Republished in several magazines, the essay went viral. Since then, various journals and art collectives including the *Afropolitan* magazine (published out of South Africa), have adopted the term Afropolitan.

Achille Mbembe has further theorized Afropolitanism. Mbembe argues that three tendencies have dominated African discourse of the past fifty years: anticolonial nationalism in its many variants, African socialism, and Pan-Africanism.[17] Over the past few decades, all three movements have lost perspective of the globalizing realities and turned into rigid, theoretical, academic discourses. According to Mbembe, the first problem arises from the equation between African and black. This association does not take into account the very complex, shifting historical reality of the African continent. In their attempt to define who the African is, political and cultural critics forget the immigration from Europe, Asia, and the Middle East. They overlook the history of the Malays, Indians, Syrians, Lebanese, and Pakistanis, who for myriad reasons including conquest, trade, and political persecutions came and settled in Africa (especially South Africa). The African continent has thus always existed at the interstices of immersion and dispersion, of the arrival and departure of various linguistic and cultural groups through slavery, economic migration, and resettlement. Mbembe names this reality "the worlds-in-movement." In opposition to different forms of "nativism," Mbembe proposes Afropolitanism, a cultural movement that positions fluidity and cultural interchange at the center of African history: "Afropolitanism is not the same as Pan-Africanism or *négritude*. Afropolitanism is an aesthetic and a particular poetic of the world. It is a way of being in the world, refusing on principle any form of victim identity—which does not mean that it is not aware of the injustice and violence inflicted on the continent and its people by the law of the world."[18] Unlike Selasi, Mbembe does not place the origin of Afropolitanism in the 1960s, instead integrating it into a long-term history of the continent.

Afropolitanism has also incited sharp criticism, particularly in relation to the capitalist commodification of the term and its reduction to product consumption. In fact, Mbembe ends his essay by associating the figure of the Afropolitan with the new art professional, underscoring a specific class belonging. He further places the center of "a new form of African modernity" in Johannesburg, due to its "multiple racial legacies, a vibrant economy, a liberal democracy, a culture of consumerism that partakes directly of the flows of globalization."[19] The problematic associations here are many, namely between globalization, consumption, and Afropolitanism. The assumption that liberal democracy serves as a vehicle for a less oppressive transnational identity goes unquestioned.

To what extent are transnational cultural movements like Afropolitanism serving transnational capital, which, for the past three decades, has also encouraged a dissociation from the nation? In guise of an answer, Stephanie Bosch Santana analyzes Binyavanga Wainaina's address, "I am a Pan-Africanist, not an Afropolitan," delivered in 2012 in the UK at the African Studies Association conference, to outline the limits of Afropolitanism: "Afropolitanism has become the marker of crude cultural commodification—a phenomenon increasingly 'product driven,' design focused, and 'potentially funded by the West.' Through an Afropolitan lens, 'travel is easy' and 'people are fluid.'"[20] Bosch Santana uses the example of the *Afropolitan* magazine, which includes articles about fashion, carpentry, and gardening as well as numerous product advertisements. The section on lifestyle is juxtaposed to business articles on female entrepreneurs, explaining how to be money savvy. In a 2015 issue, the features and columns section included debates on the South Carolina massacre and an article on African women's history. The juxtaposition between lifestyle and current events mobilizes contemporary African diaspora politics to market and sell an Afropolitan lifestyle. Along with Bosch Santana's piece, other critical articles appeared, including "The Afropolitan Must Go"[21] and "'Afropolitanism': Africa without Africans (II)," which argues that Western art criticism continues to favor African artists living in Western countries at the expense of artists and art produced on the continent.[22] This discourse still links globalized art to New York and Paris and undermines the importance of "place" as a concept. It further ignores the unequal transnational mobility of people with European/US vs. African passports. In 2011, a collection of essays entitled *Negotiating Afropolitanism: Essays on Borders and Spaces in Contemporary African Literature and Folklore* tried to recuperate the term, positioning Afropolitanism as an overcoming of "afro-pessimism," the assumption that the continent and its populations are trapped in the never-ending cycle of poverty, corruption, and violence.[23] In opposition, Afropolitanism presents a new "way of being African in the world,"[24] one that contributes to the creation of global culture rather than serving as its negative consequence. The collection aims to return the discourse on Africa to Africa by engaging in concrete examples of the practice of Afropolitanism on the continent, thus responding to the "Africa without Africans" critique.

Condé preserves the multifaceted view of Africa promoted by Afropolitanism while underscoring class and gender dynamics within the movement. The novel rethinks the extent to which this new cosmopolitan culture has led to increased communication among marginalized cultures. In *Death of a Discipline,* Gayatri Chakravorty Spivak argues that *Hérémakhonon* underscores "the lack of communication within and among the immense heterogeneity of the subaltern cultures of the world" as an "important infrastructural problem of the restricted permeability of global culture."[25] Communication as a problem persists in the twenty-first century. In *The Story of the Cannibal Woman,* in an increasingly cosmopolitan Cape Town, Rosélie's patients, mostly survivors of African civil conflicts, seek her help because they are oftentimes unable to relate their experience. A disjuncture characterizes the flows of the cosmopolitan class and those of war refugees, as the political and social precarity of the refugees confronts the multicultural lifestyle of the Afropolitan class. The refugees in the novel speak through Rosélie (a member of the Afropolitan class). This dynamic could be interpreted as a meta-commentary on the novel itself, since it is through Rosélie and by extension through Condé that the reader receives these accounts of precarity. In other words, precarious experiences are continuously mediated by Afropolitan works of art and Afropolitan characters. At the same time, the reader is introduced merely to bits and pieces of different refugee stories. There is thus an attempt to preserve the opacity (a concept I will discuss at length in chapter 4) of different characters and acknowledge the impossibility of telling their stories.

At the birthday celebration for Bebe Sephuma, a young poet and president of the Defense of the Negress Association, Rosélie encounters Cape Town's cosmopolitan class. She meets Bebe's partner Piotr, a Swedish artist who, like Bebe, wants to bring art to the people. With the help of a photographer, Piotr covered the city's buses with global images: "le marché de Cocody avant que les flammes l'aient dévoré, un autobus londonien bondé de sikhs enturbannés, les jonques et les restaurants flottants de Hong-Kong, la mosquée de Djenné, une caravane de chameaux traversant le désert en direction des mines de sel de Taoudénit" (74) ["the market in Cocody before it went up in flames, a London double-decker filled with turbaned Sikhs, the junks and floating restaurants of Hong Kong, the mosque at Djenné, and a caravan of camels crossing the desert on their way to the salt mines at Taoudenni" (57)]. The chosen images point to the infinite heterogeneity of the contemporary world. At the same time, they share a common characteristic, they all represent "traditional" modes of living. As such, they offer an escape from the "hypermodern" to the "premodern." Entirely uprooted from their local cultural and historical contexts, these images convey an entirely dehistoricized relation to the cultural diversity of the world. The artistic project glorifies the diversity of the globalized present, yet it is entirely devoid of the material historical conditions that have created it. This is cosmopolitan and comparative thinking gone awry, framing globalization as a mere juxtaposition of various (and variously exotic) cultural elements without any serious analysis of the power dynamics that have brought them together. Once again, the narrative points to a temporal and representational disconnection. South Africa's attempt to join the global community is predicated upon an "overcoming" of historical violence and participation in a snapshot global culture.

IS THERE A PAST TO THE NEOLIBERAL PRESENT?

Condé's Atlantic is caught in a disjuncture where the past, marked by the history of the Atlantic slave trade and apartheid, coexists with the globalized present and its ideology of progress and development. The repressed Atlantic past, including the South African apartheid and the slave trade, continually haunts the postmodern eclectic mixture of people and cultures, supposedly beyond the question of national belonging and racial affiliation. Shocked by the fact that a former prison, Robben Island, could become a tourist destination, Rosélie comments: "Que faire du passé? Quel cadavre encombrant! Devons-nous l'embaumer et, ainsi idéalisé, l'autoriser à gérer notre destin? Devons-nous l'enterrer, à la sauvette, comme un malpropre et l'oublier radicalement? Devons nous le métamorphoser?" (142) ["What do you do with the past? What a cumbersome corpse! Should we embalm it, idealize it, and let it take over our destiny? Or should we hurriedly bury it as a disgrace and forget it altogether? Should we metamorphose it?" (120–21)]. The novel contends with these three options. On the one hand is the idealization of the African past and the overdetermination of the Atlantic present as an endless repetition of the Middle Passage. On the other, the insistence on a "postracial" present of reconciliation promotes a disavowal of the past's present. South Africa serves here again as a metaphor for the world. It strives to bury the past, under a glorification of liberal democracy and free markets, supposed to substitute past inequalities with a free market of lifestyles. Yet the past continues to resurface. Simone, Rosélie's Martinican friend, believes that the South African people are unsuccessfully trying "de se purger de ses frustrations et de renaître, baptisé de sang neuf sous le soleil" (66) ["to purge their frustration and be born again in a baptism of blood under the sun" (51)]. But there also exists a third option: metamorphosizing the past. Throughout the novel, Rosélie wavers between these different possibilities. Immediately after Stephen's death, Rosélie does not want to leave Cape Town, claiming that she has no present aside from their past together. Her attachment to the past and her inability to live in the present mirror South Africa's unsuccessful attempts to inter the past. However, Rosélie's painting at the end of the novel, the *Cannibal Woman*, gestures toward the third option: a refusal to either live in the past or to bury it. Instead, she finally decides to face the past in order to contribute to a shaping of a different present through art.

The novel begins with a reference to the Atlantic slave trade and the question of memory. The description of a dormant Cape Town is interrupted by sirens from ferries transporting tourists to Robben Island, "ex-île-camp de concentration metamorphosée en attraction touristique internationale" (11) ["once a concentration camp, now transformed into an international tourist attraction" (1)]. One of Rosélie's patients is Dawid Fagwela, a former Robben Island prisoner, now a tourist guide: "Ce n'est pas tous les jours qu'un prisonnier politique se transforme en guide touristique, c'est-à-dire qu'un homme voyage de l'enfer au paradis, en l'espace d'une vie" (38) ["It's not every day that a political prisoner turns into a tourist guide and travels from hell to paradise in a single lifetime" (25)]. Like most of her clients, Dawid has trouble sleeping; he often wakes up in terror, uncertain whether apartheid has ended. The transformation of Robben Island into a tourist site raises the question of the commodification of historical memory.

Preventing historical erasure through the commemoration of slavery and apartheid is a crucial task. At the same time, in the novel, the museification of the prison turns it into a site of visual and physical consumption, creating a strange dialectic between the absence and presence of the past. It is still there, in the form of a museum, yet it is contained within the closed-off space of the tourist infrastructure, at a distance from the everyday reality of Cape Town. Robben Island is immediately placed in a comparative Atlantic context through an analogy with Thomas Jefferson's house in the United States: "En Virginie, elle avait visité Monticello, demeure du président Thomas Jefferson. Touche finale à la couleur d'époque, des Africains-Americains engoncés dans des casaques vendaient des souvenirs dans les communs abritant une boutique" (119) ["She had visited Monticelli, Thomas Jefferson's house in Virginia. The finishing touches to historical color had been the African-Americans ensconced in smocks selling souvenirs in the slave quarters' gift shop" (98)]. The African American souvenir sellers, in an analogous manner to the ex-prisoner tourist guide at Robben Island, serve as markers of "authenticity" of the histories that the museum aims to preserve. The present (i.e., living subjects) is used to authenticate a past that is supposedly entirely distinct from the present and can only be accessed through the sanctified museum form. In other words, the present is there to grant access to a past that is supposedly otherwise inaccessible. This configuration creates a strange dialectic where a present body represents an absent history.

Andreas Huyssen explains the role of museums in our contemporary times: "Memory and musealization together are called upon to provide a bulwark against obsolescence and disappearance, to counter our deep anxiety about the speed of change and the ever-shrinking horizons of time and space."[26] Whether museums can respond to our need for spatial and temporal anchoring is questionable, since "musealization itself is sucked into the vortex of an ever-accelerating circulation of images, spectacles, events, and is thus always in danger of losing its ability to guarantee cultural stability over time."[27] Our anxiety stems from the unprecedented speed of change but also our conflicting relationship to the past and the future. While the museum preserves the past, it also establishes clear boundaries with the present. Tourists can observe the past in a noninteractive and detached manner, as something that once took place, but that no longer directly affects their lives. The movement is multifold: memory and museums respond to our inability to "keep up" with continuous transformations by giving access to a more "stable" past. Yet, they also mark a rupture with the past. South Africa, in the novel, positions the neoliberal present as an "overcoming" of apartheid. Rosélie's relationship with Fiéla offers a different mode of comparative thinking, one grounded in a dialogic relationship between the past and the present.

Race, class, national belonging, or interracial marriage complicate Rosé-lie's friendships with other female characters. Only with Fiéla, whom Rosélie has never met, can she identify. Fiéla's stepson accuses her of having killed his father. Her trial becomes a media sensation. It is, however, a silent trial as Fiéla does not utter a word. Fiéla is ultimately sentenced to fifteen years, yet, on the day of her prison transfer, she commits suicide, without, once again, saying a word. Rosélie begins to conflate her story with Fiéla's; in one of her many imaginary dialogues with the South African woman on trial, she says: "Ne me cache rien. Tu le sais bien, quand tu dis 'je,' c'est 'nous' que tu signi-fies" (105) ["Don't keep anything from me. You know full well when you say 'I' you mean 'us'" (86)]. When Fiéla commits suicide, Rosélie wonders whether, in the spirit of complete identification, she should follow the same route. In the end, she decides not to : "Fiéla, tout bien réfléchi, tu ne m'as pas donné l'exemple. Tu as choisi de mourir. Or, ce n'est pas mourir qu'il faut mourir. C'est vivre qu'il faut vivre. S'accrocher à la vie. Obstinément" (349–50) ["Fiéla, all things considered, you didn't set an example. You chose to die. But it's not a question of dying. It's a question of living. Clinging to life. Obstinately" (309)]. Instead, Rosélie resolves to stay in Cape Town and return to painting. Though she previously had trouble naming her paintings, a new title emerges quickly: *Cannibal Woman*. In this respect, the ending diverges from *Hérémakhonon*, where Véronica, entirely disappointed by her experience in Africa, returns to France. As Kathryn Lachman argues: "Condé narrates Rosélie's progressive transformation from a broken, dependent, grieving woman into a determined artist and medium in full possession of her personal history and experience."[28] This progressive transformation, it is important to note, happens compara-tively, in relation to someone else's story. Yet, it is when Rosélie decides not to follow Fiéla's fate that she completes the painting. In other words, only once she differentiates herself from Fiéla can she tell their story. Rosélie moves away from a full identification with the past, and with Fiéla, toward an understand-ing of the present and of herself as a product of interconnected (hi)stories. These histories shape her present, yet, ultimately, they do not determine it.

Mireille Rosello introduces the term "post-cannibalism" to characterize *The Story of the Cannibal Woman*. The novel, Rosello argues, refuses to instru-mentalize cannibalism. It doesn't idealize cannibalism, it doesn't return the accusation against a broad category of the West, and it rejects the idea that it cannibalizes other texts. On the contrary, it "insists that *all* the characters, including the narrator, are cannibals, but cannibals who wish they weren't so and who can be saved from their cannibalism by each other."[29] Rosélie and Stephen compare themselves to cannibals who wish they were not cannibals, and who have been saved from their cannibalism by each other. Other characters judge Rosélie's relationship with a white man, unable to perceive the generative dimensions of this peculiar connection.

Throughout the novel, Rosélie refuses any national, political, racial, or gender affiliations. When Manuel Desprez, one of her friends, asks whether she will return home now that Stephen is dead, she responds: "Chez moi? Si seulement je savais où c'est. Oui, le hasard m'a fait naître à la Guadeloupe. . . . À part cela, j'ai vécu en France. Un homme m'a emmenée puis larguée dans un pays d'Afrique. De là, un autre m'a emmenée aux Etats-Unis, puis rame-née en Afrique pour m'y larguer à présent, lui aussi, au Cap. Ah, j'oubliais, j'ai aussi vécu au Japon" (43) ["Home? If only I knew where home was. Chance had it I was born in Guadeloupe. . . . Apart from that, I have lived in France. A man took me to Africa, then left me. Another took me to the United States, then brought me back to Africa, and he too left me stranded, this time in Cape Town. Oh, I forgot I've also lived in Japan" (30)]. Throughout the novel, Rosélie yearns for a world with no national and racial divisions: "Peut-être son rêve d'un monde où les différences seraient abolies reflétait-il son dénue-ment? Trahissait-il un désir d'aligner tout le monde sur la même tabula rasa qu'elle?" (293) ["Perhaps she dreamed the world would be one because of her own destitution? Did it betray a desire to align everybody on the same tabula rasa as herself?" (258)]. Rosélie's desire for a world with no differences echoes South Africa's attempt to simply forget and compartmentalize its history. As the plot unravels, Rosélie realizes that this is neither possible nor necessarily desirable. Rather, a different mode of historical understanding and historical possibility emerges. Toward the end of the novel, Rosélie states: "On a beau faire, le monde est un linge mal repassé dont on ne peut corriger les faux plis" (329) ["Whatever we do, the world is like badly ironed laundry, impossible to get the creases out" (290)]. This is a fairly different understanding of the world from the one where national belonging, race, and gender simply do not mat-ter. It is one where the "creases" are durable but can also serve as grounds for comparison and solidarity. Her decision, at the end of the novel, to remain in South Africa is a refusal of her initial attitude of national detachment. Instead, Rosélie decides to embed herself, and her art, in a specific historical and geo-graphical context. This is not, however, an opting for the local in opposition to and defiance of a more cosmopolitan lifestyle. Rather, it is a more histori-cally and geographically grounded understanding of the globalized present.

The transition from the personal to the historical and political also occurs in regards to Fiéla. Initially, Rosélie bases the identification to Fiéla on per-sonal circumstances: both abandoned by their husbands, both left to strive for themselves. As time passes, Rosélie begins to understand Fiéla's story in relation to the history of South Africa. Lewis Sithole, the inspector in charge of the case, comments: "Le ministère public est sur les dents. Il veut qu'on la juge au plus vite et que nous en fassions un exemple" (104) ["The public prosecutor's office is under enormous pressure. They want us to bring it to trial as soon as possible and make an example out of it" (85)]. Furthermore, in front of the courthouse, while Fiéla's trial is in process, random passersby express their anger: "Affreux, affreux, affreux! C'est une honte pour notre pays!" (233) ["Terrible, terrible! It puts our country to shame" (203)]. Rosélie begins to realize that the history of the Atlantic and of neoliberalism unfold through and on the female body. South Africa's entry into global neoliberalization is predicated upon its adoption of certain norms of global "stability" and "propriety." Fiéla's supposed cannibalism is seen as an obstacle to South African progress, toward a modern (and "civilized") nation, and thus as a source of national shame. We can read this moment comparatively with another scene in the novel, where Stephen's mother hopes that he and Rosélie will not have any children because mixed-race children would be a shame for the family. The comparison with Fiéla stems from this shared experience of shame, from an understanding that female lives are often perceived as an obstacle to national development. Yet this is not a predetermined comparison; Rosélie's life does not end like Fiéla's. Instead, Rosélie's and Fiéla's stories become part of an interweaving network of past and present experiences that shape a continuously metamorphosizing Atlantic.

ATLANTIC WANDERINGS

Few contemporary writers are more concerned with the history of the Atlantic than Caryl Phillips, who has claimed it as his home: "I have chosen to create for myself an imaginary 'home' to live alongside the one that I am incapable of fully trusting. My increasingly precious, imaginary, Atlantic world."[30] Phillips has anchored his life and storytelling in this precious, imaginary, Atlantic world.

The Atlantic Sound (2000) is an explicit rethinking of the Atlantic paradigm. The book recounts Phillips's travels along the Atlantic slave route to Liverpool, England; Accra, Ghana; and Charleston, United States. A prologue and an epilogue frame the narrative; in the former, Phillips undertakes the journey from the Caribbean to England whereas in the latter he travels to the Negev desert in Israel. Newspaper and law reports; references to figures like W. E. B. Du Bois, Langston Hughes, and Richard Wright; and visits to slave castles in Ghana punctuate these travel narratives. The eclectic assemblage of characters parallels the multiplicity of destinations, as we encounter a nineteenth-century trader from the Gold Coast in Liverpool, a young Ghanaian immigrant who gets deported from England, and a white federal judge in South Carolina who has joined the movement for civil rights. *The Atlantic Sound* is a continuation of Phillips's reflection from the 1980s and '90s, including his essay *The European Tribe* (1987). In *The European Tribe*, Phillips explores the conditions of growing up black in England and the resulting "double consciousness." He returns the European gaze, as he "'tribalizes' the European, decentering him/her from the self-ascribed position of 'Universal Subject of Knowledge,' and turning him/her into an object of study."[31] However, whereas *The European Tribe* focuses mostly on the relation between the old continent and its black population, the encounter with the United States and the African American literary tradition allowed Phillips to extend his thinking beyond the European framework. *The Atlantic Sound* examines the "high anxiety of belonging" in the age of global neoliberalization.

Phillips uses this expanded focus to experiment with form and genre. The book describes the narrator's journey to different destinations including England, Ghana, the United States, and Israel. The narrative combines past and present travels, historical figures with invented characters. As such, it is difficult to categorize. María Lourdes López Ropero characterizes it as a "postcolonial travelogue," a new way of approaching travel literature.[32] Whereas Phillips is indeed rethinking the travelogue as a genre, and blurring the distinctions between diaspora, immigration, and travel, he rejects the postcolonial paradigm: "The postcolonial label . . . seems to me to be redundant for geographical reasons—as I said before, it's complicated by North America and by other parts of the world, too. It's also been complicated by the fact that we're not really living in a postcolonial age—we're living in a *post*-postcolonial age— so what new word do we use, what new groupings do we get? I don't really know."[33] In his 2001 collection of essays, *A New World Order*, Phillips similarly claims that the colonial and postcolonial models have been replaced with a twenty-first-century world, which cannot resist "the claims of the migrant, the asylum seeker, or the refugee." This world is home to no one, since it promotes "one global conversation with limited participation open to all, and full participation available to none."[34] *The Atlantic Sound* is a search for new groupings, a new world order mix-genre form, combining, as Rae Ann Meriwether notes, "fictionalized history, historiography and travel narrative."[35]

The prologue of the book, entitled "Atlantic Crossing," initiates the decentering of the postcolonial St. Kitts–England relation. The book does not begin in Phillips's native island nor even in the Anglophone Caribbean, as Phillips undertakes his voyage in Guadeloupe. From Guadeloupe, Phillips travels to Dover, via Costa Rica and Guatemala. This contemporary Atlantic crossing is set against the journey of his parents, which followed the postcolonial route. In this expanded Atlantic space, new connections emerge. In fact, German officers on the ship are exploiting the Burmese crew, pointing to new power relations. Wallace, a seventy-year-old retired lawyer from Connecticut and Phillips's fellow traveler, comments upon this arrangement: "He is worried about the Burmese crew for they appear to be treated as slaves. 'They work seven days a week for about a year, then they get a pissy four months off in Burma, then back on for a year.' He explains to me that they are Buddhists. 'You know, kind of passive'" (8). While the notion of slavery immediately enters this new Atlantic context, it is also questioned as an appropriate framework. The comment is, first of all, made by a character that Phillips dislikes. The narrator further qualifies the comment by saying that they *appear* to be treated as slaves. In other words, while slavery is introduced as a comparative framework, the narrator distances himself from what risks being an ahistorical comparison that does not consider in-depth either the legacies of slavery or the situation of the Burmese crew. The remark is followed by another problematic association, that between Buddhists and passivity. We cannot use past frameworks to understand the present, the narrative suggests. During his later trip to Ghana, the narrator has an even stronger reaction when on Ghanaian television, an African American man states, "Those of our ancestors who are still enslaved in the Americas should not be forgotten" (186). This remark angers the narrator: "Who on earth is he talking about? This continual rush to overstatement is causing me to suffer from diasporan fatigue" (186). In both cases, the narrator questions "overstatements," comparisons made too easily by erasing the ambiguities of the transition from the past to the present.

At the same time, in a "local disco-cum-brothel" in Limon, Costa Rica, a bartender explains to the narrator that a week prior, "While one of the *Horncap*'s sister ships was docking, a rope that secures the ship to the quayside snapped and killed one Burmese crew member while another Burmese man lost his arm." After telling the story, the narrator remarks, the barman "shakes his head as though the sad story does not have any contemporary meaning. It has already passed into history" (11). The detail of the lost arm returns us to an association with slavery and slave punishment. Phillips thus does not exclude the possibility of thinking comparatively or across categories. Like the Middle Passage, like his parents' crossing, the violence endured by the Burmese crew is quickly relegated to the past, no longer considered relevant. While the three events bear significant differences, the relation to them is similar: they are quickly forgotten. Ultimately, Phillips poses a question similar to Condé's: how can we preserve the memory of the past, yet not conflate the present with the past? This question will guide his travels.

During his trip to Ghana, Phillips attends the annual Panafest, a festival that celebrates the intellectual and artistic achievements of the Pan-African world. Like Condé, Phillips critiques the idea that one can find lost roots and heritage by traveling to Africa. He expresses his frustration with the "people of the diaspora who expect the continent to solve whatever psychological problems they possess. People of the diaspora who dress the part, have their hair done, buy beads, and fill their spiritual 'fuel tank' in preparation for the return journey to 'Babylon.' They have deep wounds that need to be healed, but if 'their' Africa fails them in any way, if 'their' Africa disappoints, then they will immediately accuse 'these Africans' of catering to the white man. The same white man that they work for in New York, or Toronto, or even Jamaica. Do they not understand? Africa cannot cure. Africa cannot make anybody feel whole. Africa is not a psychiatrist" (215). The nonengagement with the present, the understanding of history as static, the attachment to old solutions and models, exasperate Phillips.

Yet, a different mode of cross-cultural engagement emerges from Phillips's encounter with Dr. Robert Lee, an African American dentist from Charleston who moved to Ghana in 1956. Phillips is initially worried that Dr. Lee "had stayed on past his time" (151), turning into an "African-American 'fossil'" (151). Ultimately, he concludes that Dr. Lee is the least fossilized man he has met. Dr. Lee explains that he settled in Ghana in the 1950s because he believed he had something to offer, a skill, dentistry: "Me, I never pretended to be anything other than what I am. An American living here, but you know you can get tired of translating in your mind. But at least I can do the translating" (153). Thinking about diasporic relationships through the notion of contribution stands in stark contrast to the attitude of African Americans who come to the Panafest to retrieve something from Africa. According to Dr. Lee, diasporic relationships are built through a process of translation and learning (Dr. Lee mentions that his son is in New York City learning to be an American), grounded in the understanding of contemporary power relations and one's own position within them. Preexisting expectations and assumptions generally fail (including Phillips's assumptions about Dr. Lee), yet, translation can serve as a "poietic social practice that institutes a relation at the site of incommensurability."[36] In *The Atlantic Sound,* this practice extends within but also beyond the African diaspora to, for instance, the Burmese crew.

At the Panafest, Phillips meets a group of Hebrew Israelites, African Americans influenced by the Marcus Garvey return to Africa tradition, who in 1969 have settled in the Negev desert in Israel and have formed a community composed of nearly two thousand members. In the epilogue to the book entitled "Exodus," Phillips travels to Israel to visit them. As he meets the families who have immigrated from Chicago, Washington, and New York in this desert setting that includes the flags of Israel and the desert city of Dimona, African American jazz, polygamy, and vegan food, Phillips concludes: "They have created a New World Order. . . . They tell me they have come home. To a world that does not recognize them. To a land they cannot tame" (270). Phillips questions this paradigm of return. James Clifford argues that "the centering of diasporas around an axis of origin and return overrides the specific local interactions (identifications and 'dis-identifications,' both constructive and defensive) necessary for the maintenance of diasporic social forms."[37] Phillips similarly insists on the importance of locally building and transforming diasporic relationships, instead of searching to restore lost connections. The myth of the return to Israel further prevents the acknowledgment of the violence of the Israeli state and the development of an identification between the African American and Palestinian populations. The book thus ends with, yet again, a moving away from the simple solution of return: "Remember. There were no round-trip tickets in your part of the ship. Exodus. It is futile to walk into the face of history. As futile as trying to keep the dust from one's eyes in the desert" (275). It is futile to walk in the face of history, trying to reach or recreate the past.

Like Condé, Phillips rethinks the history of the Black Atlantic in light of contemporary connections. In his interview "Other Voices," Phillips recounts his experience growing up black in England and receiving support from white teachers of immigrant origin: "So I began to understand issues of class and other forms of group solidarity, for these guys with weird names, who weren't English, seemed to be on my side. They were white, but they were on my side, so I didn't really believe that race was the thing."[38] Positing one facet of one's identity as a precondition of belonging precludes us from noticing other moments of connection. At the same time, his experience growing up black in England and his encounters with American and African diaspora writers have shaped his vision of the Atlantic. The two are not mutually exclusive. Phillips underscores the importance of the Black Atlantic paradigm for understanding his own experience while also gesturing toward connections that exceed that framework. For Phillips, affiliations are continuously fluctuating through space and time. He criticizes the petrification of identities and an enclosure into pregiven, past forms. The solution to present problems, like in Condé's novel, cannot be solved with a return to a romanticized past. Yet, I would not identify this position as mere skepticism or a rejection of cross-cultural thinking. I thus agree with Meriwether that Phillips "highlights spontaneous moments of affective or cognitive connection."[39] His mention of his

THE ATLANTIC REVISITED • 47

white schoolteachers underscores the fact that affiliations occur, sometimes in unexpected places. However, it is not enough to presuppose them theoretically; they need to be empirically built.

The ending of *The Atlantic Sound* can be juxtaposed to a moment from *Color Me English: Migration and Belonging Before and After 9/11*, published in 2011. The collection of essays begins with Phillips's memory of his time in an all-boys grammar school in the center of Leeds. He recalls the arrival of a Muslim student, Ali, his subsequent sense of isolation and loneliness because other students bullied him. Phillips tries to help Ali when other boys throw his belongings out of the school bus. Yet, after this moment of connection, their friendship does not develop any further. Phillips regrets his inability to stand in solidarity with Ali, to establish connections across their mutual loneliness. He was unable, at that moment, to build across a shared experience of nonbelonging, the mutual experience of precarity, of lacking social and economic protection. While he felt "some immigrant kinship" (6) toward Ali, their cultural differences separated them. Phillips experienced racism yet, unlike Ali, he was familiar with English cultural practices. Unable to bridge the cultural divide between him and Ali in real life, Phillips turned to writing to do so. Through fiction, Phillips believes, we can identify new, not-yet-realized connections: "I believe passionately in the moral capacity of fiction to wrench us out of our ideological burrows and force us to engage with a world that is clumsily transforming itself, a world that is peopled with individuals we might otherwise never meet in our daily lives."[40] Fiction allows for a search for an always-evolving set of Atlantic identifications—a search further pursued by Sylvie Kandé.

IMMIGRANTS, EXPLORERS, AND EPIC HEROES

Each canto of Kandé's poem offers a different possibility for Atlantic history: in the first, Aboubakar II never reaches the shores of the "New World," setting the foundations for history as it is today. A different version opens a new possibility: the expedition reached American shores and encountered Native American populations, gesturing toward the possibility of a never-recounted Atlantic history. In the final part, in an echo of past crossings, contemporary African immigrants are trying to reach European shores. *La quête* imagines the faith of those who have not survived various Atlantic crossings, and of those who have, but whose historical trace has been lost. Kandé does not seek a definite response to what has happened or even to what could have happened. Rather, she opens the Atlantic space to a multiplicity of untold stories and voices. She further envisions lateral Atlantic connections as explorers from the Mali Empire meet the indigenous populations of the Americas. They become the predecessors of contemporary immigrants, offering us a new lens for thinking about present-day displacements.

Kandé's Atlantic generates both possibility and destruction. It is a space where new, alternate histories can be constructed and invented. At the same time, it is an abyss. The angst and rage of the Atlantic swallow the bodies and hopes of those who try to defy it. The Atlantic offers unlimited promises only to turn them into a mirage and engulf those who have dared to try. In this regard, Kandé's poem echoes Edouard Glissant's notion of the womb abyss. Kandé and Glissant have crossed paths before, when Glissant wrote the postface to Kandé's work of poetic prose *Lagon, Lagunes* (2000). For Glissant, the first abyss is the slave ship's hold. In this enclosed space, countless anonymous bodies began their forced journey into the unknown. A second abyss followed:

> Aussi le deuxième gouffre est-il de l'abîme marin. Quand les régates donnent la chasse au négrier, le plus simple est d'alléger la barque en jetant par-dessus bord la cargaison, lestée de boulets. . . . Le gouffre est de vrai une tautologie, tout l'océan, toute la mer à la fin doucement affalée aux plaisirs du sable, sont un énorme commencement, seulement rythmé de ces boulets verdis.

> The next abyss was the depths of the sea. Whenever a fleet of ships gave chase to slave ships, it was easiest just to lighten the boat by throwing cargo overboard, weighing it down with balls and chains. . . . In actual fact the abyss is a tautology: the entire ocean, the entire sea gently collapsing in the end into the pleasures of sand, make one vast beginning, but a beginning whose time is marked by these balls and chains gone green.[41]

The ocean was a physical abyss for all those who, considered surplus cargo, were thrown overboard. The symbolic abyss extends further, into the space and time of memory. It not only engulfs those who have directly experienced the Middle Passage; it continues to have power over generations to come, through the memory and imagination of everything that has been left behind, that has been lost, and that occurred during the journey. It is a place of unrepresentable violence. Yet the abyss is also a womb. Michael Dash explains that Glissant replaces the figure of Mother Africa with that of a slave ship.[42] The slave ship is also a mother, a violent womb that forever transformed the people that it carried:

Cette barque est une matrice, le gouffre-matrice. Génératrice de ta clameur. Productrice aussi de toute unanimité à venir. Car si tu es le seul dans cette souffrance, tu partages l'inconnu avec quelques-uns, que tu ne connais pas encore. Cette barque est ta matrice, un moule, qui t'expulse pourtant. Enceinte d'autant de morts que de vivants en sursis.

This boat is a womb, a womb abyss. It generates the clamor of your protests; it also produces all the coming unanimity. Although you are alone in this suffering, you share in the unknown with others whom you have yet to know. This boat is your womb, a matrix, and yet it expels you. This boat: pregnant with as many dead as living under sentence of death.[43]

The womb abyss is both the end and a beginning. This abysmal experience created enduring links between Africa, the Caribbean, and Europe. The joint experience of anonymity and the shared fear of facing the unknown formed the bonds of a collectivity yet to emerge. For Glissant, the abyss is inextricably linked to the Middle Passage. It marks a historical rupture that will render linear history impossible in the Caribbean.

The collective experience of facing the unfamiliar resonates across both texts. Images of the Atlantic as an abyss and a graveyard multiply throughout Kandé's poem, as the sailors face the realization that they will not reach the other shore. In Kandé's poem, like in Glissant's text, history advances by stepping into the unknown. The abyss faced by fourteenth-century sailors foreshadows and echoes the abyss of the Middle Passage to come. However, the poem also points to the fact that the Middle Passage was not inevitable, that different histories could have happened. Aboubakar is a prophetic character; he can foresee the horrors of the future, which he could possibly prevent by reaching the other shore. Looking at the ocean from the front of this ship, he has a vision of the abyss to come:

Car il avait vu au fond des abysses glauques
les doubles des pour-être-enchaînés-marqués-au-fer-tailladés-
[par-le-fouet-perforés-de-mille-manières-et-à-plaisir-avant-que-
[d'être-jetés-hurlant-d'horreur-muets-de-rage-par-dessus-
[bord-à-la-grâce-du-requin. (71)

For he had seen at the bottom of the gloomy abysses
the doubles of the to-be-chained-up-branded-slashed-
[by-the-whip-perforated-in-a-thousand-ways-and-for-pleasure-before

[being-thrown-screaming-in-horror-speechless-with-rage-over
[board-to-the-mercy-of-the-sharks.[44]

He thus commits, at whatever cost, to stir history in a different direction. At the end of the first part, he does not succeed in accomplishing his vision, and the drowning bodies of his sailors become the doubles of those to be thrown overboard in the future. The Middle Passage thus seeps into Kandé's Atlantic, threatening to become the crossing of all crossings if Aboubakar does not reach the other shore. In a subsequent version of the story, Aboubakar succeeds. As the two continents "marry," his vision of the gloomy abyss dissipates:

C'est ainsi que l'Afrique et l'Amérique s'épousèrent
avant même que d'avoir connu leurs noms
Et les grands fonds glauques probablement se dépeuplèrent
des pour-être-enchaînés-et-flétris-avant-que-d'être-jetés-tristes-
    [bestiaires-par-dessus-bord-au-bonheur-du-grand-squale. (81)

And this is how Africa and America were married
before even knowing each other's names
And the vast murky waters were probably depopulated
of the to-be-chained-up-and-battered-before-being-thrown-overboard-sad-
    [bestiaries-to-the-delight-of-the-great-shark.[45]

Through the adverb "probably," the poet refuses to offer a definite account of "what could have been." The poem merely gestures toward the possibility of a different outcome. In an interview, Kandé explains this decision to circumvent the Middle Passage:

Par exemple, serait-ce que le *Middle Passage* met fin à un grand récit précédent, viable jusqu'au XVe siècle, celui du voyage de connaissance, auquel tous les audacieux, sans distinction d'origine, pouvaient librement participer ? Il y aurait eu dès lors distribution convenue des récits : d'une part, les voyages africains, au nombre desquels figurent les migrations économiques contemporaines, condamnés à rejouer indéfiniment le scénario de la Traite; d'autre part les voyages occidentaux (y compris le tourisme), construits sur le modèle de la conquête.[46]

For example, could it be that the *Middle Passage* put an end to a previous great narrative, which had been applicable until the 15th century, of travel as a quest for knowledge, a quest in which all bold men, regardless of their origin, could freely participate? There would henceforth be an agreed distribution of narratives: on the one hand, African voyages, to which belong contemporary economic migratory flows, condemned to endlessly repeat the model of the slave trade; on the other hand, Western travel (including tourism), based on the model of conquest.[47]

The Middle Passage defined and delimited all the migrations and crossings to follow, becoming the primary lens for understanding all subsequent African voyages and displacements. Erased from then on, Kandé notes, is the voyage of knowledge, not inscribed into the paradigm of conquest. Kandé clarifies that she did not want to enter the debate about the historical plausibility of Aboubakar's voyage and its various outcomes. Rather, she was interested in Aboubakar's crossing as a poetic project that seeks to surpass and redefine the limits and boundaries of human knowledge and existence:

> Avec *La quête infinie de l'autre rive,* mon propos n'était pas d'entrer dans ce débat, mais de réfléchir sur la traversée de l'océan par Mansa Aboubakar (alias Bata Manden Bori) comme projet poétique, comme hubris, comme défi à toutes les rives, à toutes les frontières, même celles qu'on dit naturelles ; en somme, comme défi à la finitude de la destinée. Toutes choses qui nous renvoient, je crois, aux préoccupations des passagers sur les "cayucos de la mort" contemporains.[48]

> With *La quête infinie de l'autre rive,* my intention was not to enter into this debate but to consider the ocean crossing by Mansa Aboubakar (aka Bata Manden Bori) as a poetic project, as hubris, as a challenge to all shores, to all borders, even those deemed natural; in short, as a challenge to the finitude of destiny. All things, which, I believe bring us to the preoccupations of the passengers on the contemporary "cayucos of death."[49]

The Middle Passage confined the destiny of millions to a predetermined narrative. It circumscribed millions of bodies into the narrow spaces of the ship's hold and the plantation, thus defining the fate of the African diaspora for centuries to come. This does not mean, of course, that within this very immobility and confinement practices of fugitivity, struggle, and defiance did not occur. But this is not the Atlantic story that Kandé wants to tell. *La quête* imagines crossings that escape the logic of the Middle Passage, questioning its historical inevitability. This is not an act of historical erasure as the Middle Passage haunts the poem. Yet, Kandé also suggests that history could have played out otherwise.

The connection Kandé introduces into Atlantic history, one that redefines the contours of the Black Atlantic, is between the Malian expedition and indigenous populations of the Americas. What if the Malian expedition had reached the other shore? And, what if instead of exterminating, colonizing, and plundering, they had simply decided to cohabit with the Native American populations? Can we even imagine a scenario where the voyage of exploration, of the discovery of new territories, is not also one of murder, the struggle for power, and the fall into social death of one of the two parties?

This is not a naïve opposition between the benevolent African explorer and the violent European colonizer. The decision of Aboubakar's fleet and the indigenous populations to cohabit in peace is achieved only after a long battle of wills between two kings and a measuring of strengths. But wisdom and peace ultimately do prevail in this version of the story. Had this happened, the poet suggests, different connections and exchanges between Africa and the Americas, sidestepping Europe, may have developed. Or maybe not. Maybe the European conquest would still have happened.

The multifarious Atlantic connections in the poem are also linguistic. Kandé's language fluctuates between highly specialized maritime terminology, neologisms, and West-African, French medieval, and Caribbean expressions. Manifold nouns describing the sea include the "ressac" (20) (the motion of the receding waves) and the "bonace" (19) (the calm of the sea after the storm). The descriptions of the boats are extremely detailed, focusing at times on the "étambot" (43) (stern post) or the "carène" (26) (hull). Aboubakar's tent is adorned with ensigns, for which Kandé uses an old French word, "gonfanons" (48). West African figures, places and expressions permeate the poem, including African storytellers, the "fina" and the "djeli" (25). On the other hand, the name of Aboubakar's opponent in the Americas is Guazabara, meaning war or warrior in the Taino language. Europe, Africa, and the Americas are linguistically enmeshed, fashioning a multidimensional Atlantic poem.

As she is rethinking the Atlantic, Kandé is also reframing the epic. In the preface, Kandé describes La quête as a "neo-epic" poem. In fact, while La quête borrows from the epic tradition, it does not reproduce all of its characteristics. The poem is dedicated to Joseph Ki-Zerbo, a renowned African historian, yet it exists at the border of history, fiction, myth, and legend. The heroes and storytellers of African epics are referenced throughout La quête. Lilyan Kesteloot explains that African epics are "very long narratives punctuated by musical accompaniment and enumerating the valorous exploits of a heroic figure." While some "are closely linked to the heroes and the warrior history of empires," others "take on a distinctly fantastical character."[50] Undoubtedly influenced by this tradition, the poet also describes herself as a "trouvère"—a medieval epic poet from Northern France—gesturing toward an enmeshment of various cultural traditions.

Kandé also takes the epic outside of the framework of national expansion and conquest. The poem begins in a traditional fashion, with a hero, Aboubakar, whose exploits will be lauded. Aboubakar is certainly an epic character, one "que tous quémandent et qui ne quémandent que Dieu" (19) ["who all beseech and who beseeches God alone"].[51] Yet, Kandé quickly shifts the focus from this male hero to a myriad of other characters accompanying him, many of them women. As El Hadji Malick Ndiaye writes in relation to Kandé's poem, "la figure du héros épique se dilue dans l'accomplissement collectif"[52] [the figure of the epic hero is diluted within collective achievement].

Unlike the traditional epic poem, La quête has no single hero; it is rather an amalgamation of multiple voices emanating from the fourteenth-century rowers and contemporary economic immigrants. The voices that emerge from the poem are not the most obvious ones. In the first canto, it is not Aboubakar himself but rather Nassita Maninyan, his *griotte*, who reinstitutes hope in the midst of despair and resignation, as she repositions the adventure as a quest for freedom and knowledge. Nassita immediately describes her role:

Je nomme leurs noms et louange leurs exploits
qu'ils ne soient demain tous oubliés
Car l'histoire est une marâtre quand la mémoire
est orpheline. (23)

I name their names and laud their exploits
so that tomorrow they be not all forgotten
For history is a wicked stepmother when memory
is orphaned.[53]

Action and narration are here placed at the same level of importance; heroic (male) exploits have no valence without someone (in this case, a woman) to recount them. Relating history through a polyphony of voices, Kandé enters, yet again, into dialogue with Edouard Glissant. In his discussion of literature and history, Glissant writes, "'Là où se joignent les histoires des peuples, hier réputés sans histoire, finit l'Histoire.' (Avec un grand H.)" ["'History [with a capital *H*] ends where the histories of those peoples once reputed to be without history come together.'"][54] Glissant further develops his concept of a prophetic vision of the past, a vision that stems from the writer's exploration of the obsessively present past, characterized by ruptures, inconsistencies, and erasures. This vision, however, cannot end with the past;

it cannot be either a "schematic chronology" or a "nostalgic lament." It must project itself into the future, or rather into the multiplicity of possible futures.

According to Glissant, the multiplicity of Caribbean histories works against the violence of universal history, leading to Caribbean transversality, or "subterranean convergence": "L'irruption à elle-même de l'histoire antillaise (des histoires de nos peuples, convergentes) nous débarasse de la vision linéaire et hiérarchisée d'*une* Histoire qui courrait son fil" ["The implosion of Caribbean history (of the converging histories of our peoples) relieves us of the linear, hierarchical vision of a single History that would run its unique course."][55] Literature and history converge as literature strives to recover and recreate these subterranean convergences. The question of historical transversality is at the center of *La quête,* though here it extends beyond the Caribbean and the Middle Passage. This transversality is both geographic and temporal. It is the convergence of the histories of people from the African continent and those of the Americas. But it is also the entanglement of past and present crossings.

The text unwinds through the linguistic echoing of past and present quests, the textual interweaving of a search for alternate endings and its often-abysmal ending. The poem begins with no clear spatial or temporal indications. It is precisely through these repetitions, echoes, and superpositions of different historical times that the poem advances. The rowing continues; no one is certain when it began and no one is certain when it will end:

une goutte de temps	a droplet of time
suspendue	suspended
au	along
fil	our
de	p
nos	a
p	d
a	d
g	l
a	e
i	s[56]
e	
s (21)	

The entire poem is this drop of time suspended at the sailors' oars, as the Atlantic becomes a time-space continuum. Kandé performs a poetics of

suspension where all final meanings and endings are suspended while waiting for new meanings and endings to come. The minimal use of punctua-
tion, the recurrence of sounds and images, and the repeated use of ellipses
fashion the transhistorical movements of oars and waves. The sailors' loss of
memory, their inability to remember what it felt like to have both feet planted
on firm soil, parallels our own memory loss of these multiple trajectories.
Like the relentless efforts of the rowing sailors, history relentlessly repeats.
Yet, this is not a mere enclosure into a prewritten narrative. As Kandé writes:
"De dénouements, il n'y en a pas moins de sept" (72) [There are at least seven
different outcomes].[57] She thus refuses to limit history to existing archives and
proven facts.

The attempt to defy natural limits is performed both by the voyagers and
the poet. Kandé's poetic writing is itself an act of defiance. By their very dis-
position on the page, the verses outline the sea and the relentless fight against
it. The writing thus obstinately confronts its own natural limit: the page.

Ah quelle pestilence monte de ce charnier sans nom
et dire que la mer
       à déchaler s'entête
          —sa vague matinale
             sans élan ni relève. (67)

Oh what pestilence rises from this mass grave without a name
to think that the sea
       is bent on dehulling
          —its morning wave
            without rush or reprieve.[58]

The regular rhythm of the verses is interrupted by a sudden swerve of
the words on the page, outlining the regular interval of the waves. The page
becomes a metaphor for the sea, as the words try to move beyond it, need-
ing to be constrained into the form of a verse. The sailors and the poet are
trying to defy their own materiality. They thus become a metaphor for one
another: the act of crossing is also the act of writing. In an interview conducted by El Hadji Malick Ndiaye at Columbia University, Kandé draws a
parallel between the figure of the writer and that of the sailor: confinement,
isolation, and monotonous repetition characterize the experience of both
writing and seafaring.[59]

Kandé further explains that her intention was not to "reenchant" and idealize a lost African past. This gesture, she suggests, belongs to a nationalist tradition and is not her primary focus. Her main objective is, rather, to propose a comparison between Aboubakar's fleet and contemporary immigrants, encouraging us to think about the present in different ways.[60] In fact, Kandé rewrites the traditional immigrant narrative, as she places contemporary immigration on the same level as historic searches for new horizons. Kandé thus questions the Middle Passage as the predominant framework for understanding the present. As she explains, since the Middle Passage, African history has been (to a significant extent) reduced to a repetition of the Middle Passage. While European travels are interpreted through the framework of conquest and the search for knowledge, African displacements continue to reenact the slaves' crossing. Lost within this paradigm are the diversity of African voyages, experiences, and intentions. Other writers and critics have similarly questioned the primacy given to the Middle Passage as a lens for understanding the present. Kandé joins Maryse Condé, who has equally argued that "not everything can be explained through slavery."[61] Stephen Best has similarly questioned the idea that "the slave past provides a ready prism for apprehending the black political present."[62] This is not a negation of the tremendous impact slavery has had (and continues to have) on the world. By searching for alternative frameworks through which to apprehend the present, Kandé strives to release the present from the clutches of the past, whose mirror image it does not always represent. There are many pasts that could have been and consequently many presents that can be.

By positioning contemporary immigrants as successors of Aboubakar's fleet, Kandé destabilizes the distinction between a traveler/explorer and an economic immigrant. Scholars have noted the colonial origins of European travel writing and its role in sustaining national and imperial identities. Mary Louise Pratt's *Imperial Eyes* is one of the most comprehensive accounts of the relation between travel and European nation-state building. Pratt examines how European travel writing produced the rest of the world for the European readership: "Travel books by Europeans about non-European parts of the world went (and go) about creating the 'domestic subject' of Euroimperialism . . . they have engaged metropolitan reading publics with (or to) expansionist enterprises whose material benefits accrued mainly to the very few."[63]

The immigrant narrative has long existed as "the other" of travel writing: if the latter is an act of exploration, expansion, and conquest, the former is its consequence, one that in media and political discourse is frequently represented as a crisis, a problem, and a tragedy. Recently, attempts have been made to displace travel writing as inherently European. The edited volume

Postcolonial Travel Writing focuses on non-European rewritings of the genre, articulating "experiences and ontologies that are often removed from dominant European or North American productions of knowledge."[64] In *Postcolonial Eyes*, Aedín Ní Loingsigh similarly argues that texts and people from the African continent

> continue to be analyzed as raw material for the literary aspirations of travel writers (for the most part Western) who journey *to* the continent. In contrast, the journeys of Africans who depart from their continent are recognized not for their contribution to the literature of travel and cultural encounter but for their historical value (e.g., slave narratives), contribution to the development of intellectual movements (e.g., Negritude), sociological importance (e.g., immigrant literature) or for their illustration of abstract and ahistorical theories of a cosmopolitan hybridity and interstitiality.[65]

Loingsigh further underscores the importance of extending "the discussion of African intercontinental travel beyond the abject conditions of the middle passage."[66] Kandé's poem gestures in a similar direction. By focusing on Malian travel expeditions, she displaces geographical exploration as strictly European. Additionally, she inscribes contemporary immigrant narratives into the same genealogy, questioning the conceptual distinction between the figure of a traveler and that of an immigrant.

For Kandé, the impulse of Aboubakar and that of the unnamed twenty-first-century immigrants to cross the Atlantic are similar. Aboubakar leads a large expedition in search of different lands in an attempt to change history and collective reality. Similarly, contemporary immigrants, this time on a raft and with very few supplies, embark on their journey driven by the desire to know and discover possibilities beyond their own social and cultural context. Both strive to overcome natural obstacles. In the case of today's immigrants, as Ndiaye notes, these hindrances are compounded by physical, economic, and ideological borders.[67] For this reason, the coast that immigrants are trying to reach is a European coast, not marked by national belonging. This is not a French coast, or maybe it is, but that detail does not change the immigrant narrative. In this manner, the poet takes the immigrant story outside of the postcolonial context. Kandé challenges the idea that economic immigrants can merely teach us about their specific socioeconomic conditions. In *La quête*, the immigrant, like the explorer, fights for the right to speak about the human condition as the poem acquires a universal dimension. It is undoubtful that contemporary immigration is linked to the history of European colonization of the African continent. Yet, *La quête* is not merely an illustration of the socioeconomic conditions of contemporary immigrants. Rather, Kandé underscores the attraction to the unknown and the refusal to accept a predetermined fate that span across centuries.

Kandé displaces the representation of immigration as an "invasion," a problem, pure victimhood, suffering, and desperation. While she acknowledges the importance of economic necessity, the voyagers explain:

> Ni pour le cuir ni pour les verres fumés
> mais pour le geste qui donnait à chacun de nous
> (nous autres ni chair ni poisson
> tripaille laissée pour compte
> sur le sable gluant du millénaire)
> la stature singulière d'une personne. (89)

> Not for the sake of leather nor for the tinted glasses
> but for the sake of the gesture that gave to each of us
> (we ourselves neither flesh nor fish
> innards cast
> upon the slimy millennial sand)
> the singular stature of a person.[68]

The immigrant existence is thus not limited to mere survival, and "economic" immigrants do not leave their countries solely for economic reasons. The crossing is also a search for dignity and recognition; this is a relentless transhistorical quest for something different and out of one's reach. This is not a romanticization or idealization of the immigrant crossing that more often than not results in death. Economic conditions that push the Malian youth to seek opportunities elsewhere are certainly recognized. Yet, survival, necessity, desire, and inquisitiveness are not mutually exclusive. Immigration is also a search for knowledge and an experience that generates knowledge.

After a patrol boat intercepts the immigrant raft, the recounting of the crossing by the survivors moves against the official representation of the event:

> Pourtant un ou deux quotidiens publieront sa photo:
> navrés deux plaisanciers scrutent la nacelle
> qui offense la plage avant d'être broyée
> Menace sur le tourisme
> annonce la manchette des journaux. (106)

> Still one or two dailies will publish its photo:
> saddened two amateur sailors inspect the nacelle

that offends the beach before it is scrapped
Tourism Threatened
reads the newspaper's headline.[69].

The media representation centers the nacelle, leaving immigrant bodies in the background. The headline foregrounds the effects of immigration on the receiving shore, ignoring the effects of the crossing on the voyagers. The mainstream assessment of the situation as a problem and a threat is countered by the various voices on the boat, explaining their decision to embark on a trans-Atlantic journey:

Si je réussis on dira que j'ai fait quelque chose
Et si je fais naufrage on saura au moins
que je suis mort d'avoir essayé:
à défaut de barsak- d'antichambre du paradis
c'est dans l'histoire que demain j'entrerai
certes anonyme parmi la foule clandestine
mais avec pour visa une valeureuse cause. (90)

If I succeed, people will say that I've done something
And if I sink it will at least be known
that I died having tried:
if I can't make it to barzakh—the antechamber of heaven
at least I'll make history tomorrow
yes anonymous among the undocumented masses
but with a worthy cause as my visa.[70]

In the same way that Aboubakar does not leave Mali in order to conquer another people or place but in search of knowledge, the desire to surpass one's mortality by entering into the historical narrative drives the contemporary migrant's decision to embark on this dangerous journey. These verses also underline the tension between the narrative voice and the anonymous silence, the individual and the collective. The poem's multiple narrators remain anonymous, thus not fully achieving the status of the epic hero. The attempt to imagine these unheard voices remains in tension with the preservation of their anonymity, their inability to come to a full subject status. The contradiction also lies in the fact that the contemporary immigrant can only enter history as part of a clandestine crowd; it is her illegality, her existence outside of legal norms and rules that allows her a place in official history. Only through her presence in an undifferentiated crowd can she attain recognition. The voices in the poem speak of this double anonymity. Anonymous because never recorded by history in their individuality, they also remain such because they echo across times, emanating from an endless plurality, one that cannot be contained by the emergence of a hero. Anonymous also, because they are too often swallowed by the Atlantic abyss.

Written in 2011, the poem references the ever-growing number of African immigrants who continue to die trying to reach Europe. Because official records are lacking, the Dutch nongovernmental organization UNITED for Intercultural Action has, over multiple years, using newspaper articles, personal stories, and coastguard reports, compiled "The List," an unofficial report of immigrant deaths since the 1990s. This incomprehensible tally rose, in 2018, to 34,361 bodies.[71] In the poem, the immigrants embark on their journey so that their efforts and accomplishments would be recounted. In this vein, they desire to join the tradition of epic heroes and kings, whose undertakings continue to be lauded. The indefinite "on dira" in the verses I just quoted becomes the contemporary equivalent of the griot, further framing history and its recounting as a collective endeavor. This desire to enter history stands in stark contrast with the rising number of unidentified bodies.

In *La quête,* the Atlantic exists as both an abysmal space, a transhistorical graveyard, and a space of endless possibilities, historical and poetic. Kandé imagines new Atlantic connections that move beyond the paradigm of the triangle and the narrative of the Middle Passage. These various histories are intertwined, as the fourteenth-century fleet and the contemporary immigrants are moved by a similar desire to venture into the unknown. Kandé envisions lateral Atlantic connections as explorers from the Mali Empire enter into direct contact with indigenous populations of the Americas. They become the predecessors of contemporary immigrants, who continue to shape diverse African traditions of travel, exploration, and displacement.

The Atlantic is at the center of Condé's, Phillips's, and Kandé's reflection on contemporary immigration. This is a newly reconfigured Atlantic paradigm, not limited to its triangular shape but remapped through a series of new, global connections and identifications. Global neoliberalization is historicized as the afterlives of the slave trade, colonization, and apartheid shape the contemporary Atlantic. Yet, these systems are also not enough to explain the multidirectional, present-day Atlantic crossings, which cannot be reduced to a repetition of the Middle Passage. The three works strive for a transhistorical model where the present stems from the past without begin determined by it. Phillips and Condé question the desire to recreate past identifications through models provided by movements like Negritude and Pan-Africanism. Afropolitanism, embraced mostly by a globally mobile elite, is also not quite sufficient, as it doesn't account for the disjuncture between contemporary immigrant flows. Yet, these authors do not give up on comparative think-ing, as they continue to imagine modes of South-South solidarity across the Atlantic via aesthetic means. There are, furthermore, multiple pasts to which the present can relate, Kandé suggests, as she circumvents the Middle Passage and inscribes contemporary migrations into a longer historical genealogy of African travels and explorations. The flows of immigrants, refugees, travelers, and explorers are no longer separate but rather intersect and in fact sustain one another. While haunted by its history of the slave trade, the globalized Atlantic is marked by emerging South-South connections.

CHAPTER 2

The Indebted Immigrant

Three months prior to his assassination in 1987, Burkina Faso president Thomas Sankara made his renowned speech against debt at the Organization of African Unity summit in Addis Ababa. In this striking denunciation of foreign debt, Sankara declared, "the debt is another form of neocolonialism, one in which the colonialists have transformed themselves into technical assistants. Actually, it would be more accurate to say technical assassins."[1] Debt, in fact, has been one of the main tools of global neoliberalization; as such, it has created new Atlantic links.

Franco-Senegalese writer Fatou Diome pursues this discussion on debt and neoliberalization in her recent novels *Le ventre de l'Atlantique* (2003) and *Celles qui attendent* (2010).[2] In Diome's work, contemporary debt operates on multiple levels: while used to justify austerity measures on the macro level, it also serves as a neoliberal tool of subjectivation. The relation to debt becomes even more complex in the case of immigrants: leaving countries that are drowning in national debt, immigrants often acquire debts in order to finance their trips. They pawn their future time chasing an idealized vision of life in Europe, and spend their lives overseas trying to prove that they were a worthy investment. This inverted logic, according to which immigrants owe the nation they have settled in for providing "opportunity," is mobilized to justify the precarious conditions of immigrant workers. National and personal debt are thus superposed, as global neoliberalization fashions an indebted Atlantic subject.

Like the works analyzed in the previous chapter, Diome's novels preserve the Atlantic geographical and theoretical framework, opening it up from a triangular to a multinodal space. While the history of slavery and colonization remain foundational, they are analyzed within the context of a globalized economy, which supersedes the predominance of the triangle. References to the slave trade are multiple; yet the current international trade in African soccer players overlies them. The relationship between Senegal and France, which still occupies a prominent place, is framed within the larger context of the global flows of capital and debt.

In *Scenes of Subjection: Terror, Slavery, and Self-making in Nineteenth Century America,* Saidiya Hartman analyses the "debt of emancipation" in the context of the postbellum United States, the responsibility of former slaves to prove that they were worthy of being freed. Hartman thus speaks of "the obligation and indebtedness of the freed to their friends and benefactors."[3] In Fatou Diome's postcolonial world, this "debt of emancipation" takes multiple forms. On the national level, Senegal is required to prove that it was worthy of decolonization. It will never be able to do so, since financial institutions control its economy through national debt. As Senegalese citizens begin to leave, becoming immigrants, they become indebted to the new country for allowing them to live on its soil. Diome's novels explore the intersections of these different dimensions of debt: the national and the personal, the financial and the symbolic. Characters articulate their relation to the global debt system, which also never fully circumscribes their experience. They thus offer the reader lines of flight, ways of reimagining "what it means to owe and to own in a period when debt is what makes our economic lives possible."[4] The relation between national and immigrant debt is of course not one of direct cause and consequence, and national debt is not the sole reason for emigration. Nonetheless, Diome advocates for a trans-Atlantic understanding of debt, which extends from the country of origin to the country of destination. Indebtedness is, in fact, an increasingly trans-Atlantic condition.

FROM SANKARA TO GREECE AND BACK

Since the 2008 financial crisis, debt, loans, and interest rates have been at the forefront of media headlines, political discourses, and social justice activism in both the United States and Europe.[5] While in the United States personal debt, mortgages, and foreclosures have been the primary focus, the "old continent" witnessed the rise of antiausterity movements and an invigorated critique of the relation between municipal debt, national debt, and austerity measures.[6] The Greek national debt crisis, which culminated in the summer of 2015, highlighted the role of debt in contemporary governance. Already at the end of 2009, Greek Prime Minister George Papandreou declared that Greece's budget deficit was about to exceed 12% of the country's GDP. In light of this acknowledgment, credit rating agencies downgraded Greece's sovereign debt to junk status, increasing the country's borrowing costs. Worried about a possible default, the EU and the IMF granted a 110 billion euros bailout in 2010, in exchange for austerity measures.[7] Five years later, after two more rounds of bailouts and reforms, Greece elected the left-wing Syriza coalition, which ran on an antiausterity platform. In an attempt to increase its bargaining power with the Troika (the IMF, the European Central Bank, and the European Commission), Greek Prime Minister Alexis Tsipras decided to hold a referendum where the population could decide whether they accepted the terms of a new bailout. *No*, was the majority response. Yet, in spite of the popular opposition to the deal, the Troika continued to insist on further austerity as the only option. The Greek government ultimately accepted the conditions of a new bailout (even more draconian than the one proposed before the referendum) in order to prevent its banks from running out of liquidity, thus ultimately negating the results of the referendum. In the end, the interests of the investors took precedence over the will of the population.[8]

In light of the Greek crisis, Sankara's speech has acquired new relevance. Whereas in the United States and Europe the major role of debt in the organization of national economies and personal lives has recently become a public conversation, in many countries of the Global South the debate has been active for decades.[9] Like many other governing techniques throughout history, debt was first experimented with in the Global South. As this question becomes prominent nowadays, since the future of the EU depends on it, it is essential not to forget that anticolonial and postcolonial movements have been fighting debt for decades. In his canonical 1950 essay, *Discours sur le colonialisme* [*Discourse on Colonialism*], Aimé Césaire argues that Europe was shocked by the advent of fascism simply because it was not paying attention to what was happening in the colonies. Fascism, according to Césaire, took root in the "New World" but was admonished only once it reached European soil.[10] Similarly, whereas the EU's blackmail of Greece has shocked many, loans, interest rates, and debt repayments have been at the forefront of neocolonial relationships for decades. In fact, around the same time as Greece, Puerto Rico was going through a debt crisis of its own. For years, Wall Street was accumulating profit over repeated loans issued (most often in exchange for bonds) to a government desperate for cash influx.[11]

As I explain in the introduction, national borrowing increased significantly across the Global South in the aftermath of the OPEC oil crisis, ultimately leading to the Third World debt crisis. The World Bank granted, for the first time in 1984, a loan to a country (Mexico), in exchange for neoliberal restructuring, including austerity measures and acceptance of the General Agreement on Tariffs and Trade (GATT). The consequences were substantial: "From 1983 to 1988 Mexico's per capita income fell at a rate of 5 per cent per year; the value of workers' real wages fell between 40 per cent and 50 per cent. . . . Food subsidies were restricted to the poorest segments of the population, and the quality of public education and health care stagnated or declined."[12] When many countries followed Mexico's example, the Brady Plan went into effect in 1989: creditors offered some debt relief (35%) in exchange for IMF and US treasury-backed discounted bonds that assured the remaining debt would be repaid. All the countries that accepted this mild form of debt forgiveness "were also required to swallow the poison pill of neoliberal institutional reforms."[13]

This was a significant victory for impersonal, economic neocolonialism, which former Ghanaian president Kwame Nkrumah already in 1965 described as the last and most dangerous stage of imperialism.[14] During colonial times, colonial powers like France had to justify colonialism and garner support at home. This required the careful construction of a "civilizing mission" whose purpose and success had to be accepted by the home population. Debt imperialism requires no justification because it consists of a set of economic reforms, "recommended" by an international group of supposedly neutral and scientifically oriented experts and presented as the only solution to an ongoing crisis. Neoliberal reforms introduced in Greece—including the deregulation of the labor market and the privatization of the energy transmission network—were presented as a necessary and nonpolitical implementation of international economic regulations. Akin to the situation in the Global South during the 1980s and '90s, Troika's technocratic, supposedly objective and scientific discourse, clouded the ideology of neoliberalism. "The EU technocrats talk as if it is all a matter of detailed regulatory measures," notes Slavoj Žižek; yet, "the denial of 'the ideological side' . . . is ideology at its purest."[15] Rather than a political choice, neoliberal reforms were passed as impersonal, regulatory measures. Economic neoimperialism relies on a "new sovereignty" of the global financial market "that substitutes (or subordinates) the old imperialist structures of the world-economy, and in this sense it could be called an Empire (*imperium*) that—much more than any military power today (i.e., with less possibilities of resistance)—has restricted the independence of States and nations."[16]

Yet, reckless government spending and fiscal irresponsibility are often cited as causes of national debt crisis. During the Greek debt crisis, the media proliferated with stereotypes of the lazy Greeks who spend most of the year vacationing. In 2015, the German tabloid *Bild* launched a campaign under the slogan: "No more billions for greedy Greeks."[17] The conversation about "poor work ethics" in indebted countries is a longstanding one. In other words, two discourses appear simultaneously: the subjective, moralizing discourse about the causes of the debt crisis and the objective, neutral discourse of the neoliberal solution. Annie McClanahan argues that "debt persistently and simultaneously occupies the logic of quantitative, scientific objectivity and of qualitative, even moral, subjectivity."[18] This is true at both the macroeconomic and the microeconomic levels.

The Third World debt crisis of the 1980s was of course not the first time in history that debt was used as a tool of (neo)imperialism. In the aftermath of its 1804 independence, Haiti was forced to pay a debt to the French government for 150 million gold francs (modern equivalent of $21 billion) to compensate its former master for the loss of its colonial properties. David Graeber, in his extraordinary work *Debt: The First 5000 Years* claims: "For thousands of years, the struggle between rich and poor has largely taken the form of conflicts between creditors and debtors—of arguments about the rights and wrongs of interest payments, debt peonage, amnesty, repossession, restitution, the sequestering of sheep, the seizing of vineyards, and the selling of debtors' children into slavery."[19] Neoliberalism has thus certainly not invented debt. However, the debtor/creditor relation has acquired new prominence in recent years.

Many contemporary discourses on debt build on the work of Friedrich Nietzsche, who wrote about the etymological and conceptual relation between *Schuld* (guilt) and *Schulden* (debts). The debt economy relies on the interiorization of the command "you shall repay." For the command to bear weight, it must act as a moral command. Debts should be repaid not simply because that is stipulated by an economic contract, but because it is the ethical choice. Subsequently, the failure to repay one's debts becomes an ethical failure, an indication of a personal inability to keep one's word, to live up to a promise, to live the life of a respectable citizen. Default awakens feelings of shame and guilt, as individual irresponsibility and unaccountability become the primary culprits. Presenting debt as a consequence of living "beyond one's means" precludes the debtor from understanding its systemic causes and identifying with a debtor class.

Failing to repay one's debt is also a failure to ascend the social ladder. A debtor asks for a loan because they find themselves in a precarious financial situation. They promise to do better, to dedicate their time and efforts to class ascendency in order to repay the debt. The loan allows the debtor to execute what their current class status does not permit them to do, but what their future status might. As a debtor defaults, they publicly admit that they failed to change their class status. This is the failure of the entrepreneurial self. Wendy Brown argues that in neoliberalism "as capitals, every subject is rendered as entrepreneurial, no matter how small, impoverished, or without resources, and every aspect of human existence is produced as an entrepreneurial one."[20] If, following Brown, we further understand neoliberalism as a system where the subject is a "bit of human capital tasked with improving and leveraging its competitive positioning and with enhancing its (monetary and nonmonetary) portfolio value across all of its endeavors and venues," the failure to repay one's debts is the failure of the neoliberal subject.[21] The debtor has not fulfilled their social role and purpose; they have failed as a social actor. By giving out a loan, the creditor invests in the entrepreneurial potential of the debtor. By not repaying one's debt, the debtor proves herself an unworthy investment, a subject unworthy of freedom and thus entirely deserving of her social position.

The specificity of the debt economy lies in its temporality. In *The Making of the Indebted Man*, Maurizio Lazzarato argues that debt is "a security-state technique of government aimed at reducing the uncertainty of the behavior of the governed. By training the governed to 'promise' (to honor their debt), capitalism exercises 'control over the future,' since debt obligations allow one to foresee, calculate, measure, and establish equivalences between current and future behavior. The effects of the power of debt on subjectivity (guilt and responsibility) allow capitalism to bridge the gap between present and future."[22] The entire debt relation is predicated on a different interpretation of the future by the creditor and the debtor. For the debtor, the loan opens up the possibility of different prospects; it serves to pay for food, education, a house, medical attention, anything that can make life easier and better, healthier or more comfortable. This is particularly visible in the case of student debt in the United States. Many debtors perceive education as a way out of poverty, an opportunity to improve one's social standing and create a future where repaying this debt will no longer be a problem (education is also advertised as such). This is similarly the case for immigrants financing their trip through debt. Debt is a conduit for change, for a better, brighter future.

From the creditor's point of view, this is not the case; debt is a mechanism that predicts and controls the future, ensuring that the future will remain exactly like the present: "For debt simply neutralizes time, time as the creation of new possibilities, that is to say, the raw material of all political, social, or esthetic change."[23] Debt sets the rhythm for the present and the future, it con-flates the two into homogenous time, punctuated solely by debt payments, thus restricting what can be thought and done.[24] It ensures that, too busy attempting to repay her debt, the debtor will not be able to challenge the sys-tem. By taking out a loan, the debtor is offering her future time as collateral; she promises to punctuate her future by the regularity of monthly payments and to make decisions that will allow this regularity to continue. The struggle between the debtor and the creditor is a struggle for who controls present and future time, a struggle for whether the future will bring new possibilities or whether it will be identical to the present.

Lazzarato's indebted man is however an abstract man, taken out of his historical and social context. While very insightful, his analysis is also total-izing. It is thus necessary but not sufficient, as he does not consider how debt operates differentially across race, gender, class, and nationality, serving to maintain these differences. Fatou Diome, however, does. In *The Belly of the Atlantic,* immigrant debt lies at the intersection of national and personal debt. Increasing national debts lead to cuts in public services and security networks, forcing more people to emigrate. Unable to pay for the expenses of emigra-tion, immigrants borrow money, embarking on this journey on credit. This is, of course, not a simple cause-consequence relationship. Still, immigrant debt connects the Global South to the Global North, as the national debt of coun-tries in the Global South is individualized through the debt of immigrants, trying to become citizens in the Global North.

Diome's novels participate, furthermore, in the building of a Francophone literary tradition that addresses debt, alongside, for instance, Congolese writer Alain Mabanckou. The narrator of *Black bazar* (2009) is an immigrant from Congo-Brazzaville, who introduces the reader to the world of the African diaspora in Paris. A successful womanizer, he is also a fervent adherent of *La Sape* (Société des Ambianceurs et des Personnes Élégantes) [The Society of Ambiance-Makers and Elegant People], a movement born out of Brazzaville and Kinshasa that embraces elegance and style.

In Mabanckou's work, the African man collects his debt from French men by sleeping with white French women. The narrator's Ivorian friend explains that he has come to France "pour faire payer aux Françaises la dette colo-niale et qu'il y parviendra par tous les moyens nécessaires"[25] ["to make French women pay back the colonial debt and that he will succeed by all means nec-essary"].[26] "All means necessary," within the context of the novel, implies all the sexual means possible. Not every French woman, however, counts as a debt repayment; race and class are in fact interconnected: "Au fond ils se payaient ma tête, surtout Yves l'Ivoirien tout court qui m'a rappelé que ce n'est pas avec une fille comme ça que je ferai payer à la France la dette coloniale."[27] ["But they were just winding me up, especially Yves the just-Ivorian who pointed out that I'd never make France pay back its colonial debt with a girl like that"].[28] By sleeping with a white woman, the black man is asking the white man to acknowledge him as a brother, to tell him "take my sister." The white woman thus serves as a conduit to the white man's approval, as Franz Fanon has already argued in *Peau noire, masques blancs*.[29] In *Black bazar,* the struggle between the black and the white man continues to be fought through the female body. The white man refuses to pay reparations and concede to the economic and psychological harm he has inflicted, leaving the black man with no other choice but to use the white woman as collateral. The sexual encounter with the white woman is thus a form of revenge, a way of claiming ownership over the white man's most precious "possession."[30] The relation between the characters' sexual escapades and colonial debt is represented in ironic terms, with the author ultimately suggesting that Africans need to stop living for and through the white man.

Diome's novels take this discussion in new directions. In *Celles qui attendent,* Diome displaces the male-centered analysis of *Black bazar* by focusing on the effects of postcolonial debt on African women. Unable to provide for themselves and their families, the women resort to microlending, thus entering the debt economy. Financial and symbolic debt inform and modify one another, as colonial relationships are transposed into a postcolonial world and restructured in light of global neoliberalization. Diome's immigrant characters trace the history and present of an indebted Atlantic.

THE INDEBTED ATLANTIC

In *The Belly of the Atlantic,* Diome addresses Franco-Senegalese relations and the contemporary configuration of the Atlantic episteme. The novel recounts the story of Salie, a young Senegalese woman, who cleans houses in France in order to finance her studies. The plot oscillates between France and Niodior, an island off the coast of Senegal, introducing us to members of Salie's family, including Madické, a younger brother, who dreams of going to France to play soccer for a French team. Distancing herself from a national framework, Diome positions her novel in a globalized Atlantic space, where the colonial power distributions have altered form. While France remains central within the Senegalese global imaginary, the entrance of new poles of power, such as the United States and Italy (as another powerhouse of European soccer), disturbs the triangular configuration of the Atlantic.

The Belly of the Atlantic encourages us to reflect on the multidirectionality of Atlantic networks. Immigration is no longer merely a facet of national iden-

tity and a source of cultural difference; the Atlantic is crossed in both directions; the act of leaving is given as much importance as the act of returning.
Those who come back influence immigration patterns when they convey, be it
orally or in writing, their immigrant lives. While sometimes perpetuating the
contemporary power constellations within the Atlantic world, these narratives
also escape the simple core/periphery, North/South binarisms.

At the beginning of *The Belly of the Atlantic,* Salie is watching a soccer
game at the request of Madické, who is unable to follow it in Niodior: "Le
29 juin 2000, je regarde la Coupe d'Europe de football. L'Italie affronte les
Pays-Bas en demi-finale. Mes yeux fixent la télévision, mon coeur contemple
d'autres horizons" (13) ["It's 29 June 2000 and I'm watching the European
Cup. It's Italy *v.* Holland in the semi-final. My eyes are staring at the TV, but
my heart's contemplating other horizons" (2)].³¹ The relation between France
and Senegal passes through the Italian soccer team and the medium of television. Madické repeatedly phones Salie to inquire about the performance of
his idol, the Italian soccer player, Maldini. Whereas Salie mentions that most
boys from the village are obsessed with French players, Madické's adherence
to the Italian team marks a break from the postcolonial France-Senegal relationship. Old colonial power dynamics are still present, yet globalization and
the entry of new poles of power such as the United States and other European countries complicate former power relations.

As she becomes acquainted with the fate of local youths who left for
Europe in order to pursue an athletic career, Salie begins to see soccer
through the lens of the history of slavery. Ndétare, the local, Marxist school-
teacher, attempts to convince Madické and his friends to give up on their
dream of playing soccer in France by telling them the story of Moussa. From
Niodior, Moussa is contracted by a French soccer team and leaves his family
and hometown to prove his worth on the other side of the Atlantic. However, after the recruiter (ironically named *Sauveur/Savior*) decides that Moussa's talents are not up to par with the other players, he becomes yet another
undocumented immigrant, with no other option but to work on the docks
of Marseille in order to repay the recruiter's investment. He is ultimately
deported to Niodior, destitute. Not being able to withstand the humiliation
and disillusionment, he drowns himself in the Atlantic.

Diome makes a rapprochement between the slave trade and the contemporary trade of soccer players: "Aussi, je declare 2002 année internationale de
la lutte contre la colonisation sportive et la traite du footeux!" (281–82) ["So I
declare 2002 international year of the battle against colonization in sport and
the trade in footballers!" (174)]. In spite of several decades of Senegalese independence, France still considers Senegalese soccer players as their property.
They increase the reputation of French teams, if talented enough, and serve

as sources of cheap and precarious labor otherwise: "En dépit des efforts de Schoelcher, le vieux maître achète toujours ses poulains, se contente de les nourrir au foin et s'enorgueillit de leur gallop" (281) ["Despite Schoelcher's efforts, the old master still buys Africa's colts, feeds them on hay and is proud of their performances" (174)]. The explicit reference to Schoelcher, the famous French abolitionist, is used to formulate a strong critique of neocolonialism where, albeit in altered forms, the old master-slave relationship persists. The proprietor-possession dynamic is intertwined with a paternalistic attitude that suggests that French teams are enabling the "development" of Senegalese players. This dynamic mirrors the French colonial ideology where economic utility was countered by (and sustained by) the "humanistic" philosophy of the civilizing mission.

As a modern form of the slave trade, soccer marks a continuity in Atlantic history. Yet, as Laurent Dubois contends, soccer has also always had multiple facets. While often used by administrators and teachers in colonial contexts to spread Western values, colonial subjects also appropriated and reshaped it into a tool of resistance. Dubois describes the conflicting nature of soccer, both "the ultimate embodiment of the promises of egalitarian meritocracy" and a reflection of the world's unpredictability, arbitrariness, and unfairness.[32] The novel's ironic tone connects the trade in soccer players to the Atlantic trade. Yet, the focus on soccer also underlines the multilayered and often conflicting dimensions of Atlantic history. The youth's admiration for various soccer teams and players reflects but also shapes the changing nature of global power relations. Through soccer stars like Paolo Maldini or Zinedine Zidane—figures who embody the belief that with hard work and talent, anything is possible in the West— Italy and France compete for the admiration of African youth. Yet, through their choices of favorite soccer players, Senegalese youth also assert their own values and beliefs. Madické's preference for Maldini challenges France as the predominant solution for Senegalese youth. Soccer and credit interweave in the novel as they point to the manifold dynamics of a globalized Atlantic space. They both represent Atlantic hopes that, unfortunately, often remain unfulfilled.

The Atlantic trade thus remains a historical and geographical framework to understand contemporary economic and political dynamics. This is not a sheer transposition of the colonial past onto the postcolonial present. Whereas the power dynamic between Senegal and France remains one of inequality and dependence, it has also adapted itself to the current functioning of global capitalism. The neoliberal economic and political doctrines that guide the international soccer world become visible in a passage summarizing the Senegalese news program:

En fin de journée, Son Excellence, monsieur le Premier ministre, s'est rendu au port autonome de Dakar pour réceptionner un cargo de riz offert par la France, afin de secourir les populations de l'intérieur du pays touchées par la sécheresse. La France, un grand pays ami de longue date, fait savoir, par la voix de son ministre des Affaires étrangères, qu'elle s'apprête à reconsidérer prochainement la dette du Sénégal. . . . Enfin, pour terminer ce journal, sachez que nos braves Sénefs (Sportifs nationaux évoluant en France) s'illustrent de plus en plus dans le tournoi des clubs français. (56–57)

At the end of the day, his Excellency the Prime Minister went to the autonomous port of Dakar to take delivery of a cargo of rice donated by France in order to help the drought-stricken people of the interior. France, a great country and our long-time friend, has conveyed through its Minister for Foreign Affairs that it is preparing to reassess Senegal's debt in the near future. . . . Finally, to end this news bulletin, I'm delighted to tell you that our valiant national sportsmen in France are distinguishing themselves in the French club league. (30)

This discourse epitomizes the superposition of a rhetoric of domination and one of aid, characteristic of the functioning of global neoliberalization. France presents the willingness to reconsider Senegal's debt as an act of generosity, stemming out of a long-term friendship between the two countries. The subtext of this decision is, of course, the IMF's liberalizing policy, where a country's foreign debt is renegotiated in exchange for structural adjustments.[33] The rhetoric of friendship obfuscates the ideology of neoliberalism.

In his speech on debt, Sankara further calls upon Third World countries to stop repaying their debt to international imperialist powers, arguing that since this debt is illegitimate, African governments are under no moral obligation to settle it. In many ways, the situation has not changed significantly since Sankara's proclamation. In order to repay their debt, governments have had to procure foreign currencies; as a result, many countries have abandoned subsistence crops in favor of export programs, cash crops, and monocultures, which create a sense of dependency on transnational corporations that control the market.[34]

In the specific case of Senegal, a Structural Adjustment Program was implemented in the 1980s, under the auspices of the United States, France, the IMF, and the World Bank. The main component of the program was the New Agricultural Policy, meant to encourage the export of local crops, such as the peanut, and restructure the state's Rural Development Agencies. The program insisted on the elimination of all state subsidies to the agricultural sector (including fertilizer subsidies), which had devastating effects on local farmers, ultimately leading to the collapse of the peanut industry. The program also had wider social consequences; between 1980 and 1989, Senegal's foreign debt grew from forty-four percent of its GNP to nearly eighty percent, leading to cuts in health and public services, and rising public sector unemployment.[35]

In *The Belly of the Atlantic,* the superposition of the discourse on debt with that of Senegalese soccer players living in France marks a relation between global neoliberalization and emigration. Senegal depends on France's donation of a cargo of rice (Senegal's own product), an obviously unsustainable solution to Senegal's economic challenges. However, this passage also introduces the question of globalization as experienced through narration. Ndétare recounts the story of Moussa to Madické and his friends; the explanation for the food shortage is obtained through a TV screen. In other words, while the effects are experienced directly, they are caused by what is happening at a distance. The novel strives to tell the macroeconomic Atlantic story in conjunction with the stories of characters who live these changes, which affect yet never fully define their lives. The two news items do not follow directly; two other pieces of news separate them: one about the weather and another about Senegalese doctors working in rural areas. The temporal delay in reading marks the complex relationship between the two pieces of information: the story of the Senegalese soccer players and that of Senegalese economic reforms are related, yet, should not be conflated. The novel in fact never posits a direct causal relation; the macroeconomic story unfolds through background details—like the news program—gesturing toward, rather than determining the connections.

The passage also underscores the various ideological discourses that circulate across the Atlantic, sometimes competing and sometimes sustaining one another: colonialism, paternalism, friendship, aid, development, and debt. The success of its soccer players counterbalances Senegalese economic "failure." In opposition to the economic situation, the national debt, and the drought, soccer players symbolize success, a domain where Senegal and France might be on equal footing. Consequently, the failure of national soccer players like Moussa becomes a national failure, adding a symbolic layer to a personal immigration story.

The news report, in combination with Moussa's story, underlines the multiple dimensions of debt. As the narrator explains, unable to pay for his trip to France, Moussa accepts the "investment" of the recruiter, a loan that will have to be repaid. Dominic Thomas notes in relation to Moussa: "The slavery topos reemerges with his realization that he has become a commodity because he has mortgaged his future for the funds he needed to travel to France."[36] In the context of the international soccer trade, black bodies are no longer acquired through purchase but through an "investment," a loan that finances the trip and stay in Europe under the promise of a financial return. The credit promises a different future to come: access to European wealth and glamor, and to the historically idealized vision of the French capital. It is often the only alternative to a life of assured poverty at home. The collateral required, however, is future time. Moussa dedicates his life as a soccer player in Paris to proving that he was a worthwhile investment. The macro and the micro situation mirror one another: Senegal's inability to repay its national debt indicates that it did not deserve independence; it can only subsist under foreign tutelage and will never acquire the designation of a "developed" country. Even though the system is designed in such a way as to prevent the full repayment of the loan, the onus is cast on the borrower, the one who ultimately was not worthy of the loan. Similarly, Moussa's acceptance of the deal to go train in France is a reconfiguration of the self as an investment, the acceptance that personal worth is valued in terms of the profit it is able to create.

As the narrative progresses, Moussa does not succeed as a soccer player (something that the recruiter might have known since Moussa was above recruitment age, and he had to falsify his birth certificate). He is thus obliged, while undocumented and under fear of deportation, to accept a minimum wage job on a boat while his recruiter collects his salary. After repaying the debt that he owes, the promise goes, he will be able to save up some money and return home. The remaining debt, however, continues to haunt him as a constant reminder of his financial and moral failure, as proof that ultimately, like his country, he was not worthy of the investment. He becomes the confirmation of the stereotype, the irresponsible, lazy, immoral Senegalese man, who does not honor his commitments. He was not worthy of the trust placed in him by the European man, of the "opportunity" given to him, of the white man's selfless intent to emancipate him, to offer him the life of a Zinedine Zidane: "Moussa savait qu'à défaut de se faire engager dans le club qui misait sur lui, il devrait lui-même rembourser à Sauveur les frais engagés, billet d'avion, pots-de-vin, frais d'hébergement, de formation, etc. Alors il se donnait à fond" (112) ["Moussa knew that if he wasn't taken on by the club backing him, he'd have to reimburse Sauveur himself for the expenses he'd incurred: the plane ticket, bribes, accommodation costs, training etc. So he gave his all" (65)]. The loan, though purely a financial deal, becomes a moral investment, an opportunity, a desire to help and emancipate.

"Debt produces a specific 'morality,' at once different from and complementary to that of 'labor.' The couple 'effort-reward' of the ideology of work is doubled by the morality of the *promise* (to honor one's debt) and the *fault* (of having entered into it)," argues Lazzarato.[37] However, while Lazzarato focuses on the indebted man as an abstraction, Diome's novel demonstrates how the indebted immigrant lies at the interstices of neoliberal capital and neocolonial ideology. Hartman's analysis of the debt of emancipation in nineteenth-century United States is useful here. Hartman argues that the "burden of debt, duty, and gratitude" was "foisted on the newly emancipated."[38] The newly freed slaves had a debt to repay to the white benefactors that supposedly freed them. They were expected to prove that they were worthy of freedom through submission, hard work, and serfdom: "Yet debt was not simply a pretext but an articulation of the enduring claims on black laborers, the affective linchpin of reciprocity, mutuality, and inequality, the ideational hybrid of responsibility and servitude, and, most important, the agent of bondage."[39] The rhetoric of freedom as gift, responsibility, and an obligation fashioned docile, indebted workers. Similarly, Moussa strives to show that he deserved the chance to work in France, the land of success. This rhetoric of opportunity effaces the commodification of black bodies for profit. The discourse of debt is strangely reversed: there is no talk of reparations; former colonial powers do not owe anything to their former colonies for years of colonization and neocolonization. Once the causes of emigration are forgotten, immigration becomes an individual choice and privilege, and thus an individual responsibility. The receiving country owes nothing to those who had to emigrate. On the other hand, immigrants owe everything to those who "gave" them the opportunity to improve their lives. The circulation of credit and debt in the novel interweaves with a neocolonial idealization of France, which reinforces the feeling of inferiority and shame. The inability to repay one's debt is also the failure to satisfy and gain recognition from the European man. Furthermore, since the common perception identifies France as the epicenter of the entrepreneurial self, the economic failure in the land of success can only be the result of personal inadequacy.

Moussa, it should be noted, is constrained by both ideological discourses and very concrete, material mechanisms. Sauveur reminds him of his choices as an undocumented immigrant: to work for Sauveur's friend or risk prison and deportation. While shame and guilt play a significant role, Moussa accepts the arrangement because of his precarious position as an undocumented immigrant. In *Dead Pledges*, Annie McClanahan challenges Lazzarato on the importance of social shame in ensuring that debts be repaid. She argues that the state has created coercive apparatuses, including "imprisonment and other forms of impersonal structural violence that operate on the debtor's body more than on her conscience."[40] In the case of Moussa, the material constraints that guarantee the entrapment in the logic of debt, and the shame and guilt associated with it, operate conjointly. They represent multiple levels of formation and control of the indebted subject. As an undocumented immigrant, his body is not only unprotected but also repeatedly attacked by different state mechanisms. Yet the shame of not having fulfilled his obligation toward both the new country and the country of origin compounds material constraints.

Finally realizing the full intricacy of the situation, Moussa decides to abandon his new job and flee. Before doing so, he receives a letter from his father reminding him of his debt to his family: "Epargne-nous la honte parmi nos semblables. Tu dois travailler, économiser et revenir au pays" (119) ["Spare us this shame among our people. You must work, save money and come home" (69)]. The French verb *devoir* means both "must" and "to owe." Moussa's father reminds him that he must do it because he owes it to his parents; there is no other choice. Diome reintroduces the notion of shame here in a transnational and transgenerational context. Moussa's failure to live up to African projections of life in France leaves him deeply ashamed. Shame extends across the Atlantic, onto his parents who are embarrassed by their son's supposed laziness and his embrace of Western individualism.

It is the promise of this symbolic debt that convinces Moussa to continue working on the boat. Debt thus becomes another sphere where the local and the global encounter, influence, and modify one another. While trapped in the cycle of neoliberal capitalist debt and forced to work illegally to repay his white savior, Moussa also needs to repay a local form of debt, one owed to his parents. Like so many other immigrant children, he is expected to send remittances. He is unable to do so due to his debt to his recruiter. His father, however, understands this inability as a sign of ingratitude and an abandonment of his cultural values. Since everyone is rich in France, the fact that they have not received anything can only be a sign of an unwillingness on Moussa's part to send money home: "-Et voilà! Mon fils, à peine en France, il a déjà changé. Regardez-moi cet accoutrement!" (113) ["You see! My son's barely arrived in France and he's already changed. Just look at that get-up!" (66)]. Moussa is thus caught between a symbolic debt expected to be repaid in material terms and a material debt with a strong symbolic value. His situation becomes even more tragic when he is deported to Senegal. At home and broke, everyone despises him. People return from France rich; if he has returned poor, it must mean that he did not do anything worthwhile while abroad. He finds some solace in his friendship with Ndétare, until stories begin to circulate about the nature of their relationship. Unable to sustain the multiple levels of shame, Moussa drowns himself in the Atlantic Ocean, thus concluding his life literally underwater.

Ndétare recounts Moussa's story to Madické and his friends, in order to dispel romantic visions of life in France. "Rappelez-vous, Moussa était des vôtres" (134) ["Remember, Moussa was your brother" (79)], he repeats, as a way of inciting the youth to identify with Moussa. He tries to frame Moussa's story as a consequence of historical and material conditions, rather than a personal failure. Ndétare encourages the local youth to see themselves as part of a collective subject, which, due to historical and economic conditions, is always already indebted. This interpretation strains against the youth's understanding, who see Moussa as an exception, rather than the rule. *The Belly of the Atlantic* addresses the difficulty in accepting debt as "a collective experience of a structural condition."[41] For the Senegalese youth, immigrant success stories are the norm, and Moussa's failure an exception. In order to identify with Moussa and accept his story as theirs, the youth would have to give up on the possibility of becoming the next Zinedine Zidane. This is no small thing to ask of them.

Moussa's story, however, may continue beyond his lifetime. It is believed that at one point in time a man named Sédar drowned himself in the Atlantic when his impotence was publicly revealed in the village. Madly in love with him, his wife followed him into the ocean. They were subsequently transformed into dolphins and remained friends of the humans. Ever since then, they have transformed every drowned illegitimate child into a dolphin and adopted it into their family. After his return from France, Moussa remembers this legend, which ignites hope that a welcoming community might exist beyond the world of the humans. Within the legend, the Atlantic exists as an alternative framework that sanctions other modes of living, as a utopian space, free from prejudices and hate.

The possible inclusion into the local legend is also Moussa's attempt to escape the logic of debt. Under the condition of indebtedness, Moussa's life would follow a predictable pattern: endless work, endless repayments, endless shame and guilt at being a failure. The only escape in this context is self-destruction. Within the legend, Moussa regains his right to an undetermined future. His story, his participation in the global trade of soccer players, and his incorporation into a local legend offer a critical perspective on current economic reconfigurations. However, the narrative moves beyond a mere critique. The possible incorporation into the local legend offers an imaginative line of flight, an escape from the structures of oppression and marginalization.

Within the legend, the loneliness of individual responsibility is transcended with the advent of a new community, the community of those unable to fulfill their obligations. Biology does not connect the family formed in the ocean; instead, they are brought together by the commonality of shame and guilt associated with their lives. Rather than being an excuse for exclusion, this becomes a reason for cohesion. Moussa imagines a future where, as a dolphin, the ocean nourishes, instead of suffocating him. He can live in and of the ocean without having to go into debt. Debt or death would, in this scenario, no longer be the only two options for him. Even if only an imaginative escape from the tragic conditions of reality, the legend still generates a vision of a different community.

Diome's Atlantic is dialectical: it is a space that both nourishes and devours, that protects and wounds, that generates life only to take it away. The title of the novel contains this ambiguity. The belly connotes pregnancy, birth, and motherhood. Yet, in the novel, it is also associated with hunger, indigestion, and vomit. Moussa's story similarly carries multiple meanings. His suicide is unquestionably tragic, and it belongs to the global context where young Africans continue to drown trying to reach European shores. Moussa seeks refuge in the Atlantic because he was unable to find it among humans; his death further links contemporary immigrations to the long history of Atlantic deaths, dating back to the Middle Passage. The fishermen ultimately recover Moussa's body, indicating perhaps, that the legend was just another Atlantic mirage. Yet, the legend continues to be retold, suggesting that a family of dolphins might exist somewhere.

The Belly of the Atlantic engages the difficulties encountered by contemporary African youth, yet it also reminds us that fiction is not merely a reproduction of that reality. Fiction also creates lines of flight, ways of reinterpreting and reimagining reality. Kathryn Lachman argues, "Diome's interest in the Atlantic may be best understood as an aspiration for deeper connections across the Atlantic, rather than as a reflection of existing Atlantic relationships."[42] In *The Belly of the Atlantic,* a comprehensive analysis of the power dynamics that lead to Moussa's death includes a potential alternative outcome of that story, one that allows for existence outside the logic of debt.

THE DEBT OF/TO THOSE WHO STAY

Many political, literary, and social science discourses have focused on the effects of immigration on receiving countries, debating whether these countries can and should integrate their immigrant populations, and whether immigration is culturally, socially, and economically beneficial.[43] Much more seldom is the topic discussed from the purview of the women and men who stay, awaiting the return of their loved ones. *Celles qui attendent* [*Women Who Wait*] takes this approach, focusing on Senegalese women who, because their sons and husbands are in Europe, have to resort to debt to survive. While *The Belly of the Atlantic* explores the connection between national and individual debt, and the ethics of obligation within the context of neocolonial relations, *Celles qui attendent* engages the consequences of local debt, acquired to mitigate the effects of emigration. When the remittances do not arrive, women seek means of supporting their families. To remedy this situation, the IMF and the World Bank have mobilized the microloan as a popular conduit to female "economic empowerment." This form of debt economics, however, often replaces and destroys local forms of solidarity economics. The novel underlines the gendered aspect of contemporary economic imperialism, its focus on women as the primary figures of "development" introduced into the neoliberal economy through debt. *Celles qui attendent* furthermore challenges the analytic division between cultural feminist issues, such as polygamy and clitoridectomy, and economic issues, like poverty and debt.

Feminists across the Global South have strongly criticized international feminism practiced in the West and advocated for a rethinking of transnational feminist solidarity. Obioma Nnaemeka maintains that "internationally, second wave feminism generated two major responses: (1) the global sisterhood approach that overplayed homogeneity and paid little or no attention to issues of difference based on race, class, culture, ethnicity, sexuality, beliefs, and so on; and (2) the development approach in its different mutations—Women in Development (WID), Women and Development (WAD), Gender and Development (GAD)—that institutionalized the helper/helped dichotomy. Both responses failed to fully account for and address the issues of hierarchy, power, and inequality."[44] Within the context of Africa and the African diaspora in Europe, mediatized political discourses have highlighted the question of polygamy and female circumcision over the past few decades, framed by the universalism/cultural relativism dichotomy, where local cultures bear the blame for gender inequality.[45] The mainstream media, but also African literary texts, have contributed to this discourse, reflecting, as Dominic Thomas argues, "a disturbing pattern, effectively displacing and shifting the responsibility for the plight of African women in the Diaspora away from the West in order to reattribute it to Africa, highlighting some of the more problematic dimensions of discourse on human rights, universalism, and hegemony."[46] To avoid this problematic reduction, a transnational analysis of gender must focus, as Chandra Mohanty phrases it, on "decolonizing feminism and demystifying capitalism." The two are inseparable given that "capitalism is seriously incompatible with feminist visions of social and economic justice."[47] National politics of the countries where they reside inevitably affect African and African diaspora women; yet, the forms of sexism and patriarchy that they experience are inflected by the circulation of capital, goods, and people in the context of global neoliberalization.

To demystify capitalism, we must demystify debt. International institutions such as the World Bank, IMF, and UNICEF, supported by a strand of neoliberal international feminism, have placed emphasis over the past few decades on women as potential capitalists and on microlending as a panacea for a whole array of economic and social issues.[48] In 2006, Bangladeshi Muhammad Yunus, a pioneer of microcredit programs targeting women and children, received the Nobel Peace Prize. The Nobel committee lauded microcredit initiatives as proof that "economic and social development from below" is possible.[49] Yet, under the guise of "female entrepreneurship," microlending programs often replace informal female support networks with the debt economy. In a recent interview, Marxist feminist Silvia Federici argues that "in the case of microfinance, banks and other financial agencies are turning the support groups that women have organized into self-policing groups. . . . This attack on communal solidarity, on the forms of cooperation people have created to strengthen their capacity for resistance, is probably the most destructive aspect of microfinance."[50] Similarly, Gayatri Chakravorty Spivak contends that "contemporary credit-baiting" is "an overdetermined script of cultural intervention: capital versus patriarchy as well as capital colluding with patriarchy."[51] Gender, race, class, and neoliberal profit accumulation create intersecting sites of oppression that exist in their mutual constitution. *Celles qui attendent* questions the separation between the cultural and the economic spheres; its gender analysis extends beyond the universalism/cultural relativism debate, embedding experiences of African women in the context of Atlantic indebtedness.

The Belly of the Atlantic already addressed the imbrication of cultural and economic questions through "the man from Barbès," a character who struggles in France, yet romanticizes immigrant life in front of Niodior youth. He flaunts his many possessions acquired abroad, including his multiple wives. The novel performs an important shift, representing polygamy not as a sign of adherence to African traditions, but as a mark of participation in global neoliberalization. As a form of social arrangement, polygamy does not exist outside of the neoliberal framework (implying that the acceptance of this framework would lead to female "progress" and more gender equality), but has been fully absorbed into the capitalist logic of exchange. The capacity to have multiple wives is, first, an indication of economic well-being since it requires financial stability. No longer a refusal of Western values, polygamy becomes suggestive of a successful assimilation into a system where buying power is indicative of success and happiness. However, this does not signify that polygamy is the consequence of capitalism. Rather, Diome suggests that a critique of polygamy conducted merely from a standpoint of human rights or modernity, without an analysis of neoliberalism, is insufficient. Tradition does not exist in opposition to modernity; it continuously evolves and adapts to the political and economic needs of the present: "Tradition is not about a reified past. It is about a dynamic present—a present into which the past is projected, and to which other traditions (with their pasts and presents) are linked."[52] Communities reinterpret and modify local traditions and hierarchies in relation to political and economic restructurings. In this instance, the practice of polygamy promotes the entanglement of heteronormativity and private property. In *Celles qui attendent,* patriarchy and capital collude within the sphere of microlending.

The novel focuses on four women—Arame, Bougna, Coumba, and Daba—belonging to two generations, mothers and wives of men who emigrated to Europe. Long-time friends, Arame and Bougna are both trapped in unhappy marriages. Unable to envision a future for their sons in their local village (and in order to be vindicated as successful mothers), they collaborate to send them to Europe. In *Celles qui attendent,* those who stay behind, living vicariously through the stories of those who return, do not experience immigration as an "in-between" cultural space but as an emptiness and a void. The novel addresses the absence created by those who departed, and the crushing uncertainty experienced by those who are left to wait.

As in *The Belly of the Atlantic,* the Atlantic extends beyond the triangle. Issa and Lamine are not trying to reach France, as one may expect, but are headed toward Spain. The specific country of destination is no longer as important as the abstract concept of Europe, gesturing toward the change in immigration patterns since the advent of the European Union. The primary goal is to reach *a* European shore, and national differences within Europe have lost some of their importance for immigrants. Arame and Bougna discuss this shift in immigration geographies:

> - Nos petits, tu crois qu'ils vont revenir bientôt?
> > - Je pense qu'ils viendront dès qu'ils auront des papiers en règles.
> > - Depuis toutes ces années, ils n'en ont toujours pas?
> > - Non, ils s'en occupent encore.
> > - Et s'ils n'y arrivent pas, tu crois que Sakoussy va les renvoyer? On dit qu'il a déjà renvoyé beaucoup des nôtres!
> > - Non, enfin, je veux dire que lui c'est en France, pas en Espagne. Cela dit, il a tellement démarché tous ses homologues que . . . (202)

> - And our children, do you think they will come back soon?
> > - I think that they'll come back as soon as their papers are in order.
> > - After all these years, they still don't have any?

- No, they're still trying to sort it out.
- And if they don't manage, do you think Sakoussy will send them back? They say he's already sent a lot of our people back!
- No, well, I mean, that's in France, not in Spain. That being said, he has solicited so many of his counterparts that . . .[53]

The utter confusion as to whether Issa and Lamine are in France or in Spain, dependent on "Sakoussy" or someone else, invites us to think about immigration not simply through the relationship between the metropole and its former colony, but within a shifting configuration of global power relations. The passage is also a parody of the European vision of Africa as a "dark," homogenous continent, without significant national and cultural differences. Here, Kathryn Lachman notes, "Spain and France merge into an undistinguished mass presided over by 'Sakoussy.'"[54] The nuances of different European national immigration policies are ironically effaced under a single preponderant consequence: deportation. This satirical reversal, as Lachman suggests, can be inscribed into the Francophone literary tradition, expressed most explicitly in Abdourahman Waberi's *Aux Etats-Unis d'Afrique* (2006) (*In the United States of Africa*, 2009). But the passage also gestures toward disjuncture in the process of global neoliberalization. The perception of global simultaneity, caused by technological advances, is experienced unevenly across the globe. The lives of characters in both *The Belly of the Atlantic* and *Celles qui attendent* are affected by global events, happening at a distance. However, information about such events is always received in a fragmentary manner—through TV, letters, phone calls, or the impersonal "on dit"—leading to a fractured understanding of trans-Atlantic connections.

To receive help in their households following the departure of their sons, Arame and Bougna convince Issa and Lamine to get married before leaving. Coumba and Daba consequently join the ranks of women whose loved ones have emigrated. The sudden absence of men transforms traditional gender roles and responsibilities; local women acquire more power but also a heavier burden to bear.[55] The novel describes Arame's and Bougna's everyday life, marked by the difficulty of providing for their families. Credit and debt immediately enter the narrative through the figure of Abdou, the local shopkeeper, a recurrent character in Francophone African literature and film. The only place where locals can acquire goods on credit is his shop. Lacking disposable currency, the villagers implore Abdou to exchange food for a promise that a payment will come. More often than not, this task is assigned to women, who assure Abdou that their husbands or sons will eventually pay. Abdou has no other choice but to, somewhat reluctantly, become the local creditor:

- Non! La boutique ne fait pas de crédit! On achète ou on dégage ! C'est simple, non?

C'était simple en apparence : ces mots, il les pensait, s'en gargarisait, les goûtait, les formulait, les reformulait avec l'application de qui prépare une plaidoirie, mais lorsqu'il se trouvait en situation de les sortir, tout devenait si complexe qu'il ne lui restait plus qu'à servir ses clients désargentés sans desserrer les dents. Après quoi, il restait à méditer sur son sort. (22)

- No, the store doesn't offer credit! You buy something or you get out! It's simple, isn't it?

It was simple only on the surface: he believed these words, he reveled in them, he tasted them in his mouth, he shaped and reshaped them with all the diligence one might apply to preparing one's case in court, but when he found himself in the situation where he needed to utter them, everything became so complicated that all he could do was help his penniless clients without opening his mouth. After which, he was left pondering his fate.

A creditor/debtor relation sustains the local economy. Thus, the novel does not merely idealize a local solidarity economy, one that with the intrusion of the IMF and the World Bank is replaced by a debt economy. Diome's ability to deconstruct the opposition between the local and the global, demonstrating how local traditions adapt themselves to economic and political restructurings is precisely what makes her fiction powerful. Nonetheless, there are significant differences between debt within the village and microloans extended to local women. Unlike Moussa's soccer recruiter, Abdou stands at the interstices of what David Graeber calls a human economy and a money economy.[56] The relation between Abdou and the local population in fact illustrates how certain characteristics of human economies have been transposed into money economies. Within the context of the village, Abdou is the primary creditor. Yet, what makes this relation different from the locals' relation to microlending institutions is interdependence.

In the village, Abdou is the primary creditor. However, his reliance on the village differentiates his position from that of a microlending institution. Abdou, Arame, and Bougna exist in a relation of mutual dependence: Arame and Bougna are evidently dependent on Abdou, given that he is their main supplier. However, the opposite is also true; strongly grounded in the community, with locals as his only customers, Abdou has no other choice but to operate a system based on debt and trust, predicated on the idea that the community will continue to function in this manner indefinitely. When survival depends on mutual reliance, credit has to be extended, and debts have to be repaid: "On ne prêtait pas seulement par générosité, mais pour avoir soi-même la garantie de pouvoir compter, à son tour, sur celui à qui on rendait service, si d'aventure la situation évoluait défavorablement" (139) [We didn't lend solely out of generosity, but in order to have the guarantee of being able to count on the person that we helped, if the situation were to deteriorate]. An underlying equality maintains this system. Interdependence assures the survival of the community, guaranteed by a similar degree of access to resources. If enough customers had enough money to always pay for their purchases, Abdou could rely on them, turning away those less fortunate. Only within the context of a relatively equal distribution of resources can the entire village (including Abdou) survive (not in a luxurious way) from this type of arrangement. Mutual dependence assures local cohesion. In other words, social relationships, and the willingness to help others because others will also provide help, play a significant role in this debt and credit system. Credit is possible because locals live in a system of mutually beneficial reciprocity, but it also serves to further build and maintain these relationships, leading to the "creation and mutual fashioning of human beings."[57]

These informal economic and social structures should not be idealized, and Niodior does not exist outside of capitalist modes of production (which should not be idealized either). The power distribution between Abdou and the rest of the population is certainly unequal. Abdou, we may assume, is also dependent on his suppliers, given that he does not produce what he sells, a dynamic that forces him to generate profit in order to remain solvent. Nonetheless, the debtor/creditor relationship changes significantly after Arame and Bougna resort to microcredit.

The two mothers turn to creative ways of survival, initially by selling seafood and wood for heating. This venture does not generate enough money so Bougna proposes a different business undertaking: they could sell doughnuts and peanuts in front of the local school. The new business temporarily alleviates their daily struggles, yet it fails as a long-term solution. A microlending institution, however, appears to save the day. Arame and Bougna sign on the dotted line, without fully understanding the conditions of the loan nor the concept of accruing interest rates, mostly enthralled by the amount of cash they will receive. Uninitiated into the capitalist business logic, they use most of the credit for their daily needs, infusing their business only with the meagre leftovers. An infinite spiral of credit, debt, and compiling interests ensues. Unable to pay the interests on their loan, Arame and Bougna borrow more money from distant relatives and local creditors:

A la fin du mois elles écumaient les marchands du coin ou leur parentèle, réunissaient de petits emprunts pour obtenir le montant du versement imposé. Après avoir difficilement honoré leur engagement les premiers mois, les retards s'accumulèrent, les dettes aussi. Outre leur dette au Crédit Mutuel, elles avaient maintenant des kyrielles de petits prêts à rembourser à des créanciers encore plus impatients que le banquier officiel. Dans l'esprit des défenseurs du microcrédit, qui croyaient agir pour leur bien, 2%, ce n'était rien, mais dans leur contexte à elles, c'était beaucoup. Arame et Bougna avaient certes mis du temps, mais elles avaient fini par se rendre compte qu'un bénéfice de 2% multiplié par un nombre incalculable de pauvres restait pour la banque une manière d'engranger du profit, aussi efficacement que ceux qui prêtent aux riches, moins nombreux, à des taux plus élevés. Le capitalisme humanitaire n'existe pas. (182)

At the end of the month they trolled all the stores in the neighborhood and all of their relatives, collecting little loans to obtain the amount required. After having—with difficulty—honored their commitment for the first few months, the payments began to run late, debt began to accumulate. In addition to their debt with the Crédit Mutuel, they now also had a plethora of little debts that they owed to creditors who were even more impatient than the official bankers. In the mind of microcredit advocates, who believed they were acting for the greater good, 2 per cent of this was nothing, but for these women, it was huge. It had taken Arame and Bougna a little time, yes, but they had eventually realized that a 2 per cent profit multiplied by an incalculable number of poor people was still a way for the bank to rake in profits, as effectively as it did with the money it loaned to rich people, who were less numerous, but at higher rates. Humanitarian capitalism does not exist.

Arame and Bougna thus transition from a form of credit grounded in social relations to an impersonal and anonymous one. Once a bank has replaced Abdou, social relationships disappear under the abstraction of financial capital. Étienne Balibar argues that two characteristics distinguish neoliberal debt: "One is that the same credit institutions (banks) subsidize both the production and the consumption of the same goods (e.g., housing), which means that, in a sense, they are *selling to themselves* at a profit through the mere intermediary of indebted industrials and consumers. The other is that debts are not only discounted, but also transformed into derivatives, which are *debts of debts*."[58] The passage underlines the oxymoron inherent in the concept of humanitarian capitalism; supposedly focusing on the "human," it replaces social networks and connections with anonymous and highly abstracted financial tools. Once they are dispossessed of their social resources, Arame and Bougna enter a cycle of debt that will never be repaid.

Unable to find a solution, Bougna decides that their daughters-in-law, Coumba and Daba, must seek work. She encourages Coumba to, on the days that she is not in charge of cooking, find work washing and ironing clothes for wealthier families. The microloan thus leads to a larger restructuring of family and social relations; female solidarity is broken as the women attempt to transform each other into profit-generating sources to repay their outstanding debts. Within the struggle for survival, human relationships are slowly instrumentalized.[59]

The belief that if women begin participating in capitalist development models, the entire family and the entire community will follow guides the microfinance philosophy. The proliferation of microfinance programs targeting women has recently caused protests across continents. Mujeres Creando, a Bolivian anarcha-feminist collective, gained worldwide attention in 2001 when, on behalf of people indebted to microfinance institutions, they occupied a Bolivian banking supervisory agency. Together with Deudora, a group of women from low-income neighborhoods, they protested for three and a half months in front of the agency. This popular mobilization enabled Deudora to reach an agreement with financial institutions, winning partial debt cancellation.[60] The No Pago movement in Nicaragua, with an estimated ten thousand members, has similarly advocated nonpayment of outstanding microfinance loans, arguing that microfinance institutions charge high interest rates, increasing rather than mitigating the financial burden of borrowers.[61]

Silvia Federici explains how microfinance transforms social relations into "social capital": "The World Bank and other financial institutions have realized that social relations are crucial, they see them as a 'social capital' and they use them, manipulate them, co-opt them to neutralize their subversive potential and domesticate the commons. . . . This is more than an attack on people's means of reproduction. It is an attack on the bonds that people have created on the basis of shared resources."[62] David Graeber similarly explains that the premise of Yunus's Grameen Bank in Bangladesh was that credit "is a human right." Simultaneously, "the idea was to draw on the 'social capital'— the knowledge, networks, connections, and ingenuity that the poor people of the world are already using to get by in difficult circumstances—and convert it into a way of generating even more (expansive) capital, able to grow at 5 to 20 percent annually."[63] *Celles qui attendent* engages the subjective experience of this process. There is not, however, a binary opposition between a perfect female solidarity before the entrance of microfinance institutions and a total destruction in its aftermath. Polygamy and power differentials within the family structure already complicate solidarity between the four women. Arame and Bougna's accomplishments are equated to the accomplishments of their sons. Bougna thus feels inferior to her cospouse whose son is a civil employee in Dakar; in order to prove herself, she sends Issa to Europe. Similarly, Arame and Bougna want their sons to marry before leaving in order to share the female burden of housework. The local family arrangements thus already encourage female competition. As such, they do not exist in complete opposition to neoliberal restructurings. Rather, the novel tries to point to ways in which local traditions and global economies work dialectically to promote patriarchy and prevent female solidarity. The indebted female subject is but the most recent incarnation of the capitalists' manipulation of gender for profit.

Diome, it could be said, is a didactic writer. In both novels, she proposes a clear solution to the youths' attraction to the mirage of Europe. In *The Belly of the Atlantic,* Sali sends Madické money to open a local store in Niodior. In *Celles qui attendent,* Issa's and Lamine's lives ultimately follow two different paths: Issa gets married in Europe and returns home with his white wife and mixed-race children to the outrage of Coumba. He continues to uphold his polygamous marriage across two continents, spending most of the year in Europe with his European family and the summers in Senegal with Coumba. Lamine, on the other hand, returns home; he forgives Daba for cheating while he was gone and invests everything he earned abroad into his family home and a local business. There is no doubt as to which solution Diome prefers. The message in both novels is clear: stay where you are, build local autonomy and self-sufficiency, and forget about the false European promises. However, beyond this didacticism, the novels also propose new ways of theorizing the Atlantic, immigration, and debt in the context of global neoliberalization. They allow us to think about the overlap between local and global practices, through debt as one of the primary mechanisms for creating a precarious Atlantic subject. Debt connects immigrants and locals in countries of both the Global South and the Global North. As they acquire debts, immigrants and locals (and countries) pledge their future time, which they spend trying to prove that they were a worthwhile investment. Feelings of personal failure and guilt accompany a possible default. Debt is one of the neoliberal mechanisms that transforms subjects into human capital, defining personal worth through a return on investment. However, the novels also offer alternative ways of thinking about owing and owning in the age of global neoliberalization. Lamine could have blamed Daba for her actions; he could have claimed a debt in exchange for his forgiveness. He, however, decides on a different approach. He thus embraces a model of human relationships based on forgiveness and the nonrepayment of certain debts, where debt is no longer used as a tool of oppression and subjugation. In the case of Moussa, the relationship between debt and literary writing is even more elaborate. The act of writing can be seen as a form of debt repayment, a way of opening up a space for other presents and futures. In the following chapter, I continue to examine how immigrant bodies are used as collateral in the global neoliberal economy. I do so no longer through the lens of debt but, rather, through an analysis of multinational corporations in the context of detective fiction.

CHAPTER 3

"How to Get Away with Murder"

Multinational Corporations
and Atlantic Crimes

I borrow the title of this chapter—"How to Get Away with Murder"—from a blog post on multinational corporations and human rights, written by Lauren Carmody, a member of the University of Western Australia's international law club. The piece offers a critical overview of human rights violations of multinational (also known as transnational) corporations that often move between different national jurisdictions to avoid legal sanction. It focuses specifically on nine activists from the Ogoni community in the Niger Delta basin, who, in 1995, were executed by the Nigerian military after protesting Shell.[1] Carmody's title is a salient introduction to this chapter, which looks at multinational corporations as the protagonists of detective novels. Focusing on multinationals, Atlantic authors address the violence of global neoliberalization but also strain against the literary conventions of crime fiction, fashioning the neoliberal anti-detective novel.

In this chapter, I explore specifically *Petroleum* (2004) by Swiss-Gabonese writer Bessora and *2666* (2004) by Chilean writer Roberto Bolaño. In both novels, multinationals become a relevant site to address the imbrication of various national spaces in the age of global neoliberalization. If different geographical spaces are connected, so are the various social and economic issues. The authors link the contemporary environmental crisis to the international division of labor, as the exploitation of precarious workers parallels the commodification and destruction of natural resources. "Green capitalism" cannot be the answer to our environmental crisis, both authors suggest, because it does not address the crux of the matter: the neoliberal logic of development and progress that instrumentalizes both workers and natural resources.

Dealing with the complex relation between the national and the transnational, the authors reshape the detective novel as genre. Both novels move beyond local violence to deal with transnational networks of capitalist power and oppression. I characterize both novels as neoliberal anti-detective fiction, as they parody the assumptions of the traditional detective novel, especially its reliance on science, logic, reason, and the existence of a single culprit. In both novels, neoliberal "rationality," its obsession with progress and development, and its overt reliance on technology and natural resources, lead concomitantly to the creation of precarious subjects, the destruction of the environment, and unsolvable crimes.

FROM COLONIAL COMPANIES TO MULTINATIONAL CORPORATIONS

Any discussion of global neoliberalization would indeed be incomplete without an analysis of multinational corporations—"parent" companies with foreign subsidiaries. Multinationals drive the neoliberal economy, often accruing revenues that exceed that of countries where they do business. Their number has dramatically increased over the past few decades, from seven thousand in 1970 to seventy-nine thousand in 2006 (though the top one hundred companies still concentrate most of the wealth).[2] The *Global Justice Now* campaign group published a report in 2015, stating that the revenue of the world's ten largest corporations amounts to $2.9 trillion, surpassing China's tax revenue. Of the one hundred major global economic players, the report states, sixty-nine are corporations and only thirty-one are countries.[3]

That they operate across borders is not enough to define a multinational; as Paul Baran and Paul Sweezy argue, the primary characteristic of a multinational is that "its management makes fundamental decisions on marketing, production, and research in terms of alternatives that are available to it anywhere in the world."[4] The more corporations extend multinationally, the more dissociated top executives become from the production process. Headquarters thus focus primarily on finance, delegating production, labor, and sometimes marketing to the subsidiaries. The proliferation of multinationals has led, as Franco Berardi explains, to "the dissemination of the labor process into a multitude of productive islands formally autonomous, but actually coordinated and ultimately dependent."⁵ This fragmentation frequently masks transnational relations of production.

The concept of the multinational corporation is not entirely new. European colonial powers protected the interests of companies like the British East India Trading Company or the French East India Company, frequently granting them monopoly over trade with colonial territories. Yet, Giovanni Arrighi argues, we should not overstate the equivalence between colonial (joint-stock) companies and contemporary multinationals:

> Joint-stock chartered companies were part-governmental, part-business organizations, which specialized *territorially,* to the exclusion of other similar organizations. Twentieth-century transnational corporations, in contrast, are strictly business organizations, which specialize *functionally* in specific lines of production and distribution, across multiple territories and jurisdictions, in cooperation and competition with other similar organizations.⁶

For Arrighi, there is a crucial difference between the two: while the chartered companies cemented the power of nation-states, contemporary corporations undermine it. By 1970, multinational corporations had become "a world-scale system of production, exchange and accumulation, which was subject to no state authority and had the power to subject to its own 'laws' each and every member of the interstate system, the United States included."⁷ In fact, through a variety of mechanisms, multinationals undercut national authority. They often benefit from tax exemptions in both the country of origin and the country of operation, leading to "double non-taxation."⁸ Through investor-state dispute settlements (ISDS), which allow them to sue countries that interfere with their operations in independent arbitration courts, they increasingly challenge the sovereignty of nation-states, operating oftentimes as a state within a state. Multinationals have also played a significant role in shaping Europe's Single Market agreement, NAFTA, and the Uruguay Round of the General Agreement on Tariffs and Trade (GATT). Economists Herman Daly and Robert Goodland ascertain that "the deregulation of trade aims to erase national boundaries insofar as these affect economic life."⁹ In light of these developments, in the 1990s, the denomination "transnational corporation" began to replace the multinational, suggesting that corporations are increasingly spreading their decision-making processes across their affiliates, no longer relying on a single national home. In 2008, the *Economist* published an article praising the "stateless multinational," a firm "seamlessly integrated across time zones and cultures" that no longer depends on a single national home.¹⁰

Yet, it should also be noted that the majority of the top one hundred MNCs still have their headquarters in the Triad: the United States, the EU, and Japan.[11] These corporations heavily invest in the Global South. In fact, since the mid-1980s, corporate investment in the Global South has outpaced national development aid, due to "global labor arbitrage"—to borrow a term from Intan Suwandi and John Bellamy Foster—"a system of unequal exchange based on a worldwide hierarchy of wages, sharply dividing center and periphery."[12] In other words, multinationals profit from lower wages in the Global South, as well as looser health and environmental regulations. In the Global South, governments have been "queuing up to attract multinationals," the *Economist* notes, making their countries attractive by privatizing public sector industries and lowering taxes and tariffs. To justify these measures, governments portray multinationals as "the embodiment of modernity and the prospect of wealth: full of technology, rich in capital, replete with skilled jobs."[13] Thus, while the power of multinationals extends beyond states, states still play a significant role in creating and maintaining favorable conditions for foreign investment. In turn, once the profits are repatriated, multinationals contribute to economic and social inequalities between countries. This "subcontracting" system also allows corporations to defuse responsibility, often blaming their foreign subsidiaries for poor labor, health, and environmental conditions.

Alain Badiou speaks of a "diagonal relation" between states and "financial concentrations of power":

> Not only have states largely become what Marx already thought they were, namely "the delegates of capital power" (but I don't know whether Marx ever imagined the extent to which, over the last thirty years, reality would prove him right); not only are states the delegates of capital power, but there is increasingly a kind of discordance between the scale upon which large firms exist and the scale upon which states exist, which makes the existence of large firms diagonal to that of states. The power of the great industrial, banking, and retail conglomerates coincides neither with the state sphere, nor even with that of coalitions of states. This capitalist power crosses over states as if it were at once independent of them and mistress of them.[14]

Multinationals operate within but also across and beyond nation-states, traversing and transecting state power. This diagonal relationship between states and corporations has created cracks within national sovereignty, spaces that fall between national and transnational responsibility, where precarious subjects reside. It has also become the focus of several contemporary trans-Atlantic novels. *Petroleum* focuses on Elf-Gabon, a local subsidiary of a French oil company. It traces the history of the company from its colonial incarnation as the Société des pétroles d'Afrique-Équatoriale française (SPAEF) to the privately owned multinational corporation that it is today.[15] A relation between colonial companies and contemporary multinationals definitely exists, the novel suggests in a humorous fashion.

Roberto Bolaño's 2666 takes place all over the world. The longest part, however, deals with the murders of women working (mostly) in *maquiladoras,* manufacturing or export assembly plants in northern Mexico, the majority of which are foreign-owned. The proliferation of maquiladoras along the US–Mexico border is explained by the fact that Mexican labor is inexpensive and, courtesy of NAFTA, taxes and custom fees are low. Alicia Gaspar de Alba notes that "Mexican women workers have become as expendable as pennies in the hungry slot machine of transnational capitalism. . . . The tragedy of the dead women's lives did not begin when their bones were dumped in the desert, but when they first set foot inside a *maquiladora.*"[16]

Bessora's and Bolaño's novels posit multinational corporations as formative sites for global precarious subjects. The oil ship and the maquiladora carry an ambivalent association with a specific national context, as their main purpose is to serve the global flows of capital. Bessora's oil ship is stationed off the coast of Gabon, yet it belongs to a multinational French corporation. Speaking about Total, Badiou notes: "Thus we see that large firms—for example the largest French firm, Total—pay no tax in France. So in what does their 'frenchness' lie? Well, their headquarters are somewhere in Paris, but . . . the French state, as you can see, does not really have any hold, even on concentrated poles of power that proclaim their French nationality. What is in progress is a victory, a vast and ramified victory, of transnational firms over the sovereignty of states."[17] These competing sovereignties but also competing visions of the colonial past and the neoliberal present are at the center of Bessora's novel. Bolaño's maquiladoras similarly demarcate the blurry line between the national and the transnational.

In *Petroleum,* corporate multiculturalism presents itself as a new world, a new era, and an ideology that has replaced colonial power relations now relegated to the "place of memory." In fact, two discourses are imbricated and juxtaposed. The discourse of corporate multiculturalism positions the corporation as a world of its own, bound only by a contractual purpose, dissociated from local history and not responsible for local society. But the reader is also exposed to what Bessora calls the "mémoire bléssée" [wounded memory] of oil, a collection of oral memories, stories, and myths, which attempt to place the corporation into a long history of colonial and postcolonial resource extraction; a history which has deeply shaped and continues to shape Gabon.

In *2666*, maquiladoras employ Mexican workers but also female immigrants from other Central American countries trying to reach the United States. Often without documents or family ties in Santa Teresa, these women are murdered without anyone to identify or claim their bodies. The novel traces transnational circuits of neoliberal violence, identifying an array of forces that have created disposable bodies that require no accountability. Both novels focus on spaces that fall into the cracks between national and international responsibility, creating nonaccountability zones.

OIL, SHIPS, AND MULTINATIONALS

Born in Brussels to a Gabonese father and a Swiss mother, Sandrine Bessora Nan Nguema (aka Bessora) has lived in Switzerland, France, Gabon, and the United States. After graduating from the Faculty of Business and Economics of the University of Lausanne, she pursued a career in finance before dramatically changing course. After a long stay in South Africa, she enrolled in a doctoral program in anthropology in Paris and published her first novel in 1999. In 2001, she obtained the Prix Fénéon for her novel *Les taches d'encre* (2000). The Grand prix littéraire d'Afrique noire was awarded to her in 2007 for her novel *Cueillez-moi jolis Messieurs* . . . . Perhaps unsurprisingly, the question of finance, and especially the relation between finance and language, plays an important role in her literary work. Referring to Bessora's first two novels, Susan Ireland argues: "In both of these zany works, humor is Bessora's main strategy for making serious social commentary. The wide range of comic devices used in the texts—farce, irony, intertextual allusions, pastiche, parody, quid pro quos, and every kind of word-play imaginable—produces a generically hybrid form, a metafictional novel."[18] While in *Petroleum* Bessora no longer focuses on African immigrant communities in Paris but rather on the international business community in Gabon, humor and parody remain her main weapon. These literary devices are, however, combined with an extensive knowledge of the history of oil extraction in Gabon (Bessora completed a PhD thesis in anthropology entitled "Mémoires pétrolières au Gabon" [Oil memories in Gabon]). The Ocean Liberator, a drillship belonging to the Elf multinational, is a microcosm where the class, race, and gender dynamics of a fossil-fuel economy are accentuated.

Petroleum begins with a prophecy of a new beginning. The Ocean Liberator is drilling deeper than ever before in an effort to uncover the remaining sources of oil in Gabon. Onboard the ship, we encounter an array of characters, including Médée, a young French geologist, who was recruited from British Petroleum because she had thus far never failed to successfully locate the resource that the omniscient narrator suggestively names "black Gold." After a mysterious explosion on the ship, which takes the life of Etienne, the second in command, a profiler from Paris arrives to help solve the crime. The main suspect is Jason, the local cook and Médée's love interest, who disappeared after the accident. Jason grew up with Louise, capable of communicating with local spirits, who are deeply angered by the geologists' continuous profanation of the local land and water. In the early 1990s, he joined protests against Elf, holding a sign that threatened to blow up Port-Gentil if Elf does not leave. Shot in the back when the French army intervened, he nearly died. Alidor Minko, a former union activist now the director of the company's public relations, is also deeply involved in the investigation.

Ocean Liberator exists at the intersection of different people and capital flows, as it belongs to a French company, is situated off the coast of Gabon, and employs Gabonese, French, British, Italian, and Filipino workers. The organization of the company is in fact ironically described as an adventure in multiculturalism, where the expat manager/national worker duo has replaced the now outdated colonizer/colonized pair. Multiculturalism, the narrator suggests, is but a euphemism for neocolonialism. The novel also offers an ironic take on the "immigrant problem." If a problem exists, Bessora suggests, it stems from expat managers acting as modern-day colonizers.

As of late, the term expat has come under scrutiny. A blog post on *SiliconAfrica.com* entitled "Why Are White People Expats When the Rest of Us Are Immigrants?" went viral when republished on multiple websites including the *Guardian, Alternet,* and *Wearechange.* In the article, Mawuna Remarque Koutonin notes that the term expat, unlike the term immigrant, carries no derogatory connotation: "What is an expat? And who is an expat? According to Wikipedia 'an expatriate (often shortened to expat) is a person temporarily or permanently residing in a country other than that of the person's upbringing. The word comes from the Latin terms ex ('out of') and patria ('country, fatherland')." In light of this definition, one would expect the term to apply to all nations and races equally. However, this is not the case. The term expat is reserved primarily for white professionals: "Africans are immigrants. Arabs are immigrants. Asians are immigrants. However, Europeans are expats because they can't be at the same level as other ethnicities. They are superior. Immigrants is a term set aside for 'inferior races.'"[19]

Koutonin cites the *Wall Street Journal* blog, which, in a featured story, "In Hong Kong, Just Who Is an Expat, Anyway?," similarly concludes: "Some arrivals are described as expats; others as immigrants; and some simply as migrants. It depends on social class, country of origin and economic status. . . . Anyone with roots in a western country is considered an expat. . . . Filipino domestic helpers are just guests, even if they've been here for decades. Mandarin-speaking mainland Chinese are rarely regarded as expats. . . . It's a double standard woven into official policy."[20] Koutonin ultimately proposes the effacement of the word expat and a more democratic assignment of the immigrant status. This clear-cut opposition between European expats and non-European immigrants could be complicated by, for instance, the panic in British public discourse when Romanians and Bulgarians finally received the right to work in the EU.[21] Although white and European, Romanians and their fellow Eastern Europeans seldom fall into the category of expats. Nonetheless, the debate underscores the race and class undertones of "immigrant" as a term.[22]

In *Petroleum,* the immigrant and the expat meet on the Ocean Liberator. For this reason, in this chapter I focus on Bessora's *Petroleum* rather than her earlier novels. It may seem counterintuitive to include *Petroleum* in a study on immigrant fiction. Bessora's first novel *53cm* (1999) or *Les taches d'encre* (2000) are much more obvious choices. However, these novels focus predominantly on race relations in a European country still marked by its colonial past. I have chosen *Petroleum* precisely because of Bessora's depiction of the drillship as a globalized workplace. Like Condé, Bessora places a country from the Global South at the center of immigration rather than just emigration. The novel thus encourages a different engagement with the concept of immigrant labor, given that the "problematic" figure is no longer the worker from the Global South living in Europe or the United States, but European and American expats, working in a country of the Global South.

THE GLOBALIZED WORKPLACE

The choice of the ship gestures toward a transhistorical understanding of the Atlantic. At the basis of the Atlantic economy, there has always been a ship. Paul Gilroy thus claims that "ships immediately focus attention on the middle passage, on the various projects for redemptive return to an African homeland, on the circulation of ideas and activists as well as the movement of key cultural and political artefacts: tracts, books, gramophone records, and choirs."[23] Bessora replaces the slave ship with the oil ship, adding new dimensions to the metaphor. The Ocean Liberator gestures toward the history of French colonialism in Gabon, but also toward neocolonial circuits of corporate power. Unlike most ships, the Ocean Liberator is stationed. It is a space where transnational flows of people, capital, and resources intersect and encounter their own contradictions. The focus is no longer on the Middle Passage or the redemptive return, both of which fixate the African continent in its past. Rather, the diagonal (shifting) relationships between Gabon, the Ocean Liberator, and Elf delineate the transformation of the colonial past into the neoliberal present. The past is present, yet it exists in a dynamic relationship with the social reality that it shapes.

On the Ocean Liberator, Médée's and Étienne's endless calculations and predictions guide the process of oil extraction. The entire staff of the ship is at the same time supported by the material labor of Jason, the cook. Bessora traces the entire international chain of labor, which originates with natural resource extraction in Gabon and ends in financial speculations on Wall Street. The abstractness of the financial market and its supposed capacity for infinite expansion collide with the concrete and finite nature of both material labor and natural resources, leading to the current economic and environmental crisis.

The choice of a drillship as a site of reflection about the contemporary division of labor is significant, as it gestures toward neoliberal power distribution. On board the Ocean Liberator, local workers, in charge of the physical extraction of oil, are located on the bottom floor of the ship, under the constant supervision of foreign technicians, located straight above them: "Au sommet, les directeurs et cadres très supérieurs. . . . Au milieu, un agrégat d'agents techniques et administratifs, classe moyenne à deux vitesses, la blanche et la noire, avec ascenseur dans le premier cas. . . . En bas, les classes laborieuses strictement indigènes. . . . Marne à engraisser les deux premières" (9) [At the very top, the senior executives and directors. . . . In the middle, an aggregate of technical and administrative agents, a sort of two-tier middle class, white and black, with an elevator for the former. . . . And at the bottom, the always indigenous working classes. . . . Marl that fattens up the first two].[24]

This passage epitomizes Bessora's use of humor and word play to describe contemporary power relations. The spatial organization of the city and the barge reveal the power dynamics that the official discourses, like corporate multiculturalism, deny. Bessora, throughout the novel, ironically comments on the intersections of class and race. Corporate "meritocracy" has supposedly replaced colonial divisions, yet it somehow still follows old racial hierarchies. To describe local workers, located at the bottom of the corporate pyramid, Bessora uses a geological term that not every reader might recognize: *marne/marl,* a sedimentary rock made of clay and lime. In the rest of the paragraphs, the upper and middle classes are compared to plastic and sandy clay. Through these geological terms, Bessora roots the narrative in the material and natural reality of Gabon, establishing, simultaneously, a parallel between natural and

human resources. The geological metaphor conjoins the exploitation of natural resources and the exploitation of local labor, both used to maintain a transnational class and race hierarchy. Often used as a fertilizer, marl enhances
growth and production, just like local workers.

If workers are compared to natural rocks, nature is also continuously per-
sonified. The act of drilling is thus compared to an act of sexual penetration,
with the discovery of petroleum as the final ejaculation. While drawing on the
familiar topos of the female land raped by the male colonizer, Bessora com-
plexifies gender dynamics. The penetration is performed by a female character, Médée, in the name of a company. Petroleum is the child of the earth and
varying fathers: Ocean Liberator, Elf, or perhaps even Médée. The discovery of
petroleum is equated to the act of giving birth. Yet this creation of new life also
brings death, maintaining Gabon in the neocolonial trap. Binaries exist in a
relation of mutual constitution, including the colonizer and colonized, the expatriate and the national, men and women, life and death. Médée's position is similarly ambiguous: she is simultaneously birthing new life and releasing death.

The specificity of the oil industry is emblematic of contemporary forms
of labor organization. In *Carbon Democracy: Political Power in the Age of Oil,*
Timothy Mitchell explores the relation between carbon energy and modern
democratic politics. He explains how the rise of the oil industry and its progressive replacement of the coal industry enabled a new form of labor politics:
"An important goal of the conversion to oil was to permanently weaken the
coal miners, whose ability to interrupt the flow of energy had given organ-
ised labour the power to demand the improvements to collective life that had
democratised Europe."[25] Spending most of their days in the mines, with no
supervisors nearby, coal workers enjoyed a certain degree of autonomy. They
also controlled the transportation of coal and, thus, were in a position to significantly disrupt the system. This led to several significant miner strikes in
both England and the US in the 1940s and '50s. The shift to oil entailed closer
supervision of workers and significantly curbed their political power. Sharing
their workspace with their supervisors, oil workers no longer benefited from
spatial autonomy. Oil pipelines, which require very little worker supervision,
have been a lot less affected by labor actions.

Spatial autonomy (and the lack thereof) are central in the novel. On the
one hand, the economic domain is continuously expanding through space.
The novel thus outlines the progressive expansion of Elf throughout the
national territory of Gabon, in constant search for oil. This spatial extension
contrasts with the confined spaces within which the managerial class operates.
The characters rarely find themselves in open spaces, as most of the narrative

unfolds in private spaces such as the boat, the Elf-Gabon office building, and the company's apartment complex. When the plot takes us out of these private spaces, the city is still navigated through the enclosed space of a private car or cab. In other words, the class and racial segregation of spaces is contrasted to the extension of economic power across all of these spaces. The corporate elite shapes places that it never enters:

> Elf bâtit son boulevard entre la compagnie forestière et la société pétrolière. Il est parallèle à un vieux canal qui autrefois séparait la ville blanche, interdite aux Noirs, des villages africains. En ce temps-là, la cité blanche prospérait en bordure de la baie qui, de siècle en siècle, vit naître et mourir des cases à sel, des entrepôts d'esclaves, des maisons de commerce, des filiales de compagnies concessionnaires, des parcs à bois.
> Le canal séparait deux races.
> Le boulevard sépare deux classes, dont l'une est noire. (123–24)

> Elf built its boulevard between the forestry company and the oil company. It runs parallel to an old canal that used to separate the white part of town, off limits to Black people, from the African villages. During that time, the white city prospered all along the bay, which century after century saw the ebb and flow of so many salt bunkers, slave warehouses, trading firms, concessionary subsidiaries, logyards.
> The canal separated two races.
> The boulevard separates two classes, one of which happens to be Black.

In an ironic tone, the passage articulates a transhistorical understanding of capitalism and the inextricability of race and class. A class division has replaced the colonial racial division, yet, in fact, not much has changed aside from semantics. Bessora also points to the inextricability of different domains of reality: natural resources, industry, and urban development. The shift in natural resources—from wood to oil—marks the different periods of Gabonese history. These distinct realities are historically and spatially connected by Elf, which operates across them. The boulevard and the canal run in parallel, as do colonial history and the neoliberal present. By tracing the semantic, spatial, and resource shifts (from the colonizer to the expat manager; from the canal to the boulevard; from wood to oil), the narrative places the present into a historical context. Behind or under the corporate discourse on multiculturalism, progress, and development are the "salt bunkers, slave warehouses, trading firms, concessionary subsidiaries, logyards."

GLOBALIZATION, ECOCRITICISM, AND ANTICAPITALISM

The novel depicts a more-than-a-century-long history of "progress" and "development," founded on the continuous extraction of resources, which has come to its point of exhaustion. In fact, Médée is recruited by Elf precisely because existing oil reserves have been depleted. She is meant to fulfill the geologists' prediction that, in spite of scarcity, untapped oil resources will be discovered: "Après un long périple, l'Or noir rencontrera la faille. Son voyage s'achèvera par trois mille mètres de fond. Le Libérateur le délivrera des entrailles de la terre" (7) [After a long journey, the black Gold will reach the surface. Its voyage will have spanned three thousand meters in depth. The Liberator will deliver it from the bowels of the earth]. Written in 2004, the novel inscribes itself into a growing global environmental movement that has pushed back against the principle of extraction, production, and consumption. *Petroleum* is set in our contemporary moment in history, where planetary resources are being depleted at an unprecedented rate. Economic and social paradigms of infinite growth have also come to a halt, as they have stumbled against the finitude of our planet. Mitchell argues that the relative accessibility of oil, since the 1950s and '60s, has enabled the predominance of the economics of growth.[26] Due to its continuously declining price, relative profusion and easy transport, oil appeared inexhaustible. Furthermore, economic growth, measured usually in terms of GDP, did not, until fairly recently, need to take into consideration the depletion of energy resources. Nowadays, however, it has become evident that oil resources are limited. We are no longer operating from a position of abundance and accumulation, but rather, from one of exhaustion and lack. The novel raises the question of where we go from here: Are the notions of exhaustion and lack emblematic of an unavoidable collapse or apocalypse? The neoliberal answer has thus far been a refusal of the paradigm shift. The liberatory act, within the context of Elf-Gabon and the Ocean Liberator, is the discovery of untapped resources meant to postpone the apocalypse caused by the lack. It thus promotes the same logic of capitalist expansion into unconquered markets, including the depths of the earth.

While it is not without referential dimensions, the discourse of depletion/exhaustion like that of discovery/progress is a discourse that reflects various kinds of ideological and sociopolitical investments. It has thus been used to justify austerity measures and cuts to public services across the globe.[27] Furthermore, in his analysis of the oil industry, Mitchell argues that from the beginning oil companies have promoted the concept of scarcity in order to keep oil prices high.[28] The environmental crisis is, thus, inseparable from the many political discourses that claim it. *Petroleum* poses precisely the question of alternative framings.

Petroleum shifts back and forth between the present moment, identified both as the end of a paradigm and an open space for the imagination of alternatives, and a historical account of oil exploitation in Gabon. Myth, fiction, and historical facts entwine as Bessora unravels the history of Gabon through the history of Elf-Gabon. The latter, it turns out, has a very controversial history, including, among other episodes, the trial of its top managers. Until its privatization in 1994, the company belonged to Elf-Aquitaine, which, the prosecutors argued, "worked as an unofficial arm of France's murkiest diplomacy."[29] When it expanded into the African continent in the 1960s and '70s, Elf paid bribes to African officials and funneled money into French politics. The secretive and illegal nature of Elf affairs seems to condone its portrayal in the form of detective fiction.

The focus on Elf is, however, significant beyond its historical accuracy. Departing from the established novelistic paradigms of national/regional history, *Petroleum* stages the history of a multinational company. As opposed to fictions that mention the economic dimension only insofar as it affects the lives of characters within a national setting, here the political and social dimensions are mentioned only insofar as they affect the life of the company. Ocean Liberator exists as a world onto itself. Even though on Gabonese territory, the company operates almost entirely independently from the Gabonese government and the Gabonese people. The oil is extracted, the profits repatriated, the stocks traded on an international market. The novel further points to the inextricability of political and economic dimensions and presents us with a world where all dimensions of life have been overshadowed by the economic sphere.

As the Ocean Liberator is under investigation, the narrative takes us into the world of the "divinités maritimes" [sea deities]. We learn that Jason grew up with Louise, a local woman initiated into the secrets of the spirit world. The novel then oscillates between the contemporary reality of Gabon and Elf-Gabon and that of the legends and stories that Louise used to recount to Jason, introducing him to various mythical creatures, including the mermaid-like sea deity, Mamiwata. According to local memories and stories, the conflict between the local spirits and the Western "explorers" reaches far back into history, but now the spirits have finally risen up against the desecration of their habitat. In 1962, as Louise attempts to initiate Jason into the secrets of the "other world," she wonders: "Maintenant, les casques orange fouillaient les eaux; les génies aquatiques, sujets de Mamiwata, demanderait-ils leur comptant?" (192–93) [Now, the hard hats were rummaging through the water; would the water genies, disciples of Mamiwata, ask for their share?] On many levels, the novel thus represents a binary structure: the city is divided into two classes/two races, while it is simultaneously divided into two worlds, the world of the spirits and the world of the mortals. Yet, in Bessora's fiction, every binary structure is quickly deconstructed.

Petroleum contrasts the exploitation of natural resources by multinational companies to a more local and anthropomorphic understanding of nature. The latter treats nature as a source of knowledge and power, the former, as a commodity. Thus, for instance, in 1926 Zéphyrin, Louise's uncle, leads foreign explorers in their search for oil, even though he knows that this will anger the forest spirits. When the prospectors disregard his warning not to cut down a tree deemed sacred, they disappear in an abyss created by the tree. The local perspective in the novel, it could be argued, attempts "to envision individuals and groups as part of planetary 'imagined communities' of both human and nonhuman kinds," which, according to Ursula Heise, is one of the main characteristics of "eco-cosmopolitanism." Heise further distinguishes between an apocalyptic and a risk perspective: "In the apocalyptic perspective, utter destruction lies ahead but can be averted and replaced by an alternative future society; in the risk perspective, crises are already underway all around, and while their consequences can be mitigated, a future without their impact has become impossible to envision."[30] The notions of risk and crisis drive the plot of *Petroleum*. Yet the novel also connects this crisis to the global division of labor, pointing to the contradictions inherent in the term "green capitalism."

The term "green capitalism" has been used to refer to the expansion of alternative energy markets and the proliferation of eco-friendly products. While these eco-markets may address the depletion of natural resources, they are already highly transnationalized and operate along the same laws of neoliberal capital accumulation. For instance, in a State of the Union address, former President Barack Obama declared: "The nation that leads the clean-energy economy will be the nation that leads the global economy, and America must be that nation."[31] Here, clean energies are simply presented as a new, unexplored market that the planet will soon depend on. Market ideology and its labor politics are never questioned. Unless we begin to relate the question of natural resources to the question of labor, it is highly unlikely that labor politics of the clean-energy industry will be equitable.

Petroleum challenges the concept of green capitalism precisely because it combines a representation of nature with the analysis of a transnational workplace. The exploitation of natural resources in the novel is related to different modes of worker control and exploitation. The question of sustainability is thus concomitant to the question of labor politics. The narrator, for instance, ironically states: "Or, l'écologie est le premir souci d'Elf. Comme les droits de l'homme" (33) [Well, environmentalism is Elf's primary concern. Just like workers' rights]. An explicit link is made here between human rights (and by extension worker rights) and the rights of nature. The same logic of commodification extends to people and natural resources alike. Thus, Flavie Minko, Alidor's daughter who is conducting anthropological research on the Ocean Liberator, wants to talk to Médée about her "human resources." The novel mocks the Western dichotomy of nature/culture, where man stands outside of nature, whose role is to facilitate his advancement. Not only is this opposition problematic, it is also not actually upheld. In Western culture, Bessora suggests, people and nature are more interconnected than one might think. Neoliberalism equates them by treating them both in equally materialistic terms; both are merely resources meant to sustain economic growth and development.

The question of lack pushes anticapitalist critique further than a mere incrimination of companies. The fact that oil reserves may be reaching their limit points to the end of an entire paradigm. The logic of development, growth, and consumption has come to a halt. The depletion of oil could thus be an opportunity to challenge this model of unlimited growth and the economic discourse that prioritizes prices and markets over questions of resource distribution and social equality. In this vein, the novel aligns with postcolonial ecocriticism. Graham Huggan, in his work *Postcolonial Ecocriticism: Literature, Animals, Environment,* describes "postcolonial writers as both 'underground' critics of mainstream development processes and unacknowledged legislators for alternative, often community-oriented, styles and modes of development that are uncoupled from neoliberal principles of market expansion and economic growth."[32] Bessora's originality lies in the fact that she does this within the context of a multinational corporation and the detective novel.

Bessora, furthermore, does not simply valorize the world of the spirits as opposed to the corporate world. Rather, she places the capitalist belief in progress (through oil) and the local belief in Mamiwata on the same plane. Both have the status of myths. Ireland argues that "as reflexive texts, Bessora's novels can perhaps most accurately be described as a type of historiographic metafiction, a term coined by Linda Hutcheon to characterize works that reintroduce historical context into metafiction in order to rethink 'the forms and contents of the past.'"[33] In fact, in *Petroleum,* Bessora returns to colonial history and the history of resource extraction in order to question the role of colonial discourse in sustaining a neoliberal reality. The narrator explicitly states that everything began with the "adhésion collective à la légende pétrolière" and the "adhésion collective à la légende coloniale" (239) [collective adherence to the oil legend; collective adherence to the colonial legend]. The myth of Western superiority depends on the myth that oil companies will bring prosperity. A third myth is introduced: the myth of the Golden Fleece. Bessora's Médée is named after the character from the Greek myth who helps Jason on the Golden Fleece quest. She tells us: "Le pétrole est la toison d'or et Elf est son gardien" (245) [Oil is the Golden Fleece and Elf is its guardian]. From the colonial to the neoliberal age, the struggle for resources continues, and oil is the substance that assures power.

By reducing the capitalist logic of progress supported by oil to the status of a myth, Bessora underlines what Gayatri Spivak calls the "worlding" of "the Third World," a process by which the violent cultural and economic domination of the West is obscured under the civilizing mission paradigm.[34] In contemporary times, the civilizing mission has become the development mission: corporate domination is obfuscated under the promise of oil-driven growth. The discourses of corporate multiculturalism, technology, history, and myth are intertwined and reversed in the novel. Mythical language is often mobilized when describing the work of the geologists. As already mentioned, the geologists' prediction that new oil will be found is likened to the prediction of an oracle. Médée's skills are also often described in supernatural terms: if Louise is Mamiwata's priestess, Médée is the priestess of oil. Concomitantly, local memories and stories are enriched with specific historical details, including exact years and geographical locations. In others words, the economic and scientific discourse of the geologists and managers is endowed with mythical characteristics, whereas the local oral tradition grounds the reader in concrete historical reality. The oppositions between myth and history, science and the supernatural, are thus narratively deconstructed.

BOLAÑO'S UNACCOUNTED SUBJECTS

Before moving to Europe in 1977 (and eventually settling in Spain), Bolaño spent most of his life between Chile and Mexico. *Nocturno de Chile* (2000), the first of Bolaño's novels translated into English (*By Night in Chile*, 2003), is a monologue of a sick and aging priest, who over the course of a single evening, remembers all the important people and events of his life. In his posthumous novel, *2666* (originally published in 2004 and in English translation in 2008), Bolaño's perspective broadens, exploring twentieth-century global history and reaching a very wide audience. The novel won the 2008 National Book Critics Circle Award for Fiction and was short-listed for the Best Translated Book Award. *Time* awarded it the honor of Best Fiction Book of 2008, while the *New York Times Book Review* listed it among their "10 Best Books of 2008." Bolaño's acquired international fame and the creation of the "Bolaño myth" have been widely discussed. Sarah Pollack suggests that Bolaño's success in the United States is partially due to the marketing of the writer as a renegade artist, one who embodies the image of a Latin America where all political, sexual, spiritual, and literary fantasies are easily satisfied.[35] Critics have further maintained that whereas he fiercely criticized the global capitalist system, Bolaño also profited significantly from that same system. His novel *2666* addresses many of these questions: the creation of the myth of the author, the roles of fiction, readership, and literary criticism in the age of global neoliberalization.

Divided into five parts—"The part about the critics," "The part about Amalfitano," "The part about Fate," "The part about the crimes," "The part about Archimboldi"—*2666* deals with an extraordinary array of characters and locations, all revolving around the themes of violence, evil, and fiction. The first three parts of the novel follow a group of European academics, a Chilean philosopher, and an African American journalist, whose quests all lead them to Santa Teresa, a possible literary mirror of Ciudad Juárez. The profuse female homicides that occurred in Santa Teresa between 1993 and 1997 are the focus of part 4. In the final part, we finally learn about Archimboldi, the mysterious writer that the academics sought in part 1. The stories and paths of these different characters intersect as they all begin to wonder about the why and the how of the Santa Teresa crimes. Though these different parts could be read independently, together they form a rhizomatic portrait of global neoliberalization and its violence.

CONGEALING GLOBAL FLOWS

The first part focuses on four literary critics—the French Jean-Claude Pelletier, the Italian Piero Morini, the Spanish Manuel Espinoza, and the English Liz Norton—in pursuit of Benno Von Archimboldi, an almost mythical German author whose trace has been lost. The critics follow Archimboldi all the way to Santa Teresa, where continuous femicides interrupt their scholarly quest. The critics' pursuit of knowledge (of an absent author) thus encounters the materiality of female workers' bodies. The violence of global neoliberalization culminates under the supervision of multinationals, yet it also reverberates across places and times, beginning significantly earlier in the narrative.

Before reaching Santa Teresa, Pelletier and Espinoza, both in love with Norton, come to visit her in London, hoping that she will finally choose one of them. As they are driving in a cab, they begin to discuss Norton's relation to her former lover. The discussion develops under the gaze of a Pakistani driver whose comments lead to a violent confrontation. The driver's remark that London is like a labyrinth offsets the argument:

> Algo que llevó a Espinoza a decir que el taxista, sin proponérselo, coño, claro, había citado a Borges, que una vez comparó Londres con un laberinto. A lo que Norton replicó que mucho antes que Borges Dickens y Stevenson se habían referido a Londres utlizando ese tropo. Cosa que, por lo visto, el taxista no estaba dispuesto a tolerar, pues acto seguido dijo que él, un paquistaní, podía no conocer a ese mentado Borges, y que también podía no haber leído nunca a esos mentados señores Dickens y Stevenson, y que incluso tal vez aún no conocía lo suficientemente bien Londres y sus calles y que por esa razón la había comparado con un laberinto, pero que, por contra, sabía muy bien lo que era la decencia y la dignidad y que, por lo que había escuchado, la mujer aquí presente, es decir Norton, carecía de decencia y de dignidad, y que en su país eso tenía un nombre, el mismo que se le daba en Londres, qué casualidad, y que ese nombre era el de puta, aunque también era lícito utilizar el nombre de perra o zorra o cerda, y que los señores aquí presentes, señores que no eran ingleses a juzgar por su acento, también tenían un nombre en su país y ese nombre era el de chulos o macarras o macrós o cafiches. (102)

Which led Espinoza to remark that he'd be damned if the cabbie hadn't just quoted Borges, who once said London was like a labyrinth—unintentionally, of course. To which Norton replied that Dickens and Stevenson had used the same trope long before Borges in their description of London. This seemed to set the driver off, for he burst out that as a Pakistani he might not know this Borges, and he might not have read the famous Dickens and Stevenson either, and he might not even know London and its streets as well as he should, that's why he'd said they were like a labyrinth, but he knew very well what decency and dignity were, and by what he had heard, the woman here present, in other words Norton, was lacking in decency and dignity, and in his country there was a word for what she was, the same word they had for it in London as it happened, and the word was *bitch* or *slut* or *pig*, and the gentlemen here present, gentlemen who, to judge by their accents, weren't English, also had a name in his country and that name was *pimp* or *hustler* or *whoremonger*. (73)[36]

The cab can be theorized as a contact zone, where class, race, and gender dynamics are staged and reworked. The driver's comment begins as a reaction to Espinoza's analogy between his and Borges's depictions of London. Why would this reference to Borges, followed by one to Dickens and Stevenson, anger the Pakistani to such an extent? The cab driver's antagonism stems from the critics' inability to relate to his personal experience other than through a reference to a highly Westernized world literature canon (Borges is of course Argentine, but Norton immediately inscribes him into the Western tradition by claiming that the same literary trope already appeared in Dickens and Stevenson). For Norton, Espinoza, and Pelletier, the Pakistani's presence and opinions are significant only as far as they fit into their own academic interests, illustrating or emulating the literary canon. In fact, when Espinoza makes his remark, he is not addressing the cab driver, but Pelletier and Norton; the cab driver serves only as a medium for his literary reflection. In what follows, the driver opposes his personal experience to a more "literary" reading of his comment, arguing that London is a labyrinth for him because he is not very familiar with the city. He further insists that as a Pakistani he might not have read Borges or Dickens, commenting on the Eurocentric focus of the critics' literary references.

Espinoza is confident that the driver could only have quoted Borges "unintentionally," as this framework of literary references is only accessible to an educated elite that of course includes the four critics but could never include a taxi driver. The driver, aware of the implication of Espinoza's statement, tries to suggest that his knowledge does not encompass these references, because they are not universal, as Espinoza assumes, but culturally specific. By reading the driver's comment in relation to Borges, Dickens, and Stevenson, Espinoza not only reaffirms his very Eurocentric position but also erases the economic and social factors that may have brought the driver to utter such a comment. He is not interested in dynamics that could lead a Pakistani to feel entrapped in what he perceives to be an urban maze. In other words, his estrangement in the city of London stems from his immigrant status. Yet, it also raises the question of the circumstances that would lead a Pakistani to work as a cab driver in London, a question that of course never crosses Espinoza's mind.

As he states that he might not know Borges or Dickens but is quite familiar with the notions of decency and dignity, the driver attempts to shift the conversation from a culturally specific content (a content he does not have access to) to what he perceives as a more universal content (a conversation that he could be a part of). Espinoza and Pelletier, erasing the context surrounding the conversation, hear only the comment addressed to Norton. They then ask the driver to stop the car, pull him out on the street and start beating him "hasta dejarlo inconsciente y sangrando por todos los orificios de la cabeza, menos por los ojos" (103) ["until he was unconscious and bleeding from every orifice in the head, except the eyes" (74)], all the while shouting: "Métete el islam por el culo, allí es donde debe estar, esta patada es por Salman Rushdie. . . . Esta patada es de parte de las feministas de París (parad de una puta vez, les gritaba Norton), esta patada es de parte de las feministas de Nueva York" (103) ["Shove Islam up your ass, which is where it belongs, this one is for Salman Rushdie . . . . This one is for the feminists of Paris (will you fucking stop, Norton was shouting), this one is for the feminists of New York" (74)].

Espinoza and Pelletier immediately associate the comment with the driver's adherence to Islam, an adherence that he himself has never proclaimed. The verbal violence of the driver against women generates the physical violence of male Europeans against the non-European other: white men are protecting a white woman against a brown man. The justification of violence toward the racial or cultural other through the defense of women's rights is hardly a new trope, but here it appears in relation to the European academic culture and its liberal politics. Espinoza and Pelletier immediately position themselves against Islam as secular defenders of feminism and women's rights, located only within the outlines of the West, represented here by the metropolitan centers of Paris and New York.

However, Bolaño is careful not to merely position European racism against a benevolent other. The driver's comment about Norton is hardly justifiable, but it exists within a larger, multinational framework of class, race, and gender. Furthermore, as academics, Espinoza and Pelletier subtly avoid the theory of the "clash of civilizations." The reference to Salman Rushdie complicates what could otherwise be a simplistic opposition between a secular, progressive Europe and a reactionary, religious Middle East. Espinoza and Pelletier are here probably alluding to *The Satanic Verses* (1988)—where, interestingly enough, London also appears as a labyrinth—and the fatwa issued against Rushdie by Iran's religious leader, Ayatollah Khomeini, in the aftermath of its publication. The situation is thus multilayered: white men are also defending a brown man against another brown man. Espinoza and Pelletier are displacing a liberal West/reactionary East opposition onto a reactionary/liberal opposition that supposedly exists independently of race and gender, thus claiming their own universality. They can thus position themselves as members of what Jean Baudrillard calls the "democratic feudality," "a minority that considers itself the holder of moral and universal ends."[37] The global framework emerges out of violent social interactions and within the narrow space of a cab. The cab thus becomes a place to explore critically the tensions inherent in the Western belief in its own universality, as there is a contradiction between the assumed universal reach of Western values and the fact that only a selected few, such as Espinoza and Pelletier, fully understand what these values are.

Norton attempts to separate the three men, arguing that this behavior will only make the driver hate the English. She is not putting into question the opposition between the liberal European "us" and the conservative non-European "them," but merely commenting on the fact that violence will slow and deter the spread of liberal values. After the incident, Espinoza and Pelletier regret what had happened, "por más que en su fuero íntimo estuvieran convencidos de que el verdadero derechista y misógino era el paquistaní, de que el violento era el paquistaní, de que el intolerante y mal educado era el paquistaní, de que el que se lo había buscado era el paquistaní, una y mil veces. En estas ocasiones, la verdad, si el taxista se hubiera materializado ante ellos, seguramente lo habrían matado" (110) ["even though deep inside they were convinced that it was the Pakistani who was the real reactionary and misogynist, the violent one, the intolerant and offensive one, that the Pakistani has asked for it a thousand times over. The truth is that at moments like this, if the Pakistani had materialized before them, they probably would have killed him" (80)]. In moments like those, they probably would have killed the Pakistani because he was reminding them of their own reactionary attitude, performed in the name of tolerance. The comment of the narrative voice, which reveals an attitude that Espinoza and Pelletier do not seem aware of, creates a complex process of mirroring, identification, and disidentification. Espinoza and Pelletier can only formulate their identity in contrast to that of the reactionary, violent other. This opposition is maintained through violence whose very presence invalidates it. Identity, within the context of global neoliberalization, is not prefigured. Rather, it is the result of social relations that congeal global dynamics into the space of a cab.

This scene also portends the violence to come in Santa Teresa. I do not say this in order to equate the violence committed by the critics to the proliferation of beaten, raped, and disfigured bodies of Santa Teresa women. Rather, the novel joins and disjoins different instances where, globally, violence is permitted. Grant Farred argues that "the maquiladora is the über-rhizome of death, linking one unknown, overinhabited place (the city that promises 'almost full employment') with every other unknowable space of potential violence against women."[38] I would suggest that the entire novel is an über-rhizome, geographically and temporally relating distant moments of violence, without necessarily conflating them. These instances connect to form a fragmentary totality that remains (and will always be) unfinished.

Connections extend through space but also through time. In the last part of the novel, we learn that Archimboldi served as a German soldier on the Eastern Front during World War II. Nazism, the Holocaust, mass murders of maquiladora women, and perhaps even Islamophobia and the war on terror, if we add the cab scene to the mix, are thus rhizomatically brought into relation. This is not an ahistorical conflation. Ángeles Donoso Macaya suggests that "la novela articula una conexión posible—y lo posible no es lo mismo que lo *probable*—entre dos formas de violencia hasta entonces inconexas"[39] [the novel articulates a *possible* connection—and what is possible is not the same as what is *probable*—between two forms of violence until then unconnected]. The complex process of inverted and distorted mirroring that occurs in the cab reveals the formal structure of the novel as a whole. Espinoza and Pelletier would have killed the Pakistani because he becomes the mirror image of their own violence; they are, ultimately, what they accuse him of being. Bolaño has similarly described Ciudad Juárez as a mirror, "el espejo desasosegado de nuestras frustraciones y de nuestra infame interpretación de la libertad y de nuestros deseos"[40] [the restless mirror of our frustrations and our infamous interpretation of freedom and our desires]. This process of mirroring occurs repeatedly in the novel: between Archimboldi and Bolaño, Bolaño and the narrator Arturo Belano, the killings of Jews and of Santa Teresa women. As a mode of representing and apprehending reality, it exists in contrast to the critics' search for pure and accurate knowledge, proposing instead a model of comparative thinking. The four academics are looking for Archimboldi because they believe he is the only one who can provide them with answers about his life and his work. They do not realize that answers about Archimboldi can be found in the cab and in Santa Teresa, all connected through the notion of sanctioned violence over precarious bodies. They do not realize that answers about Archimboldi reside in their own violence.

GLOBAL WASTE

Oscar Fate, an African American journalist sent to Mexico to report on a boxing match, notes that Santa Teresa represents "un retrato del mundo industrial en el Tercer Mundo" (373) ["a sketch of the industrial landscape in the Third World" (294)]. Guadalupe Roncal, a journalist from Mexico City, claims that the secret of the world is contained in the murders. This secret, ultimately, will never be revealed—perhaps, because we already know it.

Many of the women murdered are not from Santa Teresa, exemplifying massive rural-urban immigration, a result of the destruction of traditional agriculture and the development of maquiladoras along the border. These victims are rarely described in relation to their familial ties and geographical origins, which often remain unknown. Emphasis is frequently placed on their clothes, in some cases Nike sneakers and blue jeans, products that symbolize American culture and the American way of life but also epitomize the fact that this lifestyle is produced in the Global South. Two things anchor the murdered women in the reality of the contemporary globalized world: their presence in the maquiladoras as disposable, inexpensive labor and their consumption of goods produced primarily for someone else. The association of these women with Nike shoes and blue jeans establishes more than just their identity as consumers in a capitalist world. By wearing these products, they are trying to emulate the lifestyle that they are manufacturing. Their deaths, however, illustrate the fact that this lifestyle will always only be produced for the other side of the border. They become the mirror image of the American way of life, a life that requires death.

Many female bodies are found in an illegal dump called El Chile, a narrative detail that furthers the connection between consumption and death. This association unravels in a passage where an American investigator, Albert Kessler, invited to solve the murders of maquiladora workers, drives by El Chile:

> Kessler volvío a mirar el paisaje fragmentado o en proceso de fragmentación constante, como un puzzle que se hacía y deshacía a cada segundo, y le dijo al que conducía que lo llevara al basurero El Chile, el mayor basurero clandestino de Santa Teresa, más grande que el basurero municipal, en donde iban a depositar las basuras no sólo los camiones de las maquiladoras sino también los camiones de la basura contratados por la alcaldía y los camiones y camionetas de basura de algunas empresas privadas que trabajaban con subcontratos o en zonas licitadas que no cubrían los servicios públicos. (752)

> Kessler looked out again at the landscape, fragmented or in the constant process of fragmentation, like a puzzle repeatedly assembled and disassembled, and told the driver to take him to the illegal dump El Chile, the biggest illegal dump in Santa Teresa, bigger than the city dump, where waste was disposed of not only by the maquiladora trucks but also by garbage trucks contracted by the city and some private garbage trucks and pick-ups, subcontracted or working in areas that public services didn't cover. (602)

El Chile serves as a metaphor for Santa Teresa, a place where local and transnational waste is dumped, including the bodies of Santa Teresa women. The passage gestures toward the complex economic reality of Santa Teresa, the relation between the shrinking public sector and the expanding influence of multinational corporations. El Chile is an illegal dump; created on land that could be either public or private, it contains the waste of both sectors. It exists within the bounds of Santa Teresa, yet the city does not manage it. Multinationals use it, but they do not claim it. This pile of trash represents a specific framing of the conflicting relation between the private and the public, the national and the transnational, within the context of global neoliberalization. The public no longer monitors and balances out the private, acting rather in a complimentary manner. In fact, the private and the public spheres collude as they use one another to displace responsibility for unwanted spaces and unwanted lives.

Like in Bessora's novel, this passage establishes a connection between labor exploitation and environmental destruction. The novel deals with the question of the environment from the purview of excess rather than lack. If in today's political and environmental discourses, we hear a great deal about lack—the exhaustion of resources, the extinction of species, the scarcity of space, food, and potable water for an overgrowing population—*2666* underscores how lack and excess always exist in a dialectical relation. Global neoliberalization is depicted in its production of excess, which it no longer fully controls. El Chile reappears throughout the novel as both a political space and an aesthetic object. The constant piling of trash, originating from different places, is the result of the logic of capitalist accumulation, yet, at the same time, escapes its grasp. The tension between containment and overflowing persists; the system produces its own waste, which it attempts to discard, but which threatens to engulf it as the pile becomes too large to manage.

Both novels link the destruction of the environment to the production of disposable subjectivities. Here, environmental destruction is interlaced with the destruction of the female body, and even more specifically, to the migrant female worker. It is not surprising that the dead maquiladora workers appear in El Chile, a space that belongs to no one and for which no one is accountable. The presence of these bodies, among the waste of El Chile, disrupts the supposed separation of the public and the private, the national and the transnational. The police interpret these murders as "private" incidences conducted by individuals, but the corpses emerge within a space that is neither public nor private, covered in trash that is both public and private. The same ideology of growth and development has led to the creation of trash and of precarious labor (mobile, transient, deracinated, and unprotected). In its extreme reiteration, the bodies of female workers, literally, become trash.

Like *Petroleum*, Bolaño's narrative places the question of the environment within the context of our current ideology of growth and progress, developments that rely on the production of precarious (often migrant) labor. In other words, questions of environment, progress, and disposable subjects overlap. To take responsibility for a growing pile of trash, one also needs to take responsibility for an exploitative labor system. As Silvia Federici argues: "We need to overcome the state of irresponsibility concerning the consequences of our actions that results from the destructive ways in which the social division of labor is organized in capitalism."[41] A reorganization of production and reproduction must follow the reappropriation of resources.

Bolaño's garbage dump serves as a metaphor for the novel itself: the assembly and disassembly of fragments, the continuous piling up of details, descriptions, and characters. Kessler remarks that Santa Teresa is a puzzle constantly assembled and disassembled, as are the world and the novel. This self-reflexive gesture can lead us to wonder whether the endless descriptions of raped and murdered female bodies in Santa Teresa are the literary equivalent of this accumulation of trash. If these bodies produce an excess of the system of constant commodification and exchange, what is its linguistic equivalent? In fact, the descriptions of the murders proliferate in *2666*. In a matter-of-fact, journalistic style, the novel exposes us to all the gruesome details: the broken spleens, the anal rapes, the bruised bodies. In some cases, suspects are apprehended and explanatory theories offered, yet nothing stops the murders. Descriptions accumulate with no end in sight, mirroring the growing pile of El Chile and raising the question of the role of detective fiction in the age of global neoliberalization.

GLOBALIZATION AND THE DETECTIVE NOVEL: SOLVING NEOLIBERAL CRIMES

Bessora's *Petroleum* and Bolaño's *2666* are contemporary takes on the long literary tradition of crime fiction. In *Petroleum*, an explosion devastates the Ocean Liberator, a barge drilling for petrol off the coast of Gabon. The crime is an Atlantic one, taking place on (and perhaps against) the ocean. The attempt to solve it drives the plot: Was it a deed of the aquatic spirits, angered by the continuous desecration of their residence? Did Étienne, who had cancer, commit suicide after finding out Flavie Minko was his daughter? Toward the end of the novel, we learn that Alidor Minko was planning an attack two days after the explosion that occurred. Did his plan go awry? Not all the characters agree. And in the end, the exact answer might not be crucial. Bolaño (and Maryse Condé in *The Story of the Cannibal Woman*, it should be noted) similarly embraces the medium of detective fiction, begging the question of the relation between global neoliberalization and the rise of the global crime novel. The crimes in Bessora's and Bolaño's novels have one thing in common: there is no single culprit. No one (and everyone) is ultimately responsible for them.

Detective fiction has a long tradition, beginning, in many literary histories, with Edgar Allan Poe's three Dupin mysteries (*The Murders in the Rue Morgue, The Mystery of Marie Rogêt,* and *The Purloined Letter*) published in 1841–44. In *Mayhem at the Crossroads: Francophone African Fiction and the Rise of the Crime Novel,* Pim Higginson identifies five characteristics of traditional crime fiction that appeal to Francophone African writers: "an urban setting and a threatening alterity, the ambiguity of the law, a vexed literary status, trans-Atlantically mobile evolution, the vernacular."[42] Within the African context, he contends, detective novels allow African authors to distance themselves from the French aesthetic models taught in colonial schools. He further characterizes African crime fiction as "a novel literary-ideological enterprise—one that refuses existing socio-political conditions while steering clear of intrusive didacticism and/or excessive idealism."[43]

Contemporary authors from across the Atlantic have chosen the detective novel as their preferred literary form. In *The Cambridge History of Latin American Literature,* Gustavo Pellón identifies the detective novel (particularly in its hard-boiled iteration) as an important tendency of the post-boom era.[44] Glen Close, in *Contemporary Hispanic Crime Fiction: A Transatlantic Discourse on Urban Violence,* traces the development of the genre through trans-Atlantic literary and publishing connections between the United States, Spain, and Latin America. The focus on crime in Latin American fiction, he argues, relates to the "uncontrolled growth of cities" on the continent and the "new urban violence of the neoliberal era."[45] Thus, from different sides of the Atlantic, the focus on global neoliberalization has transformed crime fiction.

While Bessora's and Bolaño's novels draw from these Atlantic traditions, they also take the genre in new directions. Neoliberalism is certainly at stake, yet, this is not quite the urban violence that Higginson and Close describe. Bolaño's femicides take place within an urban setting; Santa Teresa is a growing city, as women from across the country and the region arrive looking for work, or with the intention of crossing the border. However, this is only one piece of the equation. Santa Teresa is prominent less for its urban status than for being the place where multinationals, the state, the police, workers, immigrants, and the intellectual class collide. In the novel, all roads lead to Santa Teresa, the exemplary and horrific product of global neoliberalization. Santa Teresa resembles what Alain Badiou calls an "anarchic zone" where "all true state power has gone" and "the whole petty world of firms can operate without any overall control."[46]

In *Petroleum,* we are similarly in an urban setting—Port Gentil—but the fact that the crime takes place on the Ocean Liberator and not in the city, is crucial. Bessora and Bolaño take the Atlantic crime tradition into the realm of what I call the neoliberal anti-detective novel. According to Stefano Tani, the anti-detective novel "frustrates the expectations of the reader, transforms a mass-media genre into a sophisticated expression of avant-garde sensibility, and substitutes for the detective as central and ordering character the decentering and chaotic admission of mystery, of nonsolution."[47] Frustration is very likely to occur in 2666 after hundreds of pages of murder descriptions to which no resolution is offered. Any theory presented by the police—serial killer, domestic violence, dissatisfied brothel customers—fails to explain and solve all the murders.

In *Petroleum,* Bessora takes anti-detective fiction into the realm of colonial history and the neocolonial present. Georges Montandon, the French profiler, is a caricature of the traditional investigative mind. He knows nothing about Gabonese history or society. His supposedly objective profiles contain a proliferation of neocolonial stereotypes about the Gabonese people and their nationalism. In a comical manner, his supposedly logical reasoning leads him to identify almost all the characters as potential political terrorists. At the very beginning of Montandon's search, Médée attempts to offer a clue: "La clé est dans le temps, dit-elle. Ce qui s'est passé sur le navire, c'est . . . C'est la mémoire que vous devez questioner" (125) [The answer lies in time, she says. What happened on the ship, it's . . . It's memory that you should question]. Because he refuses to consider local memories as valid evidence and to understand the crime as systemic and historical, Montandon will not be able to solve it. The supposed universality and objectivity of Western logic is brought into question, as Montandon continuously "misses the point." His investigation is entirely undermined when he ends up in prison, accused of statutory rape. Through science, logic, and reasoning, Montandon cannot even save himself.

Montandon's inquiry into individual motivations is contrasted with the novel's work of historiography. The crime could be understood as an individual act or it can be interpreted as a result of complex historical and geographical connections. Only the reader could undertake a parallel work of investigation: peeling multiple layers of reality to understand the imbrication of forces that shape present-day Gabon. As Médée is driving to the company's headquarters, she passes an intersection between the boulevard President-Bongo, the avenue Charles-de-Gaulle, and the boulevard Elf-Gabon: "Bongo, de Gaulle, Elf-Gabon. Aucune pancarte n'indique les noms de ces avenues. On peut comprendre que ces réalités cadastrales soient cachées car il n'y a pas de quoi pavoiser. Oui, ces réalités sont invisibles" (87) [Bongo, de Gaulle,

Elf-Gabon. There are no signs marking the names of these avenues. It's understandable that the cadastral reality is concealed, because there's nothing to crow about. Yes, this reality is invisible]. These realities are invisible because they are unacknowledged. However, they are also invisible because the flows of capital that connect them are not always tangible; there are missing links that explain the relation between the Gabonese authorities, foreign governments, and the multinationals. In a similar manner, whereas the reality of the oil extraction and the politics of Wall Street are inevitably linked, the power networks that connect the two are not immediately visible to workers on board the Ocean Liberator.

To unearth these unacknowledged realities, the reader must pay very close attention to Bessora's meticulous choice of vocabulary, her innuendos, quid pro quos, and irony. In this particular passage, realities are characterized as cadastral. A *cadastre* is a public register, recording land allocation and ownership, often for the purpose of taxation. The *cadastre* is precisely that which is missing, a public record and acknowledgment of who owns Gabon. Etymologically, the word *cadastre* originates from the Greek *katastikhon,* meaning "line by line." This line-by-line record of ownership over the country's resources is erased from the public space. It is, however, still present in the local memories and Bessora's carefully chosen words. That the three boulevards intersect is no coincidence. They represent three forces—the French government, the Gabonese government, and the multinationals—that have historically colluded to divide Gabonese resources. The intersection of the three boulevards gestures toward this complex imbrication of causes. Who is to be held responsible for the current situation: the national government, the colonial past, France's neocolonial politics, or the unregulated markets? This is a network of causes and consequences, past and present that surpasses the crimes of traditional detective fiction and the capabilities of a traditional detective. The recent explosion is hardly the only crime in the novel; the history of Gabon is marked by multiple past and present crimes. Understanding them requires a collective venture into the colonial past and our global neoliberal present.

At the end of the novel, Médée and Jason's love story finally begins, yet there is no return to the social order like in traditional detective fiction. In fact, there can be no return to the social order because the social order is responsible for the crime. At the very end, the earth crumbles close to Jason and Médée, possibly representing another one of Mamiwata's punishments. The water and forest spirits may not have been appeased, and the social order may never be restored.

If *Petroleum* is a metafictional historiography, it is also a metafictional autobiography. As Marie Carrière notes, Étienne Girardet resembles Bessora's father, who worked as deputy director general of Total-Gabon. Flavie Minko, anthropologist and daughter of an Elf executive, becomes Bessora's double (Total-Gabon was the fieldwork site of Bessora's anthropology thesis).[48] Bessora thus alludes to her own complicity in the reality that she criticizes: she is a binational daughter of an oil executive and is somewhat of an expat in Gabon. The author is always already implicated in the reality that she denounces; the only possible mode of critique is thus metafictional. This simultaneous complicity of the author and the reader is similarly underlined in *2666*.

In his analysis of Bolaño's fiction, Edmundo Paz Soldán draws an analogy between the writer and the detective, both engaged in a never-ending search for the origin of evil: "Se trata de algo más visceral, del escritor que entiende el arte como una aventura vitalista, y en otras ocasiones del narrador y del poeta como detectives en busca del 'origen del mal,' y por ello condenados desde el principio a la derrota"[49] [It's about something more visceral, the writer who sees art as a kind of vitalist adventure, and at other times of the narrator and the poet, like detectives in the quest for the 'origin of evil,' and thus doomed to fail from the very beginning]. In spite of its unlikely outcome, literature must conduct this quest. Bolaño similarly explains that literature is a dangerous enterprise that requires the courage to venture into the dark and jump into the void. It is a constant struggle, where, from the beginning, the writer is condemned to failure: "La literatura se parece mucho a la pelea de los samuráis, pero el samurái no pelea contra otro samurai, pelea contra un monstruo, generalmente sabe, además, que va a ser derrotado. Tener el valor, sabiendo previamente que vas a ser derrotado, y salir a pelear, eso es la literatura"[50] [Literature resembles a battle between samurai, but a samurai doesn't fight another samurái, he fights against a monster. Besides, he generally knows that he will be defeated. To have the courage, despite already knowing that you will be defeated, to go out and fight, that is literature].

In *2666*, everyone searches for the origin of the Santa Teresa murders. Who is responsible: the state, the multinationals, the local drug cartels, or a serial killer? All of them would be a possible answer. The failure of the police investigation in the novel rests on the fact that the police and the media refuse to acknowledge different global and local power dynamics that render certain lives more prone to murder. Instead, they try to explain the crimes through the figure of a serial killer. After the arrest of Klaus Haas (Archimboldi's nephew, it turns out), presumed to be the psychotic murderer, we learn that "la ciudad se dio un respire. . . . Ciertamente, hubo muertos. . . . Las muertes habituales, sí, las usuales, gente que empezaba festejando y terminaba matándose, muertes que no eran cinematográficas, muertes que pertenecían al folklore pero no a la modernidad: muertes que no asustaban a nadie. El asesino en serie oficialmente estaba entre rejas" (675) ["the city got a break. . . . True, there were deaths. . . . There were the usual deaths, yes, those to be expected, people who started off celebrating and ended up killing each other, uncinematic deaths, deaths from the realm of folklore, not modernity: deaths that didn't scare anybody. The serial killer was officially behind bars" (540)]. In this opposition between folklore and modernity, the figure of the serial killer becomes the embodiment of modernity. Whereas deaths from the realm of folklore are associated with petty arguments and impulsive actions, a result of exuberant displays of emotions, modernity is associated with the serial killer, a figure living outside the norms of society and morality, engaging in murder for no particular reason aside from the emotional thrill. Yet, I would also argue that modernity creates and mobilizes the figure of the serial killer in order to displace the responsibility for the marginalization and violence that it creates. Within this framework, society skirts accountability since the violence is not generated from within it (and in this case from within the global economic order), but from outside of it, from a clearly identifiable sociopath who simply does not comply with the supposedly nonviolent societal norms. Following this logic, once this nonsubmissive element is removed, society can and will return to its harmonious, peaceful existence. By blaming a serial killer, the state is desperately trying to claim its sovereignty, even though within the context of neoliberal finance and organization of labor, its sovereignty has been long compromised.

The figure of a sole killer furthermore raises the question of serialization, where murder is conceived as a repetitive gesture of ultimate consumption. But the underlining relation is the one between reading and consumption. As a reader, we are consuming hundreds of pages of murder descriptions. The novel begins with a quotation from Charles Baudelaire's poem "The Voyage": "An oasis of horror in a desert of boredom." In Baudelaire's poem, throughout his voyage, the poet discovers that "the world, monotonous and small, today, yesterday, forever, gives us back our image: an oasis of horror in a desert of ennui!"[51] We are this oasis of horror, but the horror also easily turns into boredom. The novel 2666 reproduces the horror of boredom and the boredom of horror through sequences of descriptions that span several hundred pages. Consumption, commodification, boredom, and destruction are here caught in a web of mirroring. El Chile is the result of overproduction and overconsumption. Similarly, female bodies are commodified in maquiladoras and consumed through rape. Commodification and consumption continue through the acts of reading and writing. The final destruction of the female bodies takes place, perhaps, once the reader becomes frustrated and bored with the endless horrific descriptions.

Bolaño's *2666* uses repetition and serialization, the very methodology of the evil that it denounces, Ángeles Donoso Macaya argues, thus formally conveying violence through fragmentary reiteration. Yet, according to Macaya, the narrative also eventually names the unnamed women, turning serialization into singularization.[52] I would add that the novel underscores the necessity of naming at the same time as it emphasizes its impossibility. While the naming is necessary to avoid anonymous serialization, it participates in an act of commodification and consumption. The act of naming leads to the creation of the novel, a product that ultimately brought fame to a male author. After being consumed, who knows, the novel might end up in El Chile, returning us to the initial point.

Yet, this does not mean that nothing can be done, and that the novel, being a commodity, should not be written. Rather, a denunciation of violence invites a self-reflexive gesture toward one's own role in this violence. Juan Velasco and Tanya Schmidt argue that "by emphasizing the complicity of multinationals, the media and the police, *2666* creates an image of ourselves and the complicity of readers as we look at 'un oasis de horror en medio de un desierto de aburrimiento'" [an oasis of horror in a desert of boredom].[53] This is not a moral incrimination of the reader, or a deterministic comment on human nature. Like in *Petroleum,* there is an acknowledgment that when violence is systemic, we are always already implicated. For this reason, the crimes contain the secret of the world; the secret is the world-as-is, which forms precarious bodies that it does not protect against violence.

No longer addressing immigration, precarity, and violence within a single national setting, contemporary Atlantic authors consider situations and genres in which one is constantly trying to trace accountability, responsibility, causation, on a global scale. The multinational corporation becomes a perfect setting within this context. It is a space that condenses the power dynamics of global neoliberalization, a space where state and corporate power collide and conjoin. It is also a crossroads for locals, immigrants, and expats. The diagonal relationship between state and corporate power creates spaces frequently neither under national nor international supervision, facilitating the creation of a precarious international labor force, one that no one is accountable for.

Focusing on multinationals, contemporary Atlantic authors like Bessora and Bolaño address the network organization of the neoliberal power configuration, while refashioning the detective novel. Global neoliberalization relies on a form of fragmentation, which renders it difficult to identify the exact center of power. The international division of labor has divided the process of production and distribution into various pieces that seem autonomous yet are utterly dependent. The neoliberal anti-detective novel encapsulates this fragmentary understanding of reality, which results from a fragmentary nature of globalized production.

The traditional detective novel opposes two individuals: a criminal mind and a rational mind. The detective, through empirical observation, logical reasoning, and deductive capabilities, manages to apprehend the disordering (individual) element and return society to the status quo. The problem in the neoliberal anti-detective novel is that the status quo is the culprit. In other words, the police and the investigators cannot solve the crime because the question they are asking no longer suffices. The crucial query is no longer merely which individual committed the crime, but who (in plural) allowed for these crimes to happen? Who is responsible for creating a status quo where certain bodies are disposable? This is a significantly more complex question, particularly given that the author and the reader are included in the answer. As long as bodies are deemed "killable," killers will appear. The individual perpetrator is no longer the cause of social disarray, but its symptom.

The novels shift the focus from individual punishment to systemic indictment. A medic in Santa Teresa asks: "¿Cómo me voy a responsabilizar de esta mujer si ni siquiera sé cómo se llama?" (448) ["How can I take responsibility for a person when I don't even know her name?" (357)]. The question could be rephrased in the following manner: who is accountable for this internationalized labor force? Responsibility is diminished as local authorities, the state, multinational corporations, and international organizations lay the blame on one another. The passage further dwells on the relation between identity and responsibility. Rights and protection depend upon participation in a specific category of identity: citizen, tourist, academic, and so on. By creating subjectivities that do not fall within these categories, the system eschews responsibility. The novels reframe questions of responsibility and accountability. Instead of searching for individual perpetrators to punish them, in what seems to be a never-ending chase, we may need a collective ethics of precarity, collective responsibilization for the human and natural destruction we perform in interconnected ways.

CHAPTER 4

Trans-Atlantic Opacity

"Nous réclamons pour tous le droit à l'opacité" ["We clamor for the right to opacity for everyone"], Martinican writer and philosopher Edouard Glissant writes in *Poetics of Relation*.[1] Glissant rejects the notion of transparency, electing an aesthetics of opacity, which does not strive for full comprehension or explanation. Opacity is at the basis of his understanding of Relation; Glissant invites us to "Non pas seulement consentir au droit à la différence mais, plus avant, au droit à l'opacité, qui n'est pas l'enfermement dans une autarcie impénétrable, mais la subsistance dans une singularité non réductible" ["Agree not merely to the right to difference but, carrying this further, agree also to the right to opacity that is not enclosure within an impenetrable autarchy but subsistence within an irreducible singularity"].[2] The act of comprehension, according to Glissant, can constitute an act of violence if it endeavors to bring the other back to the same, the known. While it does not prevent a relation from forming, opacity precludes the reduction of the other to familiar norms and categories. Opacity respects the irreducible difference of the other, no longer considered an object of knowledge. Relation, for Glissant, can occur only between two equal subjects, who respect each other's right to difference, and who protect this difference from being fixed. To stand in solidarity with the other, we do not need to understand them fully, claims Glissant.

Alongside Glissant, other Francophone authors, including Marie NDiaye and Leila Sebbar, have reverted to a writing of opacity, posing the question of political and ethical possibilities that emerge out of this relation to fiction.[3] In this chapter, I explore opacity in the work of three contemporary Atlantic writers: Puerto Rican Yolanda Arroyo Pizarro, Franco-Senegalese Marie NDiaye, and Mexican Yuri Herrera. Placing the reader in front of opaque, immigrant subjects, these authors propose new ways of conceptualizing immigration.[4] Instead of underscoring the difficulties of integration and assimilation in the new country and the formation of new cultural identities, they focus on the interdependent and intertwining lives of the many Atlantic subjects who remain opaque. "Des opacités peuvent coexister, confluer, tramant des tissus dont la véritable compréhension porterait sur la texture de cette trame et non pas sur la nature des composantes" ["Opacities can coexist and converge, weaving fabrics. To understand these truly one must focus on the texture of the weave and not on the nature of its components"], writes Glissant.[5] The authors in this chapter similarly explore interlacing Atlantic opacities, underlining the economic, political, and formal structures that bring these lives together. The characters in these novels remain opaque: sometimes to themselves, sometimes to each other, and sometimes to the reader. The psychological opacity of characters interlinks with elements of unreadability built into the writing.

All three authors consider Atlantic migrations within a regional framework. In Arroyo Pizarro's *Los documentados* (2005) [*The Documented*], characters migrate between the neighboring islands of the Dominican Republic and Puerto Rico. Yuri Herrera engages the extended North American space and the US–Mexico border. Finally, NDiaye represents migrations from the hexagon to Guadeloupe, within the context of a decentralized France. Though NDiaye and Herrera may not have ever met, or been directly influenced by one another, their novels, *Rosie Carpe* (2001) and *Señales que precederán al fin del mundo* (2009) [*Signs Preceding the End of the World*, 2015], as well as their literary careers, bear striking resemblance.

Both narratives focus on young women in search of their brothers. Rosie Carpe travels from Paris to Guadeloupe in the hope of finding her long-lost brother Lazare. Makina, the protagonist of Herrera's novel, unofficially crosses the US–Mexico border in order to convince her brother to return home. The brother, whose name is never revealed, moved to the United States several years prior to retrieve a piece of land the family believes it owns. A common formal feature to these two works is the absence of psychological explanation. Both protagonists are opaque and impenetrable, offering us little ground for identification. Geographical breadth replaces this lack of character depth; the novels do not depict a complex interior, focusing, rather, on the protagonists' constant movement between various geographical locations.

Well, this is nothing new, the reader might object. Decentered, deconstructed, destabilized subjects are a well-recognized literary trope. In fact, the lack of psychological explanation is often associated with the aesthetics of the Nouveau roman, a literary movement of the 1950s and '60s associated with, among others, Nathalie Sarraute, Alain Robbe-Grillet, and Michel Butor. Nathalie Sarraute has explained that her writing strives to escape "la clarté mortelle du déjà connu" [the lethal clarity of the already known].[6] Similarly, Alain Robbe-Grillet has written that the coherence and unity of characters is but an illusion of the realist novel.[7] However, the contemporary move to opacity takes place within a different sociopolitical context. Precarity and opacity undergird the aesthetics of a globalized Atlantic and a formal resistance to global neoliberalization.

Opacity operates on multiple levels in contemporary Atlantic narratives, as it performs several, related functions. Fundamentally precarious, these characters cannot be represented in coherent, transparent ways, because they have no coherent, stable ground to stand on. In the case of Arroyo's and Herrera's undocumented immigrants, constant flight is their only mode of survival, and they cannot afford to be exposed. The impossibility of stability and coherence, however, also becomes a refusal of stability and coherence. These characters are not fighting precarity with a longing for transparency and stability; rather, they appropriate it, turning it into a poetics of opacity.

The characters analyzed in this chapter escape full explanation and full understanding; they exist beyond and under any stable category. They are not seeking recognition, because complete recognition and representation imply an inclusion into a system that upholds precarity. Therefore, they refuse a return to stability. In *The Undercommons: Fugitive Planning and Black Studies,* Fred Moten and Stefano Harney explore the refusal to respond to the "the call to order." They define black aesthetics in terms of disavowal, refusal, and fugitivity: "We are disruption and consent to disruption. We preserve upheaval. Sent to fulfill by abolishing, to renew by unsettling, to open the enclosure whose immeasurable venality is inversely proportionate to its actual area, we got politics surrounded. We cannot represent ourselves. We can't be represented."[8] "When we refuse," Jack Halberstam explains in the introduction to the book, "we create dissonance and more importantly, we allow dissonance to continue."[9] This mode of politics, or perhaps rather, "antagonism to politics" in its contemporary form, is expressed through a refusal of representation. The possibility of fugitivity is predicated upon the preservation of opacity.[10] A demand for inclusion and integration legitimizes and returns the system to order. Fugitivity is thus not mere disempowerment, as it questions and refuses the existing frameworks of recognition. The characters I analyze in this chapter strive to maintain disorder within a trans-Atlantic framework. Their opacity and their fugitivity become their strength; because they cannot be captured, they continue to refuse the call to order, to destabilize the existing system.

By representing opaque characters, Atlantic authors also refuse to be subsumed under stereotypical modes of representation. Immigrant authors have long contended with the instrumentalization of their narratives. Often used as sociological and anthropological evidence, their aesthetic value frequently remains secondary. Subha Xavier thus writes that immigrant novels "capitalize on ethnic heritage, especially when it carries a seal of marked otherness, saddling writers with the expectations and hopes of their communities of origin as well as those of their new countries." Immigrant authors vacillate "between exploitation and resistance," trying to preserve "the autonomy of their very creative enterprise."[11] Graham Huggan has spoken of the "postcolonial exotic," which "marks the intersection between contending regimes of value: one regime—postcolonialism—that posits itself as anticolonial, and that works toward the dissolution of imperial epistemologies and institutional structures; and another—postcoloniality—that is more closely tied to the global market, and that capitalises both on the widespread circulation of ideas about cultural otherness and on the worldwide trafficking of culturally 'othered' artifacts and goods."[12] The recourse to opacity represents one of the literary strategies used by contemporary authors to navigate these expectations. The works analyzed in this chapter are not bildungsroman, coming-of-age stories that grapple with in-between spaces and double identities. They do not describe the process of growing up in a place that is not one's own, that one is supposed to integrate, while never allowed to do so fully. The immigrant subjects in these novels are opaque; they are not meant to be understood. Playing with and eschewing the demand to explain minority subjects to nonminority readers, contemporary authors represent characters who are unstable and unpredictable.

Stereotypes, Homi Bhabha argues, are "a form of knowledge and identification that vacillates between what is always 'in place,' already known, and something that must be anxiously repeated."[13] The stereotype, a primary mode of colonial discourse, fabricates a "social reality which is at once an 'other' and yet entirely knowable and visible."[14] The power of the stereotype lies in the constant repetition and reactivation of this knowledge, which attempts to reduce alterity to fixity, an objective never fulfilled because the anxiety of the unknown, which the stereotype will never be able to appease entirely, reemerges. We, thus, cannot replace the rigidity of a "negative" stereotype with a similarly firm "positive" image. To negate a stereotype, one has to repeat it, thus reactivating its power. Celia Britton remarks that "if Bhabha's analysis is correct, then opacity provides the only possible mode of resistance to the stereotype. That is, it confronts the stereotype's attempt to fix racial difference with a self-representation that cannot be fixed because it is deliberately unintelligible."[15] An opaque subject is a visible, present subject, who eludes the power of the stereotype. The opacity of the characters overlaps with other elements of formal opacity, as we shall see in the analysis of the three texts. Opacity, in fact, intersects with Samantha Pinto's "difficulty." Through formally complex texts, Pinto argues, the women of the African diaspora refuse to be reduced to "established, legible frames."[16] Atlantic writers similarly reject pre-given frames for their immigrant characters, resorting to opacity. This unintelligibility is, however, never complete, leaving room for relation.

These opaque characters encounter one another, and they encounter the reader. Opacity channels the recognition of intersecting modes of precarity while underscoring the fact that the experience of the other can never be—and does not need to be—fully explained. It is a mode of aesthetic and ethical cross-cultural thinking that refuses to presume that the other is accessible or knowable in one's own terms. Without disavowing difference, these authors build upon the shared experience of necessary flight and a refusal to return to transparency. The act of withholding, in these narratives, forms the basis of trans-Atlantic thinking and being. Diaspora, Samantha Pinto argues, "can also challenge the order of things—the way we come to recognize and interpret our specific historical and social realities—in its difficult play between the known and the unknown, between recognizable forms of being, knowing, belonging, and acting in the world and the new forms that emerge as we try to understand its shifts."[17] Trans-Atlantic solidarities exist precisely within this tension between the known and the unknown, the recognizable and the not recognizable. The globalized Atlantic, in this chapter, is not a result of sharing but of interconnected acts of withholding.

These authors thus invite the reader to engage their characters on different terms. The reader is placed in front of characters she does not fully comprehend and thus with whom she cannot fully identify. All three authors have moved away from a more traditional model where ethics and politics stem from the identification with a specific character. Rather, the reader is invited to relate to those that she cannot fully understand. An attempt to "explain" these characters is replaced by a narrative focus on the relation between characters and transnational spaces. Characters are constantly moving through space, drawing attention to transnational sites of neoliberal precarities. The encounters (among characters and between characters and readers) while no longer leading to a full identification, can lead to common acts or refusals, or disidentification, to borrow a term from Jacques Rancière. According to

Rancière, politics stems from a disidentification from certain structures that protect some at the expense of others. In the rest of the chapter, I trace precisely how these three works of fiction position us in front of opaque subjects, inviting us, not necessarily to "understand" them but rather to disidentify from power configurations that maintain us sometimes similarly, sometimes differentially, precarious.

The various levels of opacity that I just described are not identical; the authors, in fact, shift between them. In my readings of the texts, I underline how the three authors mobilize these different meanings as I trace a formal universe of interlacing opacities. Through an ethics and aesthetics of opacity, these authors represent forms of life that exceed norms of recognition and that do not strive for recognition. As such, they pose a challenge for critical discourse. How can we discuss these works and these characters without returning them to transparency? How to, rather, accompany them in their fugitivity? Perhaps an impossible task, but one worth the try.

DOCUMENTING THE UNDOCUMENTED

Yolanda Arroyo Pizarro was born in the Puerto Rican town of Guaynabo, in 1970. Her first literary recognition came at the early age of nineteen, when her story "Vimbi Botella" won the intrauniversity competition of the Bayamón Central University. In 2004, she published her first book of stories *Origami de letras* [*Letter Origami*]. Arroyo Pizarro was chosen as one of the most important Latin American writers under thirty-nine years of age as part of Bogotá39, a festival convened by UNESCO, the Hay Festival, and the Ministry of Culture in 2007. Her work frequently deals with questions of marginality, solidarity, queerness, exploitation, and resistance. *Los documentados,* of interest to us in this chapter, is her first novel, which won her the PEN Club Prize.

Los documentados is a novella about immigration to Puerto Rico, mainly from the island of Hispaniola. It deals with intra-Caribbean displacements and dynamics, which position Puerto Rico at the intersection of emigration and immigration flows. However, the scope of the novella extends beyond immigration. *Los documentados* is also a story about those with papers, the documented ones, similarly caught in a web of precarity, marginalization, pain, and suffering. Kerenhapuc (known as Kapuc), the protagonist, is a deaf girl who lives with her mother and brother in the village of Playa Tereque. Because she cannot hear and does not speak, the rest of the village considers her mentally disabled. Her father, who could not withstand the shame associated with such a daughter, left the household, abandoning the mother in her struggle to support her two children. Moving from one unsuccessful love affair to another, the mother, Karen, struggles with poverty, loneliness, and the difficulty of caring for a deaf child without adequate social services. To add to the family dysfunction, the brother, Vitito, with no clear direction to follow, becomes involved in immigrant trafficking. The novel deals with the parallel suffering of the documented and the undocumented, their inability to build solidarity around this anguish or communicate their pain. It tackles the desire of some to escape *to* what others are desperately trying to escape *from*.[18]

Kapuc's sole refuge from her family is her best friend, a large tree in the mangrove that she anthropomorphizes and calls Humberto. From Humberto's branches, she observes immigrant boats trying to reach Playa Tereque. She watches immigrants as they drown, as the police apprehend them, and as they sometimes succeed in reaching the coast of Puerto Rico. Everything she observes, she documents in her notebook, thus transforming the undocumented into the documented. The title of the novella in fact carries a double meaning: the story of the documented is the story of those who have documents as much as it is the story of those who Kapuc documents; it is about the intertwined lives of both groups as they remain in isolation.

The novella contains some exceptional descriptions of Kapuc's identification with nature, ants, dragonflies, jellyfish, as well as her relationship with Humberto, the tree. Kapuc experiences synesthesia, she makes up for her loss of hearing through strong olfactory perceptions, describing people, events, and places through olfactory memories and metaphors. The contrast between the unwavering life of the local ecosystem and the repetitive deaths of those considered human surplus traverses the novella. Kapuc's inability to hear mirrors the inability of the *indocumentados* to be heard.[19] In fact, whereas the different chapters are recounted from different points of view (Kapuc's, Karen's, Vitito's), mutism permeates the novel. The novella proceeds through interior monologues, which the characters never exteriorize. There are very few dialogues, as characters rarely communicate with one another; those who can speak do not, because there is no one to listen, leading to an atmosphere of collective mutism. The richness and complexity of internal experience and pain is opposed to the inability to share that experience with others. The multiplicity of stories overlap, circumvent, influence one another. Rarely shared, they move around and beyond each other. The novella engages the difficulty of building solidarity in a world where precarity and solitude predominate. Descriptions of unison and symbiosis with nature are juxtaposed to the brutal treatment of those who enter the island uninvited. The local ecosystem functions due to the interconnectedness of its different elements, which all contribute to the survival of the whole. While the characters, and by extension the different Caribbean islands, are similarly a part of the same system, they do not perceive their interconnectedness. Many residents of Playa Tereque survive financially because of their involvement in immigrant trafficking. Yet, they refuse to acknowledge their dependence on those whose presence they claim to be undesirable.

These multiple connections are also historical. Kapuc spends most of the time perched up in Humberto's branches. The mangrove, for Edouard Glissant, with its multiple intertwined roots, is a metaphor for the interlacing cultures and histories that shape the Caribbean. In *Los documentados,* it gestures toward the interdependent faiths of the characters and the coexisting cultural and historical realities. In fact, Kapuc mentions that Playa Tereque carries a Taino name. Karen, in Kapuc's description, frequently smells of chocolate, a drink Kapuc traces back to the Aztecs. The narrative contains multiple allusions to the cultural contributions of Afro-Puerto Ricans, the Arawak, and Spaniards. These multiple realities surface through aromas, tastes, and words. The connections are thus individual, geographical, and historical. They stand in stark contrast with the characters' fear of being "invaded" and "contaminated" by the Dominicans, with whom they are, actually, already in relation.

Different elements that create these rhyzomatic links echo across scenes. In the prologue, Kapuc and a Dominican boy named Samuel (though we only learn at the end of the novel that it was the two of them) save a man of whom we know nothing except that he has a tattoo of an unusual tree. The man in question does not reappear until the epilogue, when Kapuc's father is attacked by the dogs of a man with a strange tattoo. The scene furthermore echoes Kapuc's own experience, similarly attacked by dogs, and saved by her grandmother. Subtle resonances between scenes point to the enmeshments of all characters' lives. The image of the tree reappears here, ultimately, as a metaphor for the narrative's formal structure. These connections are planted throughout the narrative, yet, could be easily missed by the reader, adding an element of formal opacity.

The ending, however, allows for some of these relations to flourish. Samuel, around the same age as Kapuc, arrives to Playa Tereque alone. He is Kapuc's mirror image: she loves to write, he loves to draw. Humberto, Karen's coworker who is also in love with her, adopts Samuel. At the end of the novella, Vitito marries Sara, a Dominican girl he was in love with for a long time. He and his two friends stop all clandestine activities and open a tire repair shop. Karen, who for a long time refused Humberto's advances because he is an *indocumentado,* finally decides to overcome her prejudices and give this love affair a chance. Kapuc returns to school where she finally has a human friend, Samuel.

The strength of human bonds and solidarity thus ultimately overcomes loneliness, separation, isolation, and hatred.

How can a person become *illegal*? Which lives are worth preserving? How are we to document the undocumented? These are some of the questions of *Los documentados*. Undocumented immigrants are depicted in the anonymity of the crowd, through impersonal pronouns "they" and "them." Kapuc counts and documents them as she sees (and smells) them: 6, 20, 39, depending on the night. The descriptions and actions are repetitive: they arrive, they drown, they try to reach the shore, they run, they flee, they are arrested, they are deported, they escape, they never want to return.

Their anonymity deepens their precarity. When Carmelo and Raul, Vitito's friends, suggest that they should all participate in the illegal transport of immigrants, given that the business is one of the most lucrative on the island, Vitito is at first hesitant. To convince him, his friends state their case: "Mi primo hace mil pesos a la semana llevando y trayendo, y cuando le va mal o uno de los dominicanitos se niega a pagar lo acordado, lo desaparece del mapa. Total que nadie los va a extrañar si no existen, para los efectos. No tienen papeles, como quien dice nunca entraron al país" (101) [My cousin makes a thousand pesos a week ferrying back and forth, and when it goes badly or when one of those Dominicans refuses to pay what was agreed upon, he just wipes him off the map. The result is, no one is going to miss them if they don't exist, for all intents and purposes. They don't have any papers, it's like they never entered the country].[20] The passage interrogates the political, economic, and ethical frames that make life recognizable. The causal links established here are thought provoking: if they don't have papers, the don't exist, and if they don't exist, no one will miss them. Predominance is granted to the legal framework as a precondition to ethics; state recognition of these lives, it seems, undergirds the human ability to miss someone. Only an economic framework could replace the juridical: a life can be recognized only when a suitable amount of money is exchanged. Carmelo and Raul preclude an ethics that moves around and beyond state recognition, as they dismiss the possibility of missing lives that have not been legitimized.

When writing a story about those without one, Arroyo Pizarro does not take the traditional route. *Los documentados* does not document the undocumented by recounting their story, by returning them to their context, by explaining what occurred. She does not criticize immigration policies through a literary illustration of the inhuman treatment of Dominicans. "Escribo todo lo que acontece y documento todo cuanto perciben mis sentidos" (6) [I write down everything that happens and document all that my senses perceive],

Kapuc explains. In other words, she does not try to understand or to explain the situation; instead, she proposes a sensory description of undocumented immigration. The novella approaches immigration through the "redistribution of the sensible," a concept coined by Jacques Rancière. Through a sensory *décalage,* it both conveys and transforms the other's precarity.

In his "Ten Theses on Politics," Rancière writes: "The essence of politics is the manifestation of dissensus as the presence of two worlds in one."[21] Dissensus subsists in relation to its opposite, consensus. We are currently living in the time of consensus, characterized by an acceptance of the present assignment of roles and an absence of alternatives to the current "distribution of the sensible." Dissensus is an interruption, "a division inserted in 'common sense': a dispute over what is given and about the frame within which we see something as given."[22] Politics breaks with the sensory self-evidence of the order that destines specific individuals and groups to occupy positions of authority or subordination, assigning them to private or public lives. Being disrupted are not only the hierarchies of a given social order, but also, more importantly, the perceptual and conceptual coordinates of that order and the naturalness attached to it.

Aesthetic experience, through the free play of the imagination, can destabilize the "natural" distribution of the sensible. The political dimension of art, thus, does not arise solely from the representation of political events, nor is it equivalent to the writer's political viewpoints. It grows, rather, out of art's capacity to suspend normal coordinates of sensory experience and imagine new possibilities of what can be seen, said, and thought, consequently leading to a "new landscape of the possible." *Los documentados* creates, precisely, a dissensus in our sensory experience of immigration:

> Algunos me ven trepada y corren aún más, aún con mayor fiereza, aún con mayor miedo. El miedo es el mejor combustible para hacer a la gente escapar.
>
> Me pasan de largo, dándole duro a las piernas y a los brazos, mirando hacia arriba, recortando el sereno de la noche con la oscuridad de frazada. Esencia para asegurar el escape. Avanzan sus extremidades en mitad de la carrera y sudan,—algunos empapados en el pavor y la sorpresa por descubrirme,—tanto que varios se desvanecen y se caen. Se vuelven a poner de pie, sólo para volver a caerse más adelante, o regresar a recoger a alguno que otro caído más atrás . . .
>
> Entonces, en el peor de los casos, si no se ha logrado una buena coordinación, aparece la policía, y el miedo que han sentido hace un momento al observarme allá arriba trepada, cuando corriendo me han pasado de largo, es relegado a un segundo plano. Carece de la menor importancia. Entonces

da lo mismo que yo esté encaramada en el mangle, como que no lo esté. Parecería de pronto que se vuelve transparente mi cuerpo, terso como las aguavivas, y mi presencia en las alturas deja de tener todo sentido. Y me convierto en medusa. Mudo de cuerpo y me transformo en un ser de aspecto acampanado. Soy entonces una sombrilla de tentáculos colgantes con bordes que absorben todo a su alrededor y que luego entre zarpazos lapislázuli, traduce a letras el acontecer. Se mimetiza mi fisionomía en aquel celentéreo libre y traslúcido de las profundidades. Su órgano auditivo, aseguran los científicos, puede predecir la llegada de la tormenta hasta catorce horas antes de lo que puede hacerlo un barómetro común. Y sin embargo, no emite el menor de los ruidos. Justo como lo haría yo. (5)

Some people see me perched up and they run even harder, with even more ferocity, with even more fear. Fear is the best fuel to help people escape.

They just run past me, sweating all down their arms and legs, looking up above, silhouetted against the night's tranquility with darkness covering them like a blanket. A necessity to ensure their escape. They keep moving their extremities forward and sweating—some are completely soaked with dread and the surprise of seeing me—with a number of them fainting and falling to the ground. They sometimes manage to get back on their feet, only to fall down again, or to go back and try to lift someone else who has fallen . . .

So then, in the worst cases, if everything wasn't coordinated well, the police show up, and the fear that they felt just a moment ago looking at me crouched up high, when they had just run past me, that fear is relegated to the back burner. It no longer has the slightest importance. It's completely irrelevant now whether I'm perched up in the mangrove or not. Soon it'll even be like my body has become transparent like a jellyfish, and my presence up above will no longer have any meaning. I turn into a jellyfish. I change bodies and transform into a bell-shaped being. I am now an umbrella with hanging tentacles with edges that absorb everything around them and which later, through ultramarine swipes, transcribes what happened into letters. My physiognomy mimics that of some member of the Coelenterata phylum, translucent and free among the murky depths. Its hearing organ, scientists claim, can predict the arrival of a storm up to fourteen hours before a normal barometer can. And nonetheless, it doesn't make the slightest noise. Exactly as I would do it.

This, I realize, is a very long passage to quote. However, it illustrates the sensory disruption that arises out of a juxtaposition of the immigrant experience and Kapuc's subsequent symbiosis. On the one hand, we have a detailed description of the newly disembarked. They remain in the anonymity of the crowd; the reader does not know and will never learn anything about them. Instead, the novella proposes a purely corporeal description offered by an external observer. The passage depicts a proliferation of bodies, the physical expression of immigrant fear and exhaustion, conveyed through the movements of arms and legs, going at full speed yet transmitted in slow motion. These are bodies covered in sweat, bodies falling down, desperately trying to get to land, to hold on, to move on. No additional information is included. The passage exposes the corporeal experience of immigration, the proliferation of anonymous precarious bodies, with no protection, and on the verge of collapsing. The entry of the police into the scene interrupts the gaze between Kapuc and the anonymous crowd: a gaze covered in fear, but a moment of potential solidarity.

The police, for Rancière, is a "symbolic constitution of the social." Its essence is not solely in repression, but in dividing the world into clearly definable and identifiable parts, each with a specific function. The police prevents groups from altering their modes of being and doing, or exchanging the places assigned to them. As such, it defines and determines what can be seen, thought, and said. In this scene, in its quite literal presence, the police stand between Kapuc and the immigrants; they interrupt and prevent the gaze, the recognition and the potentiality of a relation. As Kapuc notes, in addition to her body, they negate immigrant bodies. Kapuc must remain in her role of the disabled child with no comprehension of the world, and the migrants must continue in their part of precarious and disposable bodies. A danger arises from the gaze, the moment of recognition between the two, which could lead to a reassignment of roles. The police intervention ultimately pushes Kapuc's body toward transparency, as it metamorphosizes into a medusa.

A description characteristic of Arroyo Pizarro's style follows, which, in the mode of magical realism, describes the slow transformation of a human body into a medusa, a being characterized by its exceptional ability to hear. The discrepancy between the barren, matter-of-fact description of the first part and the metaphorical description of the second is flagrant. The immigrant body, in its precarity, is denied the ability to transform itself, to enter into relation with the natural world, to contemplate and be part of a whole. On the one hand, we encounter the lack of access to the magical, and on the other, the power of magical transformation in light of negation, where the juxtaposition between the two creates a sensory dissensus. The reader observes the immigrants through Kapuc's eyes, through the eyes of a nascent medusa. The dying immigrant bodies become part of a larger process of natural transformation, while also exposed in their inability to transform because they are confined either to the small space of the boat or a prison cell. As they are fleeing the police, the *indocumentados* are also fleeing the reader, refusing to be captured either physically or through literary representation. Flight, the constant and never-ending flight in search of freedom, defines human life. Through the multiple discrepancies, fissures, juxtapositions, and sensations, the novella conveys precarious life on both sides of the border. Immigration is experienced through the senses, through a dissensus in the sensory experience of the world: a world that is two in one, and that thrives of the creation of precarious life.

HERRERA'S FRONTIER NARRATIVES

Yuri Herrera's first novel, *Trabajos del reino* (2004) [*Kingdom Cons,* 2017] received the Premio Binacional de Novela Joven Frontera de Palabras/Border of Words, positioning its author as one of the most praised contemporary Latin American writers. Republished in Spain in 2008, the novel also won the "Otras Voces, otros ámbitos" prize, as the best work of fiction. *Trabajos del reino* depicts the life inside a Mexican drug cartel, focusing on Lobo, a corrido composer who sings inside a "narco palace." Herrera's concise style has distinguished him as a writer and inspired Elena Poniatowska, one of Mexico's renowned authors, to write in relation to *Trabajos del reino*: "Los capítulos, sin numerar, son fulgurantes. Ni una palabra de más. La prosa es escueta, dura, certera y sabe a pólvora porque Yuri la dispara con precisión." [The unnumbered chapters are astounding, there's not a single superfluous word. The prose is terse, unerring and firm, and it smells like gunpowder because Yuri shoots with accuracy].[23]

Herrera's second novel, *Señales que precederán al fin del mundo* (2009), received equal praise. While still interested in marginalized subjectivities, in his second novel Herrera exchanges the world of drug trafficking for the experience of border crossing and a female protagonist, Makina. Discussing the differences and similarities between his two novels, Herrera states that whereas *Trabajos del reino* focuses more explicitly on the physical border, *Señales* deals with epistemological borders:

> Creo que en *Trabajos del reino* estaba más claramente la frontera. Espacial y temporalmente. Es más explícito. Pero esta última novela es más fronteriza en un sentido epistemológico. En realidad hay un sólo capítulo que sucede en la frontera. Al principio es un movimiento hasta la frontera y después

cuando la cruza y lo que ocurre del otro lado. Sin embargo podría decir que este texto es más fronterizo. Una frontera que no tiene que ver sólo con los límites geográficos o políticos. El de Makina es un personaje fronterizo. Ella es una traductora de lenguas, de realidades. Está en la frontera de distintos tipos de sujetos. Y al moverse transforma su identidad. Conforme está viajando, su identidad, que ya es inestable, se modifica. La frontera es un espacio lábil, es un espacio de intercambio donde se está gestando otro universo.[24]

I believe that in *Trabajos del reino* the border is clearer. Both spatially and temporally. It's more explicit. But this last novel deals more with borders in an epistemological sense. In fact, there's only one chapter that takes place at the border. At the beginning, there's a movement toward the border and then later the crossing occurs and then what happens on the other side. However, I could say that this text is more influenced by borders and border crossing. A border that is not limited to geographical or political concerns. Makina is a liminal character. She translates between languages, between realities. There are different kinds of subjects at the border. And by moving, people transform their identities. Thanks to her travels, her identity—which is already unstable—is altered. The border is a labile space, a place for exchange where another universe can emerge.

The border is a liminal space, where identities, languages, and places are in the constant process of fluctuation. Identity in the novel is withheld and absconded, rather than being asserted or constructed. In the United States, Makina fears that she may be in danger and thinks to call the police, only to realize: "Y para qué llamar a la policía, si la medida de la ventura es que ellos no se enteren de que uno existe" (95) ["And what was the point of calling the cops when your measure of good fortune consisted of having them not know you exist" (60)].[25] The central preoccupation is not to display one's identity but to protect it. This does not mean that what is protected is stable and fixed; the withheld opacity is continuously shifting as it enters into relation with other border elements. In *The Undercommons*, Moten and Harney conceive of blackness "as the modality of life's constant escape," which "takes the form, the held and errant pattern, of flight."[26] *Señales* similarly conceives of the border as a space—physical, ethical, philosophical—of constant flight. Identity is not constructed in relation to ties: linguistic, national, or territorial. Rather, it is defined by that which cannot be recognized, and which does not seek to be recognized. Characters on both sides of the border encounter each other as their flight patterns overlap.

In *Señales,* the name has become detached from the subjectivity, which it no longer grounds. Makina and her mother, Cora, are the only two characters with a stable name.[27] A letter (possibly the first letter of their name) distinguishes other characters, who will help Makina cross the border: señor Hache (Mr. Aitch), señor Dobleú (Mr. Double-U). The name no longer grants access to a subjectivity, which it safeguards. Señor Hache and señor Dobleú are defined by their functions, their illegal activities on and across the border; all other signs of identity are withheld. Makina's brother, who now lives on the other side of the border, does not have a name; he is known only as the brother. Likewise, Makina and Cora are often referred to as the sister and the mother. A corresponding relation extends to cities Makina travels through, which do not carry local names but generic ones, such as *Ciudadcita* (Little Town). The depersonalization of characters, who can be interpreted as archetypes, assigns an allegorical dimension to the narrative, removing it from the immediate US–Mexico context. Different gaps that the reader has to fill punctuate the narrative, as Sara Carini suggests, allowing for a more subjective relation between reality and fiction.[28]

The story, in fact, invites two possible readings. A more "realistic" one, where Makina feels close to death as she crosses the Mexico–US border, encounters an alternative reading, where Makina is dead and is crossing into the underworld. Within this interpretation, Makina's voyage takes her progressively deeper and deeper through the nine levels of the underworld (corresponding to the nine chapters of the book), known as Mictlán. Herrera comments on this ambiguity:

> La novela permite dos lecturas: una más llana, que es el viaje de una mujer en busca de una persona querida que descubre un mundo. Y otra, que es el viaje de un muerto que no sabe que está muerto. La estructura narrativa es la del descenso al Mictlán en la cultura Mexica. Es la mitología de una cultura que algunos se confunden y dicen que es la azteca, pero no. Cierto es que no hay sólo una versión de esa mitología. Yo tomé una versión de esta narrativa y tomé los nueve pasos en este descenso al inframundo. Pero para entenderla el lector no necesita estar enterado de todo esto. De todas maneras, y tal como lo comentás, en este nivel de lectura el personaje también pone en duda la estabilidad de la realidad.[29]

The novel allows for two different readings: a more superficial reading, of a woman's journey in search of a loved one and her discovery of a world. And another reading, that focuses on the journey of a dead person who does not know that they are dead. The narrative structure is that of the descent to the Mictlán, in Mexica culture. It's the mythology of a culture that a lot of people mistakenly say is Aztec, but it's not. Of course, there's not only one version of this myth. I took one version of this narrative and took the nine steps down to the mythological underworld. But in order to understand this, readers don't need to know all this background. At any rate, and like you observed, at this level of interpretation the character also casts doubt on the stability of reality.

Herrera thus introduces the indigenous myth of Mictlán into a narrative about modern immigration. According to the myth, the journey from the first to the ninth level was difficult and took four years; the dead had to pass many challenges, crossing a mountain range with the mountains crashing into each other, traversing a field with wind that blew flesh-scraping knives, and a river of blood with fearsome jaguars. A border between reality and myth is thus introduced, one that the reader may decide to cross.[30] The multiple readings available gesture toward the coexistence of multiple histories and the porousness between past and present; the space of the border is "a shifting and unsteady palimpsest of indigenous, Mexican, and *norteamericano* signs, rubbing like tectonic plates and signaling an apocalyptic rebirth."[31] The Little Town on the border, Makina remarks, "estaba cosida a tiros y túneles horadados por cinco siglos de voracidad platera" (11–12) ["was riddled with bullet holes and tunnels bored by five centuries of voracious silver lust" (5)], insinuating that multiple pasts, specifically pre-Columbian and Spanish, undergird the present of narcoviolence and migrations (and even, as we shall see, US involvement in Iraq). The reader can peel, or may decide not to, the different layers of Atlantic histories, that extend far in time and space. Herrera's unusual usage of the language—including for instance, the neologism "jarchar" (used as a synonym of "to exit" in the novel and translated in English as "to verse")—conveys this multidimensionality. In the English version, the translator explains the difficulty of finding an equivalent for "jarchar":

> The word is derived from *jarchas* (from the Arabic *kharja,* meaning exit), which were short Mozarabic verses or couplets tacked on to the end of longer Arabic or Hebrew poems written in Al Andalus, the region we now call Spain. . . . These lyric compositions served as a sort of bridge between cultures and languages, Mozarabic being a kind of hybrid that was, of course, not yet Spanish. And on one level *Signs* is just that: a book about bridging cultures and languages. (79–80)

The neologism extends the space and time of the border, across the ocean, to Al Andalus, itself a bridge between the Atlantic and the Mediterranean. The allegory thus gestures toward a fluid and transformative relation between the past and the present. It inscribes the present-day crossing of the Mexico–US border into a larger history of conflicting Atlantic border crossings. The allegory questions the linear understanding of progress and progression. Different histories and stories crisscross, leaving their mark in the most unexpected places; they also exist in a relation of relative opacity, which undergirds the epistemology of the border.

WRITING OPACITY

When asked about his intent to describe "the beauty of the arid," Herrera responded: "Si es cierta esa frase de Lezama Lima de que el paisaje crea cultura, algunas de aquellas historias surgieron directamente de cómo percibía el Mezquital. Un lugar duro, sin exuberancia, de una belleza trabajosa que exige atención y tiempo para advertir el resplandor de la tierra árida"[32] [If Lezama Lima's phrase about how landscape creates culture is true, some of these stories came directly out of how I perceived El Mezquital. As a hard place, devoid of any exuberance, that possessed a kind of beauty that you had to work for. It was an arid land that demanded time and attention for people to realize its radiance]. Here, building on Herrera's belief that "style isn't surface; style is a form of knowledge,"[33] I want to think of this stylistic aridity as a form of knowledge that preserves the other's opacity.

The very infrequent and sparse dialogues between the characters could be characterized as arid. Communication often focuses on space, particularly, one's future location. Language does not indicate where one is, gesturing rather toward where one is going. The scarcity of language operates in conjunction with an emphasis on communication. Characters exchange few words, yet, the question of the means of communication is central. Makina's brother decides to cross the border because he received a message concerning a piece of land. Similarly, Makina begins the quest for her brother in order to convey a message from their mother. Along the way, señor Hache, who helps her cross the border, gives her a package to deliver to one of his associates in the United States. Literally and metaphorically, Makina is the one who delivers messages. In her hometown, she works as a telephone operator; receiving both local and international calls, she learned to speak three languages. The interconnectedness of spaces, characters, and times exists in a dialectical relationship to the impossibility of communication. The novel centers on Cora's attempt to transmit a one-sentence message to her son and the difficulty of doing so, given that the interconnectedness of the world has produced subjects whose survival depends on the erasure of messages.

Even though Makina brings into relation the different spaces that she traverses, we know very little about her. Herrera's writing, wonderfully precise and sparse, offers very few descriptions of her. The narrative is recounted by an external narrator, denying us access to the characters' interiority. In the instances where we drift into Makina's interior monologue, we do not learn much. Makina's stunning first words—"Estoy muerta" (11) ["I'm dead" (5)]—turn out not to be true, as Makina survives the sinkhole in Little Town that provoked this statement. Or maybe they are true, if Makina is indeed on her way to Mictlán. Or they may be a prophecy. Whereas the first sentence gives us access to Makina's interiority, we are also immediately invited to doubt her statement. We are in front of a character that cannot reveal much about herself, as she is uncertain whether she is dead or alive. Following Makina's flagrant proclamation, the narrative shifts to her spatial surroundings: "Pinche ciudad ladina, se dijo, Siempre a punto de reinstalarse en el sótano" (11) ["Slippery bitch of a city, she said to herself. Always about to sink back into the cellar" (5)]. The lack of access to characters' feelings and thoughts is counterbalanced by detailed spatial descriptions and the characters' attempts to find their bearings within unknown spaces.

Similarly, whereas we are told that Makina speaks three languages, we also immediately learn that she uses all three for silence: "Makina hablaba las tres, y en las tres sabía callarse" (19) ["Makina spoke all three, and knew how to keep quite in all three, too" (11)]. Makina transmits messages, yet, she rarely speaks. She experiences multiple dangers, however, as readers, we do not know how she feels. When Makina and Chucho cross the border, they encounter a ranchero who threatens to kill them. As Chucho tries to prevent the ranchero from shooting and tells Makina to run, the narrator merely states: "Makina no estaba acostumbrada a que la gente le dijera Huye" (54) ["Makina wasn't used to having people say Run away" (34)].

As Makina crosses the border and comes into contact with US farmers, she realizes that she identifies with their language: "Hablan una lengua intermedia con la que Makina simpatiza de inmediato porque es como ella: maleable, deleble, permeable . . . un algo que sirve para poner en relación. . . . Más que un punto medio entre lo paisano y lo gabacho su lengua es una franja difusa entre lo que desaparece y lo que no ha nacido" (73) ["They speak an intermediary tongue that Makina instantly warms to because it's like her: malleable, erasable, permeable . . . something that serves as a link. . . . More than the midpoint between homegrown and anglo their tongue is a nebulous territory between what is dying out and what is not yet born" (45)]. Language is associated with impermanence and the continuous, never-ending production of meaning. In the same way that the question of the border is not resolved with a Mexican American identity, the question of language is not resolved with a heterogeneous form such as Spanglish. Rather, relation is constantly changing and continuously creating new elements. Herrera's understanding of the border intersects with Glissant's understanding of Relation, where the primary elements not only create a third element but are also themselves transformed as they enter into relation.[34] "A nebulous territory between what is dying out and what is not yet born," encapsulates Herrera's writing, his conceptualization of the border, and of immigration. It also refers to the superposition of the different histories within the Americas, some of them, like the pre-Columbian past, violently erased, only to resurface to shape the language that is spoken and the present that is lived. In relation to the story of Mictlán, Herrera comments:

> With each underworld that you cross, you are getting rid of some part of you, some part that makes you a living human being. And when you get to the last underworld, there is only silence; no others and no sounds and no life. That place is the place of *re*-creation. In this world, you didn't die and disappear, and you weren't reincarnated: you came to this place of silence to somehow be part of a re-creation.[35]

The linear narrative thus becomes cyclical, as death leads to birth, and birth leads to death. This applies to Mictlán, but also allows us to conceptualize the trans-Atlantic as a space of constant flight, death, and re-creation. Within this process, something always remains opaque, unstable, continuously in movement, evading our understanding. Immigration is, throughout the novel, represented as an experience that exceeds full comprehension, a search for something, material or immaterial, that remains out of reach. When Makina, at the end of the novel, asks her brother why he refuses to return to Mexico, he replies: "Ya peleé por esta gente. Debe de haber algo por lo que pelean tanto. Por eso me quedé en el ejército, mientras averiguo de qué se trata" (103) ["I already fought for these people. There must be something they fight so hard for. So I'm staying in the army while I figure out what it is" (66)]. Immigration is a quest for a meaning that continuously escapes us, a desire for a resolution and an explanation that is seldom found. This is not merely a futile endeavor, as new life is born along the way.

When Makina finally locates her brother in a military base, he tells her the incredible story of his life on the other side of the border. He met a family whose son had enlisted in the US army. They were terrified at the idea of their son going to Iraq and offered Makina's brother money to fight in his place. The brother joined the military and returned from the war alive, something that no one expected. The interlacing precarities and mutually constituted global cycles of death and birth are underscored in this story. Like Spanish colonialism, American imperialism relies on a hierarchy of lives, fighting to become less disposable. Makina's brother should fight in the war, the family believes, as his life is worth less than that of an American soldier. He is then allowed to stay in the US and be reborn, at the expense of, even more precarious, Iraqi lives. The privilege of citizenship is gained by extending the cycle of violence and precarity. As the histories intersect, so do the precarious lives that they beget. After she learns that her brother fought in the Iraq war, Makina asks him to describe his experience. Her brother's response questions this very gesture: "Para qué quieres saber, dijo, No lo entenderías." (100) ["Why do you want to know, he said. You wouldn't understand." (63)]. Comprehension remains suspended.

NDIAYE'S CONTRADICTORY REALITIES

Born to a Senegalese father and a French mother, Marie NDiaye was raised in Pithiviers, a town south of Paris. Her father left when she was little, severing her relation to Senegal. NDiaye thus spent most of her life in France—until recently, when out of political reasons, after Nicolas Sarkozy's 2007 election as president of France, she decided to move to Berlin, thus joining the ranks of immigrant (commonly called expats, as explained in chapter 3) writers. The reader may be surprised by my decision to include *Rosie Carpe* amidst immigrant fiction. This may seem as odd of a choice as Bessora's *Petroleum*. A much more obvious choice (if there is one at all) would have been NDiaye's later novel, *Trois femmes puissantes* (2009) [*Three Strong Women*, 2012], which won the Prix Goncourt, the most prestigious literary award in France. Maya Jaggi describes the novel in the *Guardian*: "Moving mainly between France and Senegal, this novel explores survival, inheritance and the feared repetition of history—within families, as between peoples. Its three heroines have an unassailable sense of their own self-worth, while their psychological battles have an almost mythic resonance."[36]

In the third and final story of *Trois femmes puissantes,* the Senegalese Khady Demba dies while trying to reach Europe in NDiaye's most explicit engagement with the question of immigration. While a wonderful novel, *Trois femmes puissantes* follows a more classic narrative structure. Being half Senegalese, NDiaye has for a long time contended with expectations to write about Senegal and immigration. The novel is thus much easier to "understand" and classify. Not so with *Rosie Carpe*. *Rosie Carpe* is a difficult novel, one that defies any easy categorization. It is not *about* immigration (like many novels included in this book), but it represents immigration and displacement through unusual lenses. *Rosie Carpe* represents a decentralized France; it focuses on precarious subjects moving from the province to Paris and then to Guadeloupe in an endless attempt to restart their lives. The novel challenges the representation of Guadeloupe as solely a space of emigration, depicting instead the island as a last resort for those who have been unable to find a home elsewhere.

At the beginning of the novel, Rosie Carpe, pregnant, arrives to Guadeloupe, hoping to find her brother Lazare. She has a son, Titi, whose father, Max, is the manager of a hotel in Antony where she used to work; she is uncertain who the father of her second child is. In Guadeloupe, she encounters a society devastated by poverty and racism, a brother who is living on the edge of the law, and strangely rejuvenated parents, who are trying to build a new life in this "tourist paradise."

Neglected by her parents, her brother, and Max, Rosie is a solitary and marginal character. She feels excluded and alienated: "Marie Ndiaye fait partie de ces écrivains dont on reconnaît la signature stylistique dès les premières lignes d'un roman. Une même quête, un même questionnement identitaire animent ses écrits. Sous sa plume, ses protagonistes subissent le même processus d'exclusion, d'aliénation et de nomadisation"[37] [Marie Ndiaye is one of those writers that can be identified by their style in the first few lines of a novel. The same quest for and questions about identity drive all of her texts. Under her pen, her protagonists all suffer processes of exclusion, alienation and nomadization], writes Nora Cottille-Foley. Rosie cannot successfully occupy the position of the subject or assume the "I." The subject is doubled, Rosie often refers to herself in the third person, as she feels that she is observing herself from the outside. She does not know how to position herself in History nor in the story; she plays no role in a narrative that was constructed without her will or participation. Rosie's instability as a character has led Lydie Moudileno to write that Rosie represents "the subject in disarray," who perfectly illustrates "the condition of a contemporary subject ill-equipped to interpret a reality whose logic always seems to escape her."[38] Whereas the novel in fact presents us with unstable characters, it also moves beyond a postmodern decentering of the subject and the question of identity loss, especially if we think about it in relation to immigration, citizenship, and precarity.

Like Herrera's narrative, *Rosie Carpe* poses the problem of the name, of the relation between the name and the person who carries it. We know that Rosie used to be called Rose-Marie. However, Rosie refuses to admit to the continuity between Rosie and Rose-Marie. Rosie does not depend on, does not need, Rose-Marie in order to be Rosie:

> Bien longtemps après que les années de Brive-la- Gaillarde se furent écoulées . . . elle se contentait de dire, sans regret, sans intonation:
> - Je m'appelais encore Rose-Marie à ce moment-là.
> Et il fallait comprendre, car elle ne savait pas trop elle-même et ne pouvait rien ajouter, que le pli lentement pris et lentement affermi de l'appeler Rosie, plus tard, à Paris, avait signifié et comme provoqué la fin d'une saison jaune, douce, provinciale et pleine d'aspirations. (51)

> Long after the Brive-la-Gaillarde years were over . . . she merely said without nostalgia and without intonation, "I was still called Rose-Marie at that time."
> Which was as much as to say, for she was not too sure herself and could say nothing further, that the slowly acquired, slowly engrained habit of calling her Rosie later in Paris had meant and somehow brought about the end of a soothing yellow phase, provincial and full of aspirations. (37)[39]

Thus begins the second part of *Rosie Carpe*. Whereas in the first part we were in Guadeloupe, here, we have returned to Rosie's and Lazare's childhood in Brive-La-Gaillarde, to their brief stay in Paris, and to Rosie's life in Antony. Characteristic of NDiaye's style, this passage performs a disorientation in relation to the temporality of events. While several adverbs—which connote the past or the future—are interspersed throughout this passage, they exist in relation to a not-clearly-defined present. A return to the past thus begins with a reference to the future: "Long after the Brive-la-Gaillarde years were over." At this moment in the novel, we do not know that Rosie grew up in Brive; Brive is still an empty reference point, in the same manner that "a long time after," is a very imprecise temporal indicator. How long after is "a long time after?" Furthermore, "after" does not refer to the time immediately after Rosie left Brive but rather to a time after the Brive years have gone by. This future exists in relation to a present where the years spent in Brive have already passed.

The name change marks a temporal discontinuity of the subject, appearing simultaneously as the consequence and the cause of an occurrence. She begins to call herself Rosie because the Brive years are already over but also in order to provoke the disappearance of Brive. The name change is not perceived as a loss in relation to an original name; Rosie remarks with no regrets that her name is no longer Rose-Marie. Names are associated to places, and instead of being defined by their names, characters are demarcated by their manner of inhabiting a certain space. Every movement in space requires a change of identity, and name.

The past and the future exist in relation to an unspecified present, adding to the narrative's formal difficulty. The novel thus begins in media res: "Mais elle n'avait cessé de croire que son frère Lazare serait là pour les voir arriver, elle et Titi" (9) ["But she had not stopped believing that her brother, Lazare, would be there to see them arrive, her and Titi" (1)]. What does this "but" refer to? The narrative is immediately placed into a temporal continuity that that the reader cannot access.

Like Herrera, NDiaye presents the reader with characters that question their relation to both their names and their families. Aside from their relation to specific spaces, there is very little we, as readers, know about these characters.

WHO IS ROSIE?

Aucune définition de ce que je suis censée être ne peut me venir à l'esprit. En revanche, j'entends de plus en plus d'injonctions de se définir (en tant que Noire ou métisse, métisse en France, etc.). Se définir, c'est se réduire, se résumer à des critères, et par le fait entériner ce que d'autres seraient ou ne seraient pas.[40]

There is no definition of what I'm supposed to be that comes to mind. But on the contrary, there are more and more calls to define oneself (as a black or mixed-race woman, as a mixed-race individual in France, etc.). Defining oneself means reducing oneself, being no more than a list of criteria, and as a result confirming what others may or may not be.

Rosie rarely speaks, she mostly remains silent. In fact, Carpe, Rosie's last name, in French also means "carp," a freshwater fish. "Muet(te) comme une carpe" [silent as a carp] is a common expression in French, due to the fact that a carp frequently brings its head above water, with an open mouth, without making a sound. Just like Rosie. In Paris, "Elle ne connaissait personne à qui parler. Je cherche un certain Lazare Carpe, murmurait-elle de temps en temps, surprise d'entendre sa voix, ayant prévu cette surprise et malgré tout surprise" (64) ["She knew no one she could talk to. 'I'm looking for someone called Lazare Carpe,' she muttered from time to time, surprised to hear her voice, having foreseen this surprise but nonetheless surprised" (50)]. Similarly, when she arrives in Guadeloupe, she has such a feeling of powerlessness and solitude that "elle ne pouvait soulever ses pieds ni prononcer le moindre mot" (42) ["she could not lift her feet or utter so much as a word" (32)]. There is very little dialogue in the novel, aside from the two questions that Rosie continuously poses, asking everyone whether they know her brother Lazare, or the father of the child she is carrying. Rosie likes silence, she is immensely frustrated that Max talks too much. During their encounters, Max speaks, and Rosie listens to him in silence: "Il savait des choses qu'elle ignorait. Elle l'admettait et l'écoutait parfois, engluée dans un vague dégoût mais attentive, silencieuse" (73) ["He knew things she did not know. She admitted it and sometimes listened, bogged down in vague disgust, but attentive and silent" (58)]. Max knows almost nothing about Rosie because Rosie never tells him anything: "Rosie appréciait qu'il ne lui pose aucune question la concernant. Il ne savait d'elle qu'une chose, qu'elle était Rosie Carpe de son vrai nom, et cela lui suffisait" (74) ["Rosie appreciated him not asking questions about her. He knew only one thing about her, that she was called Rosie Carpe for her real name, and that was enough for him" (59)]. In fact, Max doesn't know absolutely anything about Rosie since her real name is not Rosie Carpe. However, it is not only the protagonists who do not know each other. As the reader, we find ourselves in the same position; Rosie remains for us an impenetrable character that we cannot fully grasp or understand, a character with whom with cannot fully identify.

Though in the first two parts of the novel, through free indirect discourse, we have access to Rosie's point of view, NDiaye deconstructs the distinction between exteriority and interiority. Even though Rosie's mind is transparent, she remains opaque, because we do not learn anything through her thoughts except the fact that she cannot understand herself. She is surprised that the figure she sees in the mirror is her, Rosie Carpe; she is surprised that the life she lives belongs to her, Rosie Carpe. She is surprised to be Rosie Carpe; she is surprised to do the things she does. The reader is also constantly surprised; sometimes by her lack of action, sometimes by her actions, sometimes by her surprise. Rosie's interiority returns us to her exteriority since she feels like she is observing herself from the outside.

While there are several descriptions of Rosie, these descriptions don't amount to a precise image: "Rosie portait des vêtements larges et discrets, et elle attachait ses cheveux en une queue peu fournie, si bien que chacun devait comprendre, en la rencontrant, qu'elle n'avait aucune prétention à signifier ou exprimer quoi que ce fût" (55–56) ["Rosie wore loose-fitting, unobtrusive clothes, and she pulled her hair back in a thin plait in such a way that everyone must have realized when they met her that she had no pretensions to mean or express anything whatsoever" (41–42)]. The account thus merely indicates that nothing differentiates Rosie from anyone else; leaving the reader to wonder what Rosie Carpe actually looks like. Rosie acts in ways that we do not fully understand, and no attempt is made to elucidate her actions. When Max brings a woman to film them while they are having sex, Rosie knows that she does not want to do this; she knows that she wants Max and the woman to leave, she knows that she wants to scream, but she does not react. Why? She doesn't know: "Et Rosie tâchait d'exécuter ce qu'on attendait d'elle, ne sachant pas comment il était possible qu'elle fût incapable de le refuser, ne comprenant pas et s'absorbant dans une rêverie grise et maussade" (79) ["And Rosie would try to act out what was expected of her, not knowing how it was possible that she was incapable of refusing, not understanding, and going off into a gray, sullen daydream" (64)]. All we learn is that she doesn't want to participate in these sessions because "elle finirait par succomber d'avoir la peau si complètement froide" (78) ["she would end up dying because her skin was so completely cold" (63)]. Any psychological explanation is thus avoided and circumvented; it is not because she finds it immoral or because she is ashamed (at least, not as far as we know) that Rosie wants to scream when Max and the woman enter the room, it is because she no longer wants to be confused about seasons. She is responding to an exterior cause, to a corporal sensation; she wants the cold to end. After ten pages of filming session descriptions, we still wonder why she does it.

Marie NDiaye often resorts to ellipses, which appear in crucial moments in the novel. We follow Rosie while she is pregnant with Titi, yet, the narrative skips over Titi's birth. Soon after, Rosie loses her milk, and Max finds Titi nearly dead. After that, once again, there is a rupture. In the following scene, Rosie is already in a different apartment; Titi was taken away from her for some time, but they are now living together again. A similar situation occurs in Guadeloupe, at the end of the novel's third part. Titi almost dies when Rosie leaves him alone; Lagrand (the elegant black man who greets her at the airport at the beginning of the novel) brings him to the hospital and saves him. An ellipse follows, the next time Lagrand sees Rosie, she is living in Morne-à-l'Eau with a married Titi who is also a teacher. We learn from Titi that Rosie abandoned him and that he spent the majority of his childhood with his grandparents. Titi's birth, both of his hospital stays, and finally the moment when Rosie abandons him are all erased from the novel. How does Rosie feel when Titi is born? How does she feel when she realizes that he almost died? How does she feel when she abandons him? We don't know. Almost every time there is a need for a psychological or moral explanation, the narrative stops and a rupture ensues.

Rosie becomes particularly opaque and inaccessible in the last part of the novel. At the very end, Lagrand and Rosie are married and in their common life: "Rosie ne lui commandait rien, ne le maltraitait d'aucune façon, esquivait son regard. Elle lui semblait avoir atteint le point le plus extrême de la passivité et de l'indifférence" (334) ["Rosie gave him no orders; she did nothing to mistreat him, and she evaded his gaze. She seemed to him to have reached the farthest point of passivity and indifference" (301)]. Instead of offering us a progressive elucidation of the character, by the end of the novel, Rosie is merely a surface.

A psychological opacity of the character intertwines with the opacity of the writing. Comprehension is always differed in the novel; a temporal gap exists between the event and its grasp, both for the characters and the reader. Thus, at the beginning of the novel, when Rosie thinks that Lagrand is her brother Lazare, the reader could deduce that Rosie is black. Only after a few pages do we realize that this is not the case. Similarly, from the beginning, we know that Rosie is pregnant with a second child only to learn significantly later that she got pregnant at Max's wedding. The characters, like the reader, do not understand the meaning of events straightaway: "Plus tard encore, lorsque Rosie essaierait de comprendre quand les choses avaient commencé à mal tourner, il lui semblerait ne pouvoir mieux illustrer les premiers temps à Paris qu'en expliquant qu'ils étaient demeurés, elle et son frère Lazare, dans l'air épais de Brive" (54) ["Later still, when Rosie tried to understand the point at which things had begun to go wrong, she would feel that there was no better illustration of the early days in Paris than the explanation that they had remained, she and her brother, Lazare, in the thick Brive air" (40)]. Once again, the passage begins with a "later still," characteristic of NDiaye's style; a "later," whose "now" we don't know. Furthermore, the narrator does not tell us that at that moment Rosie will have understood but that she will have tried to understand. It is not certain that she will have understood, since comprehension is always deferred in NDiaye's prose.

Opaque characters who live in violent and strange worlds, characters with whom we cannot fully identify, proliferate in the three novels of this chapter. In Arroyo's novella, through the eyes of Kapuc, we encounter an array of opaque, precarious, migrant bodies. In Herrera's and NDiaye's novels, protagonists commit unexplainable actions without any value judgment. In all three cases, the reader is not in a position of power because she is not in a position of knowledge. She is invited to enter a space that she will never be able to own, a space that remains somewhat other, where she will feel estranged. A relation between the reader and characters founded on incomplete comprehension emerges. Relation, Glissant claims, thinks "la totalité" [totality] but not "le totalitaire" [totalitarian]. Generalization is totalitarian; it establishes universal models in an attempt to bring the world to its transparence. "Totality," on the other hand, encompasses all the world's relations that can never be fully known because they are involved in a continuous process of transformation. Relation, as Celia Britton explains, is "a dynamic process governed by principles that are themselves always being changed by the elements they govern."[41]

Glissant differentiates between "la pensée de l'Autre" [the thought of the Other] and "l'Autre de la pensée" [the other of Thought]. The "thought of the Other" encourages us to accept and respect the existence of alterity. Yet, this presence does not necessarily affect us. The other of Thought implies a recognition and a willingness to be transformed as we enter into Relation. Our relationships always change us; for this to happen, we do not need to "know" the other.[42] These authors want to establish a relation founded on opacity between the characters and the readers as they build the other of Thought. They seek modes of representation that do not transform the other into material to know and to understand. By opting for opacity, authors relinquish the traditional authorial power of omniscience, admitting that, after all, they can never know fully those that they represent. This relation is reproduced on multiple levels: within a character, between the author and the characters, among the characters, and between the characters and the reader. We do not need to fully understand alterity for it to change us and change our relationship to the structures and circumstances that render our lives interdependent (often interdependently precarious).

ATLANTIC CITIZENSHIP AND OPACITY

When asked about her obsessions, Marie NDiaye responds: "'L'étrangéité.' Le fait d'être étranger pour une raison ou pour une autre. Soit au sens propre, soit dans un sens plus figuré"[43] ["Strangeness." The fact of being a stranger for one reason or another. Either in the literal sense of foreignness, or in a more figurative sense]. Herrera, on the other hand, claims that literature can encourage the reader to reflect on her role as a citizen: "Creo, en todo caso, que la lectura sí puede tener ciertos efectos en la creación de ciertas formas de ciudadanía. Yo siempre insisto en que la literatura no hace hombres buenos o malos, pero que puede crear ciudadanos reflexivos"[44] [In any case, I believe that reading can have some effect on the creation of some forms of citizenship. I always emphasize the fact that literature doesn't make people good or bad, but it can create thoughtful citizens].

Thus, on the one hand, NDiaye has expressed her interest in the figure of the stranger, and on the other, Herrera has spoken about the relation between literature and citizenship. Of course, the figure of the citizen and that of the stranger have always existed in a dialectical relation. In order for there to be citizens, there also have to be noncitizens or strangers. The three works deal with the limits of citizenship as a conceptual framework when dealing with contemporary forms of precarity. Contemporary precarity moves within and in excess of citizenship, which is no longer a sufficient solution. Inclusion into citizenship is not necessarily the objective, but rather, a disidentification from citizenship as the condition for legitimation.

All three novels resituate ethics and politics in relation to the process of disidentification, working in conjunction with, but also across and beyond, identity politics. This, however, does not mean that categories such as race, gender, class, and nationality are no longer pertinent. In fact, the three narratives deal with the intersections of race, gender, and nationality from a transnational perspective. However, identification along any of these categories is no longer at the basis of the political, replaced by the interplay between identification and disidentification.

For Jacques Rancière, in order for there to be politics, there has to be disidentification. Identification with victims often produces feelings of fear and pity, which are not political affects. In order to illustrate this point, Rancière offers an analysis of the images of massacres in Rwanda and Bosnia: "At best our exposure to them inspires moral indignation, a powerless hatred of the torturer. It often inspires a more secret feeling of relief at not being in that other's shoes, and sometimes it inspires annoyance with those who are indiscreet enough to remind us of the existence of suffering. Fear and pity are not political affects."[45] In order to feel pity, we must be located in a safe and distant place. We feel pity for what happens far from us, and not to us. Pity is not political because, in order for there to be the "cause of the other" as a political figure, there needs to be a "refusal to identify with a certain *self*."[46]

In order for there to exist a political feeling, there has to be a "gap" in relation to ourselves, in relation to the world we live in. Through his description of October 17, 1961, Rancière attempts to explain the relation between politics and disidentification. That day, thousands of Algerians responded to a call from the *Front de libération nationale* [National Liberation Front] (FLN) and demonstrated in the streets of Paris. A brutal repression followed, and the authorities never disclosed the number of victims. In this case, political subjectivation came from a disidentification from the French state that did this in the name of its citizens: "We could not identify with the Algerians who appeared as demonstrators within the French public space, and who then disappeared. We could, on the other hand, reject our identification with the State that had killed them and removed them from all the statistics."[47] Political subjectivation does not stem from an identification with Algerians because this identification is impossible, given that it requires the transparency of the other, the reduction of the other to the same. On the other hand, the disidentification of the citizen in relation to the state, of the reader in relation to his world, leads to the construction of a political subjectivity.

In a very different context, queer activist and theorist José Esteban Muñoz has addressed the question of disidentification in the context of queer performativity. In his work, Muñoz connects disidentification to the notion of "worldmaking," because a disidentificatory moment in the present bears a utopian imprint on the future:

> Disidentification is a point of departure, a process, a building. Although it is a mode of reading and performing, it is ultimately a form of building. This building takes place *in the future and in the present,* which is to say that disidentificatory performance offers a utopian blueprint for a possible future while, at the same time, staging a new political formation in the present. Stakes are high. . . . The minoritarian subject employs disidentification as a crucial practice of contesting social subordination through the project of worldmaking. The promises made by disidentification's performance are deep. Our charge as spectators and actors is to continue disidentifying with this world until we achieve new ones.[48]

In other words, feeling sorry for the marginalized, wishing that they could have what the more privileged do, is not enough. We need to recognize that we are unfree when a system in place constrains us but also when our limited freedom is contingent upon the unfreedom of another. The disidentification from structures that grant privilege to some at the expense of others, thus oppressing us in intersecting ways, is the first step toward solidarity. In *Rosie Carpe,* the whites who move to Guadeloupe are often poor; like Rosie and Lazare, they often cannot find a place within the social hierarchy. Guadeloupe is their last resort, their last attempt to revalorize themselves. They come to Guadeloupe because there, due to the color of their skin, they are all of a sudden in power. When Lazare and his friend Abel assault a French couple, the two tourists do not expect it because they feel racial solidarity. Whereas in France, they would have felt threatened by their poverty, in Guadeloupe, race outweighs class. Questions of race and racism resurge when Rosie meets Marcus Calmette, a black man from Guadeloupe. When he invites her for a coffee, she hesitates and then finally refuses because she doesn't know how to call him other that "le Noir" ["the Black man"]. Rosie later regrets that she sided with the Carpes and the Maxs, rejecting Marcus. Alliances and solidarities shift from one side of the Atlantic to the other, creating hierarchies and interlinking precarities. Rosie Carpe is to an extent the precarious subject pushed to its extreme, what Peter Hallward calls a singular subject, one no longer able to relate to anything or anyone.[49]

In *Señales,* the relation between the state, its citizens, and its noncitizens is quite prominent. During her return from the US, Makina is stopped by the police and ordered to join a line of immigrants kneeling on the ground. The police officer lays out the first "rule" of immigration: "Si quieren venir, se forman y piden permiso, si quieren ir al médico, se forman y piden permiso, si quieren dirigirme la puta palabra, se forman y piden permiso. Se forman y piden permiso. ¡Así hacemos las cosas aquí, la gente civilizada!" (107) ["You want to come here, fall in and ask permission, you want to go to the doctor, fall in and ask permission, you want to say a fucking word to me, fall in and ask permission. Fall in and ask permission. Civilized, that's the way we do things around here!" (69)]. Following this speech, he realizes that one of the men in line is holding a poetry book, which he subsequently takes, demanding further that the man write a poem on a blank piece of paper. Noticing the man's fear, Makina interferes and begins writing: "Nosotros somos los culpables de esta destrucción, los que no hablamos su lengua ni sabemos estar en silencio. Los que no llegamos en barco, los que ensuciamos de polvo sus portales, los que rompemos sus alambradas. Los que venimos a quitarles el trabajo, los que aspiramos a limpiar su mierda, los que anhelamos trabajar a deshoras. . . . Nosotros los oscuros, los chaparros, los grasientos, los mustios, los obesos, los anémicos. Nosotros, los bárbaros" (109–10) ["We are to blame for this destruction, we who don't speak your tongue and don't know how to keep quiet either. We who didn't come by boat, who dirty up your doorsteps with our dust, who break your barbed wire. We who came to take your jobs, who dream of wiping your shit, who long to work all hours. . . . We, the dark, the short, the greasy, the shifty, the fat, the anemic. We the barbarians" (71)]. To the officer's definition and identification with "civilized people," Makina proposes a definition of "the barbarians."

However, this is not merely a counteridentity or identification. Rather, Makina points to the inextricability of different forms of experience, and the fact that "civilized" life is ultimately dependent on the labor of those deemed "uncivilized." In *Dissensus,* Rancière claims "politics as the action of supplementary subjects, inscribed as a surplus in relation to every count of the parts of society." The political subject is not a clearly identified group but the "supplementary part in relation to every count," the continuous surplus in relation to the whole.[50] In this passage, Makina identifies precisely with the uncounted surplus, the ones that can be named only through an incomplete enumeration, and whose existence activates the opposition civilized/barbarian. After reading Makina's poem, the guard walks away, pointing perhaps to his inability to identify with the "barbarians" but also to the possibility of disidentifying from his role in the construction of the civilized/barbarian dichotomy. The scene centers on a moment of writing, gesturing toward the capacity of narrative to produce moments of disidentification.

Arroyo's novella questions citizenship as the precondition for recognition. The transnational ethical gesture invites a disidentification from one's condition as a citizen, from a protection based on the exclusion of the noncitizen. Instead of trying to exclude others from structures that grant minimal protection, the novella encourages us to think comparatively about precarious conditions experienced by citizens and noncitizens alike.

The three narratives analyzed in this chapter approach immigration, displacement, and citizenship, not through questions of identity, cultural mixing, and integration, but in relation to flight and opacity. They produce a distancing between the reader and her world. The reader is drawn into a world in which she feels slightly strange, slightly alienated. A world she cannot fully understand or own. And that is nonetheless her world. A world she knows but which she cannot recognize. The reader might disidentify from this world, from a world that has produced so much violence and discrimination. What is one to do when faced with these violent and strange worlds? The question is transmitted to the reader. In this process of disidentification, or reappropriation, the political resides. From here a "political subjectivation" could be constructed.[51] This moment is merely a possibility, a creation of a potential political space. Like Muñoz suggests, this is an initial step. For literature, this is already plenty. However, it is important to note that disidentification will not inevitably lead to the building of an alternative future. It is a first step in recognizing our interconnectedness and encountering each other in a common process of flight, refusal, and disidentification. Yet, a collective imagining of nonprecarious forms of life must follow if a different world is to emerge. In the following chapter, I continue to explore questions of flight and fugitivity, and more specifically, solidarities that can develop when we flee together.

CHAPTER 5

Atlantic Undercommons

In *The Decline of American Power,* Immanuel Wallerstein defines our current moment as a period of transition: "We do indeed stand at a moment of transformation. But this is not that of an already established newly globalized world with clear rules. Rather we are located in an age of transition, transition not merely of a few backward countries who need to catch up with the spirit of globalization, but a transition in which the entire capitalist world-system will be transformed into something else. The future, far from being inevitable, one to which there is no alternative, is being determined in this transition, which has an extremely uncertain outcome."[1] A global struggle between those who wish to pursue global neoliberalization and those fighting against it marks this transition. It is unlikely, Wallerstein suggests, that the United States will give up its power easily; it will probably intensify wars, domestic and international surveillance and control in an attempt to maintain its current predominance. However, it is precisely now, when the future is highly uncertain, that any, even minor, political action can influence the outcome. The era of global transition, the decline of US power, as well as the fundamental role of Atlantic migrations in redefining power relations, are the focus of Giannina Braschi's *United States of Banana* (2011). Resistance to the US Empire and its politics of neoliberalization is headed by the Atlantic undercommons, formed through unlikely friendships and alliances, based on their shared experience of political precarity. The Atlantic undercommons participate in the creation of a literary, philosophical, and political language: foreign-speaking English.

Braschi addresses most of the aesthetic and ethical preoccupations raised by the authors in this study. The Atlantic is central to her work. In fact, most of the novel takes place in Liberty Island, under the skirt of the Statue of Liberty. The novel addresses Puerto Rican immigration to the United States, Puerto Rico's colonial status in relation to the United States, and power imbalances within the Americas. Braschi's Atlantic, however, stretches far, all the way to the Middle East, since the situation of immigrants in the United States, in the aftermath of 9/11, is conditioned by the global war on terror. If the tension between a regional and a global framework characterizes all the works studied thus far, in *United States of Banana* it reaches a new level as the Puerto Rican immigrant and the Middle Eastern war prisoner, so-called terrorist, meet in Lady Liberty's dungeon. In the context of the state of emergency, the immigrant and the prisoner of war face new forms of political precarity; more specifically, indefinite detention without a trial. Their common precarity, or, as Fred Moten and Stefano Harney phrase it, their common "brokenness of being,"[2] intensified within the state of emergency, allow for their solidarity.

The state of emergency instituted in the aftermath of 9/11 has redefined, Judith Butler upholds, the relation between sovereignty and governmentality.[3] Following Michel Foucault, Butler maintains that governmentality operates through a diffuse set of tactics, institutions, and discourses in order to shape and manage populations rather than directly punish or restrict them.[4] In the age of governmentality, no single sovereign subject decides upon these strategies. For Foucault, the two ages follow chronologically: as state sovereignty dwindles, governmentality gains force. Butler, on the other hand, argues that in the state of emergency, sovereignty has returned with a vengeance, as the state grants itself the right to both suspend law and exercise prerogative power. This sovereignty exists within the framework of governmentality because it is no longer exercised by a single subject but by a set of bureaucratic and administrative bodies.

At the center of this new power configuration is the concept of indefinite detention. Within the context of the state of emergency and heightened insecurity, the rule of law is suspended both nationally and internationally, and the concept of basic human rights doesn't hold sway: those who are identified as a potential national threat are no longer granted the basic right to trial. Bureaucrats and government officials are the ones endowed with this newly formulated sovereignty; they decide who will be tried and who will be indefinitely detained. The state thus claims its right to suspend law and operate outside of the judiciary framework. This is a strange return to the past, Butler contends, to a time of indivisible sovereignty, before the separation of the judiciary and executive branches. As the law is suspended, the belief that there is a threat and the existence of an actual threat are conflated. In the name of preemption, the opinion of those with unilateral power becomes the only proof necessary: "Law itself is either suspended, or regarded as an instrument that the state may use in the service of constraining or monitoring a given population; the state is not subject to the rule of law, but law can be suspended or deployed tactically and partially to suit the requirements of a state that seeks more and more to allocate sovereign power to its executive and administrative powers."[5] The concept of indefinite detention also adds new temporality to this freshly found sovereignty. A state of emergency is an exceptional and out of the ordinary situation. By describing terrorism as new, unexpected, and extraordinary, the state circumvents the law. Yet, at the same time, detention has no determined end in sight. While the state of emergency is exceptional, this exception could potentially be indefinite, becoming, in effect, the new norm.

The state of emergency as the new norm is a trans-Atlantic phenomenon. In the aftermath of the November 13, 2015, attacks, France also instituted a state of emergency—which the government prolonged several times—justified by a declaration of war. That France was now at war was meant to validate increased surveillance, police searches, and detentions. Like in the United States, this is an indefinite war with no end in sight, French philosopher Alain Badiou explains: "Cette fausse déclaration de guerre est surtout l'occasion d'imposer des mesures de police, des mesures de contrôle, des mesures liberticides, des mesures de restriction de tous les droits de la défense. Par ailleurs, le gouvernement, dans ce contexte, tente de se faire valoir comme un grand souverain, protecteur du pays contre la menace"[6] [This false declaration of war is in particular an occasion to impose new police measures, new freedom-destroying measures of control that restrict all the rights of the defense. Moreover, in this context the government tries to assert itself as a great sovereign, defender of the nation against all threats]. For the state to keep its extralegal powers, it has to sustain a collective atmosphere of fear and revenge, an increasingly trans-Atlantic atmosphere.

Braschi's novel takes place within this current moment of transition, marked by the collapse of US ideological supremacy, and the deployment of the state of emergency and indefinite detention. Within this context, Braschi broaches the question of resistance: what resistance is possible after 9/11? How can politics, philosophy, and aesthetics participate in this process conjointly? Widespread political precarity within the state of emergency has enabled the formation of new and unlikely friendships and solidarities. Within the novel, shared conditions of contemporary immigrants precipitate new linguistic and social modes of living. If a resistance is going to exist, it will have to question the concept of sovereignty, focusing instead on the interrelatedness of people, countries, and languages. *United States of Banana* is an aesthetic contribution to contemporary debates, including the concept of the multitude and that of the undercommons. What language do the literary multitude and undercommons speak? Braschi's work provides a possible answer.

THE BANANA EMPIRE

Giannina Braschi has lived a trans-Atlantic life. Before settling in New York City, she studied literature in Spain, France, Italy, and England. There exists, perhaps, a connection between her interest in mixed genre literature and her manifold personal proclivities: she has lived her life in multiple locations, has had multiple careers, and has cited multiple literary influences, always refraining from choosing one option. As an adolescent in Puerto Rico, Braschi already participated in a wide array of activities: she was both a tennis champion and a fashion model. In the United States, her academic career has paralleled her literary accomplishments. After obtaining a PhD in Hispanic literatures at Stony Brook, she taught at Rutgers University, the City University of New York, and Colgate University. As part of her academic research, she has written about the Spanish poet Gustavo Adolfo Bécquer, as well as Cervantes, Garcilaso, Lorca, Machado, and Vallejo.

Braschi's writing has followed a similar turn to that of other writers in this study. Since the beginning, her work has been highly experimental in style and genre. However, her early work deals more explicitly with the position and cultural production of Puerto Ricans in New York City. Her novel *Yo-Yo Boing!* (1998) does not have a traditional story line. The reader encounters a multiplicity of characters, with names reduced to a dash, who engage in conversations over a variety of topics, including New York City, sex, and immigrant cultural production. The main subject of the book is, however, Spanglish, formed through the constant code-switching between English and Spanish.

United States of Banana is also the continuation of Braschi's epic poetry collection *Empire of Dreams* (1994; published initially in Spanish, *El imperio de los sueños*, in 1988), where the questions of language, politics, and desire intermingle in the New York City landscape. Alicia Ostriker, in her introduction to the English translation, calls Braschi an heiress of Lorca, Neruda, Borges, Mistral, and Márquez, as well as "a female (and tropical) Samuel Beckett."[7] In *United States of Banana* (I will refer to it as *USofB* from now on), Braschi continues her trajectory of linguistic experimentation. The work is similarly

(if not even more) disorienting as it traverses different literary genres, including poetry, prose, and theater, and contains an intimidating amount of literary
and cultural references from Shakespeare and Calderón de la Barca, to Artaud
and Joyce. Unlike the first two books, however, *USofB* is written in English.
The three works function as a trilogy, representing the three linguistic options
for Puerto Rico: Spanish, English, and Spanglish, which mirror the three political options: independence, statehood, and colony or Free Associated State.

The novel has been described as philosophical fiction, though this denomination still does not encompass the work's complexity. I will attempt to offer
a brief summary, though it will inevitably fall short. The main plot line, if it
can be called such given that the narrator explicitly strives to destroy the concept of a plot, follows Giannina, Zarathustra, and Hamlet, as they are trying
to liberate Segismundo from the dungeon under Lady Liberty's skirt. Segismundo, an allegorical representation of Puerto Rico, has never seen the light
of day; he was imprisoned at birth by his father, the king of the United States
of Banana, for the simple crime of being born. Under Lady Liberty's skirt,
Segismundo, Giannina, Hamlet, and Zarathustra reflect on the three options
offered to Puerto Rico: wishy, washy, and wishy-washy (independence, statehood, and colony).[8]

This is the second part of the book. A reflection on 9/11 and the world
in its aftermath, constitutes the first part. Giannina, who at the time lived in
Tribeca, a few blocks from what is now Ground Zero, is running toward the
Hudson River with her editor and translator Tess O'Dwyer, as she witnesses
the fall of the Twin Towers and the proliferation of decapitated bodies. The
novel addresses the political status of Puerto Rico, distinct from other Latin
American countries, in conjunction with the global state of empire and anti-
imperial struggles. In fact, Segismundo is not alone in the dungeon; other
war prisoners, so-called terrorists and destructors of freedom (mostly from
the Middle East), surround him. The narrative revolves around the characters' search for freedom—physical, psychological, literary, individual, and
collective—which exceeds both the free market logic proposed by the United
States of Banana and the model of national sovereignty. "En *Estados Unidos de
Banana,* más que nunca soy transnacional y transgeneracional, rompiendo los
bordes de los géneros literarios" [In *United States of Banana,* I am more than
ever transnational and transgenerational, breaking the boundaries of literary
genre], states Braschi.[9]

While there is continuity in her work, the scope of *USofB* is indeed significantly broader. If the future of Puerto Rico remains at the center, the
novel also deals with the Atlantic world post 9/11, the end of the American
empire, and the role of immigrants in this transition period.[10] According to
Arnaldo Manuel Cruz-Malavé: "What is most striking in her most recent

book is the—perhaps obvious—impossibility after 9/11 of reconstructing a hegemonic privileged vantage point from which to apprehend empire in order to assault it, invert it, and occupy it."[11] Braschi deals with the impossibility of identifying a clear and stable counterposition. New modes of resistance are necessary.[12]

More than in her first two works, *USofB* contains a totalizing gesture, an attempt to write about the totality of the world, not simply by representing it but also by creating a world in its totality. The totalization, however, operates through a very fragmentary writing. *USofB* contains no single plot, no clear narrative. It is a succession of bits and pieces of often-unrelated thoughts, reflections, and fragments. Strong political statements appear within the characters' stream of consciousness. Commas, semi-colons, and dashes punctuate this stream, slowing it down, fragmenting it, and splitting it into loosely connected bits and pieces. The characters are similarly fragmentary; they appear and disappear, sometimes for merely a space of a replica. None of them appears in their original contexts; taken from famous literary and philosophical texts, Zarathustra, Segismundo, and Hamlet, do not play their original roles nor follow their original fates.

Even in their original settings, these characters already carried a seed of decontextualization: Segismundo, from Pedro Calderón de la Barca's Golden Age play *Life Is a Dream,* is a polish prince imprisoned by his father Basilio because of a prophecy claiming he would destroy the kingdom. Hamlet is the prince of Denmark, the protagonist of an English language play. Finally, Zarathustra, the Persian founder of Zoroastrianism, is also the protagonist of Nietzsche's philosophical work.[13] These three bilingual characters, whose literary lives do not correspond to their backgrounds and origins, are further decontextualized as they stand with Giannina under Lady Liberty's skirt. For Cruz-Malavé, Braschi engenders a "contradiction or even a paradoxical structure in the sense defined by Gilles Deleuze: a trope that urges us as readers to advance in two mutually contradictory senses at once."[14]

USofB operates within the increasingly popular genre of totalizing or encyclopedic fictions.[15] In *Modern Epic: The World-system from Goethe to García Márquez,* Franco Moretti categorizes Goethe's *Faust,* Joyce's *Ulysses,* and García Márquez's *One Hundred Years of Solitude* as "world texts" (referencing Immanuel Wallerstein's notion of world-systems), "whose geographical frame of reference is no longer the nation-state, but a broader entity—a continent, or the world-system as a whole."[16] These texts, bearing structural similarities to the traditional epic form, also present several discontinuities, including "the supranational dimension of the represented space."[17] They operate within the contradiction between the totalizing form of the epic and the fragmented reality of the modern world. Furthermore, according to Moretti, from the traditional to the modern epic, the protagonist suffers significant transformations. If, in the traditional epic, the hero is defined by action, in *Ulysses* he becomes pure passivity and interiority, and in *One Hundred Years of Solitude* we are confronted with a family rather than the individual.[18]

USofB strives to depict the contemporary world in its totality. However, the proliferation of foreigners, immigrants, and terrorists distinguishes it from Moretti's corpus. Joyce's metropolis could be read as "a concentrate of the world" and Márquez's Macondo, as Moretti writes, is "open to the world."[19] But the constrained space of Lady Liberty's skirt and dungeon is where all the unwanted immigrants, foreigners, so-called terrorists, and historical leaders meet to discuss globalization from the point of view of those who no longer have anything to lose: "There are two movements in the history of coloniza-tion: invasion and immigration. Emigration is a reaction to the invasion of a nation. Because they have been invaded—they will emigrate. This is about changing perspective from the point of view of the colonizer to the point of view of the colonized" (45). Liberty Island in *USofB* is not simply open to the world, or a concentrate of the world; it is a space where actual and allegorical representatives of formerly colonized countries encounter each other to dis-cuss alternatives to US domination, forming the Atlantic undercommons. This is a fragmentary totalization from the point of view of those who survived (or are still living under) colonization.

Totalization through fragmentation is, as we have already seen, also the logic of global neoliberalization. Finance capitalism, Étienne Balibar remarks, "has seen the emergence of multinational private firms whose power exceeds in several respects that of most states. . . . For such neo-capitalism, the world has become largely *deterritorialized,* but also *fragmented* into zones of unequal profitability whose value for investments is continuously changing. The idea of an ultra-imperialist phase therefore acquires a new relevance."[20] Simi-larly, Franco "Bifo" Berardi states: "In the sphere of precarious work, time has been fragmented and depersonalized. Social time is transformed into a sprawl of fractals, compatible fragments that can be recombined by the net-worked machine."[21] Financialization has contributed to the "deterritorialized and rhizomatic proliferation of economic power relations."[22] In other words, if the objective of neoliberalism is to extend the logic of the market to all spheres of human life, it does so through financialization, precarization, and the geographical dispersal of production, which create fragmentation. I am not suggesting that the fragmentary nature of Braschi's text merely repre-sents the fragmentation of global neoliberalization. The shift in perspective is the objective, Braschi explains. Multiple viewpoints in the novel intertwine as the neoliberal logic of fragmentation and totalization encounters a fragmentary resistance from below. Braschi also strives to preserve the autonomy of the literary sphere; it is through the invention of figures, words, expressions, and modes of thinking that she counters the neoliberal and imperialist logic. Resistance develops through literary and linguistic examples of unlikely friendships, undercommons, and solidarities, which arise out of the common experience of political precarity. The novel places precarious, migrant subjects at the center of the resistance to global neoliberalization (promoted by the United States of Banana) and at the center of a new language.

THE EMPIRE IS FALLING

The first part of the book "Ground Zero" deals with the breakdown of meaning in the aftermath of 9/11. A description of the mutilated body of a man in a business suit, falling from the window of the Twin Towers, opens the novel: "I saw a torso falling—no legs—no head—just a torso. I am redundant because I can't believe what I saw. I saw a torso falling—no legs—no head—just a torso—tumbling in the air—dressed in a bright white shirt—the shirt of the businessman—tucked in—neatly—under the belt—snuggly fastened—holding up his pants that had no legs" (3). The mutilated body serves as an allegory for the downfall of the US Empire. The fall of the Twin Towers has transformed New York City into a site of abjection, which, according to Julia Kristeva, is the result of the breakdown in meaning that occurs when the distinction between subject and object, self and other, is no longer upheld. The abject refers both to this collapse of boundaries and to our violent reaction to this breakdown. The abject "draws me toward the place where meaning collapses."[23] As her main example, Kristeva uses the corpse, which reminds us not only of our mortality but also of our materiality. The corpse is the body that became pure object; devoid of interiority and subjectivity, it decomposes into an infinite number of tiny particles, losing its unity and coherence. The ideological, legal, and political systems that maintain the unity of our selves are always under an imminent threat of collapse, the corpse reminds us.

USofB begins in the midst of this downfall. The system of meaning that upheld the United States of Banana domination is breaking down; from a whole and stable body, it is transformed into a series of body parts scattered on the ground. The body represented is not neutral; it is the body of a businessman, marking the interconnection between the ideological and economic foundations of Empire. This is not necessarily the end of Empire. The abject, Kristeva explains, is both the threat and our reaction to this threat. In light of its breakdown, the Empire responds and tries to reassert meaning with all the means possible. As Braschi writes:

> Finally, the empire is falling. This is the beginning of the upset.
>   What a defeat.
>   Not because they fall will you rise. Why are you gloating?
>   Because the fall will make other towers rise.
>   Okay, okay. But the towers that will rise will not be the ones that laughed when our towers fell. It's not the laughter that rises. What rises is the curtain." (15)

What will come after will not necessarily be better. The curtain rises as the normative conceptual framework that upholds the Empire breaks apart. The moment described is one of uncertainty, of rupture, and of interruption; a moment in which words are emptied of their meaning: "Preconceived notions of reality are coming down like the Twin Towers. Democracy is obsolete. It's an empty formula" (56). The American vision of the world, based on the assumption that human rights, democracy, and free markets are inseparable, no longer holds sway in the aftermath of 9/11. The Empire has pushed precarity to the point of unsustainability, creating subjects "who have too little, too little to lose" (34). The subject of resistance is a subject who claims: "I have claimed bankruptcy 20,000 times. Each time with more conviction–less guilt–and less shame" (25). It is a subject that declares: "I can hardly pay for my coffee cake" (22), and "I immigrated with another speech, with another currency" (22). It is an insolvent subject. The ethics of debt, shame, and individual responsibility that we already encountered in other novels are here losing their global reach, unsettling the neoliberal Empire. The Empire will respond, with violence and might, indefinitely detaining those that question its exceptionalism. Yet, it will also bring together the nonconforming, threatening bodies that search for new meanings. The Empire's relentless fight to maintain its sovereignty cannot be challenged from the position of an alternate sovereignty but rather from the locus of precarity and precariousness.

THE IMMIGRANT AND THE TERRORIST

Para mí el postmodernismo es un lagartijo que le cortan la cola y la cola se queda bailando [risas]. Eso es el postmodernismo para mí. O como un *chicken*, un pollo que le cortan la cabeza y todavía camina pero que no sabe donde va. Esa es la poesía del postmodernismo, que no sabe adónde va, pero mientras tanto va caminando. Yo sé a dónde voy, pero hay algo de no saber, de estar con una cabeza degollada, desmembrada. Hay algo desmembrado en el postmodernismo. Y es como que te han cortado la cabeza, o una parte del cuerpo. Y en eso, los *suicide bombers* son una metáfora muy del momento, porque tú ves los miembros de la gente tirada en el suelo, y hay que relacionarlo con la desintegración del sujeto, *the disintegration of the subject into body parts*. Si en el Renacimiento teníamos la integración del ser humano, el descubrimiento del hombre, volviendo a sus raíces del pasado, yo creo que la globalización supone la desintegración del ser humano como memoria, como historia.[24]

For me, postmodernism is a lizard whose tail has been cut off, but the tail keeps dancing on its own [laughs]. That's postmodernism for me. Or like a chicken whose head has been cut off, but the chicken still walks around without knowing where it's going. That's the poetry of postmodernism, it doesn't know where it's going, but it's going! I know where I'm going, but there's something about not knowing, about walking around with a severed head. Postmodernism has something dismembered about it. It's like if they cut off your head or part of your body. And in that regard, suicide bombers are a very timely metaphor, because you see pieces of people strewn around the ground, and you have to put that into relation with the disintegration of the subject into body parts. While during the Renaissance, we had the integration of the human being, the discovery of man, returning to his roots in the past, I believe that globalization entails the disintegration of the human being as memory, as history.

The suicide bomber embodies the dialectic between totalization and fragmentation, characteristic of global neoliberalization. The novel begins with the encounter between the immigrant and the terrorist, or rather with an immigrant witnessing a terrorist act. These two figures are intertwined; the United States of Banana has created the immigrant and the terrorist as two figures that embody its paradoxes and contradictions. Within the logic of Empire, an immigrant is always a potential terrorist; among immigrants is where "terrorists" are fashioned, when they are needed to justify the state of exception. Both are, ultimately, the consequence of Empire's military and neoliberal invasions: "The suicide bomber is an explosion of a contradiction in its paradox, victim and victimizer, yin and yang, two sides of the coin, fire bomb and fire extinguisher, prosecutor and defendant, hangman and hanged" (32). A suicide bombing is powerful because it is a pure act. The author has disappeared in the act itself, leaving only the crime and no one to take the blame. The threat has disappeared since the actor of the threat has vanished, yet it is continually present, since there is no resolution, no body to carry the guilt, to be imprisoned or disposed of. When blame cannot find a single body, blame finds many bodies; it dissipates in the crowd, involving everyone equally: "The crime against society becomes the crime of society" (33). Everyone begins to monitor everyone else, because anyone is a possible suspect. A terrorist crime could happen anytime, anywhere, to anyone, and by anyone, creating a heightened sense of insecurity, which is then used to justify exceptional measures.

"When the government proclaims war against terrorism—it proclaims war against the awakening of the masses. What the suicide bomber kills is the passivity of the masses," Braschi writes (33). The suicide bomber kills the passivity of the masses because the mass can no longer continue to exist in its anonymity; it can no longer continue to believe in its complete autonomy and sovereignty. The horror of 9/11 has proved the vulnerability of the United States, its dependency on others. The war on terror and all the security measures that ensued, including indefinite detention, represent attempts to reinstate this wounded sovereignty, to make up for the loss of control. This is but a futile and impossible task.

Yet, those indefinitely detained by the United States of Banana are not all Middle Eastern "terrorists" but also the Puerto Rican immigrant, Segismundo, whose crime is his very existence. He is, thus, not imprisoned because he acted outside the confines of law but because he exists within the confines of society. His very presence is a potential threat to the existing order. In Calderón de la Barca's play, Basilio, Segismundo's father, imprisons his son based on a prophecy that Segismundo would bring disgrace to his kingdom and kill him. It is, in many ways, a king's preemptive defense of his sovereignty. In *USofB*, a prince imprisoned by a king due to a prophecy is reimprisoned by the United States of Banana in the contemporary dungeon built for terrorists, as old and new forms of sovereignty and government intersect. In a very bizarre way, history repeats.

The newly defined sovereignty of the United States of Banana in the aftermath of 9/11 resembles that of the seventeenth-century monarch. Both have control of the judiciary, both determine who has rights and who does not. The prophecy of the Oracle is now replaced by government suspicion. In the novel, Segismundo is no longer a Polish prince, but comes "from the smallest island of the Antillas Mayores," and he was born to "the most beautiful whore of la Perla" and the governor of Puerto Rico (109). He is also accused of terrorism: "The more you push me down—and your culture has really put me down—and accused me of things I have never done–like being a terrorist—how can I be a terrorist if I have never been given a chance to exist?" (158–59). This replica underscores the contradictions of Puerto Rico's colonial status in a postcolonial world. How could Segismundo have committed a terrorist act if he was never free to do so, when he has never had the independence required? Braschi reminds us that colonialism has not fully disappeared; it is still very much alive in certain parts of the world. But this is not all. In the age of global neoliberalization and indefinite detention, Puerto Rico's "exceptional" status is extending to the rest of the Global South. The global state of exception, the novel suggests, might best be understood from the vantage point of those who were already an exception. United States of Banana describes Puerto Rico as "*a state of exception, a state of emergence, an emergent state*" (165, emphasis in the original). Braschi engages in word play here, based on the semantic proximity between emergency and emergence; as well as the state of exception and the state of being exceptional.[25] Puerto Rico's political status is no longer exceptional within the global state of exception. As an emergent state, Puerto Rico can only emerge into the state of emergency. In other words, Puerto Rico's political choices—wishy, washy, and wishy-washy—sound fairly similar, and this is not merely a question of semantics. Those who have emerged into the state of nationhood still find themselves sharing the dungeon with Segismundo, all in the name of freedom. National sovereignty may no longer be the most pressing political question, given that neoliberal Empire operates within, across, and beyond national independence. Independent or not, you end up under the watchful eye of Lady Liberty. Political debates that do not challenge the neoliberal system of values, that do not extricate freedom from the realm of economics and markets, do not amount to much. The necessary fight might not be in the name of sovereignty, but against it.

The king of the United States of Banana and Oliver Exterminator live in the crown of liberty. Oliver's job is to lead "*fumigation tours in Israel, Palestine, Iraq, Iran, Afghanistan, and Pakistan*" (111) and also to oversee "*the dungeon of liberty—a U. S. territory where the inmates don't celebrate Thanksgiving or eat turkey,*" (112, emphasis in the original) an allegorical representation of Guantánamo Bay. A certain camaraderie develops within the confines of the dungeon. As new prisoners of war from across the world enter confinement, Segismundo remarks that they brought him "thoughts and desires and an appetite to live" (114). Their numbers quickly grow, and they become a whole population, the size of the state, living in the Empire's underbelly: "If the Twin Towers hadn't fallen, I would have never met a Pakistani, Iraqi, or Iranian friend, or a Chinorican, or an Egyptian. I am thrilled to be able to talk to prisoners of war from around the world. It's becoming a gathering of tribes—a United Nations—without nations—not the whore of the US of Banana—but a think tank where new ideas are brewing in the cauldron of races and genders and religions" (118). This is the other side of the war on terror, its countereffect, the creation of a global rhizomatic network of those who no longer wish to adhere to the state of exception. *USofB* is a linguistic and philosophical revolt of those who have been stripped of their rights in the context of the global state of emergency. They are the global multitude, the global undercommons.

THE POETICS OF THE MULTITUDE

To understand Hardt and Negri's multitude, one needs to first become acquainted with the concept of Empire. Written in the mid-1990s, *Empire* was published in 2000, selling far more copies than an average academic book. Hardt and Negri argue that the age of Empire has replaced the imperialist age. If the latter was characterized by conflict between imperial nations, these nations are now cooperating to uphold the interests of the Empire, which relies on decentralized forms of power, a "global network distribution of power" that complicates the opposition between oppressors and the oppressed. This power network includes the major nation-states, supranational institutions, and major capitalist corporations (as well as major NGOs, one might add):

> In contrast to imperialism, *Empire* establishes no territorial center of power and does not rely on fixed boundaries or barriers. It is a *decentered* and *deterritorializing* apparatus of rule that progressively incorporates the entire global realm within its open, expanding frontiers. Empire manages hybrid identities, flexible hierarchies, and plural exchanges through modulating networks of command. The distinct national colors of the imperialist map of the world have merged and blended in the imperial global rainbow.[26]

Hardt and Negri end *Empire* with the entry of the multitude, an equally restructured subject of resistance. *Multitude: War and Democracy in the Age of Empire* (2004) is the sequel, dealing with the intricacies of the concept. So who is the multitude? The multitude is the alternative to Empire and in many ways its mirror image, similarly taking advantage of new modes of communication and new technologies. It takes the shape of a network, allowing for all the differences to be expressed and sustained, without the need to overcome them in a centralized form of power or a unified identity. The multitude is different from the people, the masses, and the working class. Unlike the multitude, the people is one; the unity of the people sublimates the diversity of the population. The masses do contain differences, but they are drowned and submerged into an undifferentiated whole. Finally, why the multitude and not the working class? Because historically the working class prioritized industrial workers. The multitude accounts for the shifting organization of labor in the age of global neoliberalization, including workers that produce goods but also communications, forms of life, relationships, and services. Through communication and collaborative action, the multitude produces "the common," the ability to act together while respecting each other's differences.

While certainly appealing, as a theoretical tool, the multitude also carries certain limitations. It does not take into account the labor necessary for building technology nor its environmental impacts. The concepts of the multitude and the commons are also vague, relying on equally abstract Deleuzian concepts of the rhizome, deterritorialization, and multiplicity. While theoretically engaging, the book does not offer any concrete organizing guidance nor does it truly deal with the difficulties of acting in common across race, class, gender, and sexuality. Slavoj Žižek objects: "In their social-economic analysis, the lack of concrete insight is concealed in the Deleuzian jargon of multitude, deterritorialization, and so forth. No wonder that the three practical proposals with which the book ends appear anticlimactic."[27] He refers here to Hardt and Negri's call to fight for the rights to global citizenship, a minimal income, and the reappropriation of the new means of production (i.e., access to and control over education, information, and communication). David Harvey has waged the most interesting critique of the multitude, centered on the concept of mirroring. He argues that every mode of production generates a distinct type of opposition, one that mirrors it. In the 1960s and '70s, when industrial production in Western countries represented the core of the capitalist system, primary opposition came from unions, similarly hierarchical and corporatist. Since the 1970s, a decentralized organization of capital has generated a decentralized, network-like form of opposition—the multitude (though Harvey does not actually use the term). Harvey's main argument is that "maybe what we should do is to break the mirror and get out of this symbiotic relationship with what we are criticizing."[28] USofB traces a network-like opposition to Empire. However, this multitude is one that conceptualizes and philosophizes. The novel underscores the importance of the creative process in extricating the concepts of resistance, democracy, freedom, friendship, and love from the neoliberal grasp. To exit the symbiotic relationship with Empire, we first need to learn to think and act in common, in order to conceptualize and practice nonimperial ways of relating. In USofB, the many voices of the multitude chitchat, philosophize, and debate.

In a long replica, Giannina discusses the relationship between the multitude and the poet: "Multitudes bring multiples. And to be wise is to allow all the possibilities to exist—and to exist in all the possibilities that you can imagine—and then you create those imaginations—and after you create them you watch them exist in reality. I give birth to the multitudes" (287). The role of the poet is here to multiply possibilities, options, and connections, ones that do not amount to the same, like wishy, washy, and wishy-washy. The poet searches for "the multiple networks of horizontal rhyzomatic relations that the incitement to be singular and different, not to fit, can create."[29] The multitude in the novel operates both at the level of form and content. For the latter, it is a network of unlikely alliances and friendships, the ability of Giannina, Zarathustra, and Hamlet, who have very little in common, to work together for the liberation of Segismundo: "The characters Zarathustra, Hamlet, and Giannina exemplify the unity of philosophy, literature, and politics. They encounter each other in the streets of contemporary New York, recognize each other, and don't stop walking, talking, and contradicting each other—but all dealing at the same level—no one thinking he is superior to the other," Braschi explains.[30] The three embody the multitude: they represent different countries, fields, and points of view. In the novel, they are constantly arguing, rarely able to achieve consensus. Yet, they are still able to work together and relate through their common deterritorialization and decontextualization. The multitude in the United States of Banana is a multitude of immigrants, colonized people, and political prisoners. Yet, it is also a literary multitude. At the center of Braschi's multitude is Segismundo, who has always been a literary character. In other words, Braschi does not attempt to represent the real-life multitude or reproduce the language that Hardt and Negri's multitude may speak. Her multitude is not a "stand in," it is a complement. The novel dwells on the intersections between literature, philosophy, and politics, reflecting on possible dialogues between literary, philosophical, and political multitudes:

> The halo rises when the crowd unites in one voice that becomes the voice of the individual claiming its voice through the crowd. I don't mean a leader who stands up for the rest of us. We are no longer the rest of us. We have been the rest of the world for a very long time—standing in a very long line of protestors waiting for a change—a change that never comes when I give you one dollar and you give me back four quarters. It's the economy of divisiveness. You divide them among the tribes of quarters—so they count the quarters—and they start thinking in dimes and nickels and pennies—that bring penuries—and forget they had one dollar each. (136)

The passage ultimately questions the meaning of choice. Wish, washy, and wishy-washy, Braschi writes, are the equivalent of "mashed potato, french fries, or baked potato" (7). No matter which option one chooses, potatoes constitute the meal. In other words, within the sphere of predetermined options, and reliance on leaders to offer solutions, choice is limited. There is no election in electoral politics when the options are just variations on a theme. The solution proposed has been the same for many years; its justification, that no outside to it exists. Groups and countries are further competing to be granted these options in, what Braschi calls, the economy of divisiveness. The solution cannot be found within this ideological framework: within electoral politics, representational democracy, competition, and free markets. We need to begin thinking outside of these given options.

Well, I can hear the objection, this is all good and well, but the novel is written by a single author, not by the multitude in an act of "commoning." Yes, it is true, the novel does not claim to be an authentic expression of the multitude; it suggests that challenging the conceptual framework of the Empire must come from all directions, including grassroots activism, philosophy, and, yes, works of fiction. Interdisciplinarity may be required to accept that the system is, and has always been, broken, with no possibility of repair.

ATLANTIC UNDERCOMMONS

How do we resolve to live with the brokenness of being, Fred Moten and Stefano Harney ask? Instead of trying to fix it, how do we embrace it, live in it, and create connections across our common brokenness?

First, the answer begins, the undercommons need to give up on the idea of repair, because the current system cannot and should not be repaired. It cannot be repaired because it does not even acknowledge that something has been broken. The work of the undercommons cannot be to force this acknowledgment; the undercommons should no longer require recognition, inclusion, and integration—only dismantlement, pure and total. The structures in place are isolating us, keeping us apart in our respective loneliness. For the undercommons to find one another, these barriers must be torn down. Only then will we be able to talk about what comes next. The undercommons are precisely that which escapes inclusion, which resists "the call to order."[31] They are the wild, the disorderly, and the unruly, who cannot be described directly and clearly. Fugitive planning requires a fugitive language. Harvey and Moten build on the black radical tradition, including the work of Frantz Fanon, whose aim was not simply to destroy colonialism but to end "the standpoint from which colonialism makes sense" (*USofB*, it could be argued, strives to destroy the standpoint from which Empire makes sense).[32] For that, one has to inhabit the places abandoned by neoliberalism, by rule, by order: "Can this being together in homelessness, this interplay of the refusal of what has been refused, this undercommon appositionality, be a place from which emerges neither self-consciousness nor knowledge of the other but an improvisation that proceeds from somewhere on the other side of the unasked question?"[33]

Giannina, Hamlet, Zarathustra, and Segismundo engage precisely in this undercommon appositionality.[34] Brought together because the system considers them a threat, they coinhabit their homelessness. They no longer seek repair or inclusion. In fact, this is precisely the difference between their position and that of Gertrude and Basilio, the metaphorical leaders of the United States of Banana. To appease Puerto Rico, and other Latin American and Caribbean countries, Gertrude and Basilio propose washy (statehood), full participation in the United States of Banana. They are offering appeasement through inclusion. However, *USofB* does not call for inclusion. In the tradition of the undercommons, the characters refuse the possibility of repair. The system cannot be fixed, nor should this be the goal. The system is collapsing, and what is required is the "creation of a new value" (141). *USofB* does not attempt to offer a political platform that should be followed. But as Moten and Harney argue, before alternatives can be built, the undercommons need to encounter one another; they need to escape their isolation and loneliness. This is precisely what happens in the novel: the undercommons are formed during the collapse of Empire. Braschi is interested not necessarily in a concrete model to replace the current system, but in the creative process of engendering alternatives. Challenging skepticism that maintains that, though neoliberalism is problematic, it is the sole option, is the beginning. This creative process is not a solitary process; it is a process that occurs between characters, mainly through their dialogues, exchanges, and quarrels. The novel aims to displace thought from a place of pregiven options (such as wishy, washy, and wishy-washy) to one of creative exchanges and imaginative choices.

This creative process moves against representation: "Creation is taking over representation—by representation I mean also narration, plot, descriptions—and all the paraphernalia of information for analphabetism that adds more garbage (less meaning). Creation means discovery of a new reality that exists but that has not yet been noticed. The word is alive again. The speaking word. The verbs are in revolt—a revolt of the masses against the representation that has always been the main weapon of the state" (229). Political and aesthetic representation are here linked; representation is a weapon of the state, which represents its citizens, speaks for its citizens, and decides on its citizens' interests. United States of Banana thus elects the options for Puerto Rico's "freedom." But representation is also the main weapon of the state because it has the monopoly over the meaning of freedom, democracy, and politics. The model of individual rights, democratic elections, and free markets has overtaken the meaning of freedom. Politics outside of the realm of elections and representation has become difficult to conceive. Braschi moves away from representation into creation; she wants to explode the freedom of free markets through the explosion of language. Through this eruption, the undercommons create a new language: foreign-speaking English.

ALL THE ENGLISHES

Braschi links the three linguistic possibilities for her work to the three political possibilities for Puerto Rico: Spanish, Spanglish, and English correspond to independence, colony, and statehood. In *United States of Banana*, we are in the domain of English and statehood. But this is, as Braschi, names it, a foreign-speaking English. This is a very different approach from the bilingualism of *Yo-Yo Boing!* or the bilingualism of, for instance, Junot Diaz and Ana Lydia Vega.[35] In *Yo-Yo Boing!*, Braschi writes:

> – New York es una lata de resonancias y una lata de atardeceres y sonidos-resounding-resounding-resounding.
>> – Crude is the word, raw.
>> – Como una zanahoria. Una zanahoria cruda.
>> – It's the last great European city. And the first great American city.
>> – And the capital of Puerto Rico. (129)

David William Foster writes in relation to *Yo-Yo Boing!*: "However, one of the most notable characteristics of Braschi's novel is the agile and productive use of an interlingua poised between English and Spanish."[36] Similarly, Laura Loustau contends: "En la novela *Yo-Yo Boing* Giannina Braschi plantea un bilingüismo e identidad nomádica. . . . Braschi utiliza *un code-switching* para subrayar la complejidad de vivir simultáneamente en más de una cultura y una lengua" [In the novel *Yo-Yo Boing*, Giannina Braschi depicts a kind of bilingualism and nomadic identity . . . Braschi uses code-switching to underscore the complexity of living simultaneously in more than one culture and language].[37]

In *United States of Banana*, Braschi no longer practices the code-switching of *Yo-Yo Boing!*. She includes several Spanish words, but they are few and far apart. So, then, what is a foreign-speaking English? Braschi offers an explanation: "The problem with foreign speaking English, apart from it being flawed, is that it doesn't play by the same rules—it has its own passport—it could barbarize, it could terrorize—it could plant a bomb in the Oval Office—destroy national treasures—piss and shit on the roots of the White House Lawn. Minorities will become majorities if we don't patrol the borders" (39). A foreign-speaking English is a creative destruction of English from inside the language. It is the creation of a specific rhythm through alliterations, anaphors, and assonances, through the repetitions of the harsh "r" and "z" in juxtaposition with the soft "b," "l," and "i."

Foreign-speaking English flows in unpredictable directions; it uses sentence structures that sound awkward in English because they have been imported from a different language. The fragmentation of sentences, the pauses, the repetitions of the same elements create the effect of a stammer, the hesitation of someone who does not speak the language well. Braschi's foreign-speaking English is a thoughtfully crafted poetic stutter. The passage cited above is emblematic of her style and the frequent personification of language, which becomes not only a protagonist but also a political actor. Braschi's work is metafictional; in the process of creating this new language, she describes its role and purpose: to function as a terrorist threat to the language of Empire. The lexical field of terrorism is applied to the language itself; to barbarize means to brutalize as well as to use barbarisms, which are forms or constructions that do not correspond to standard language use. Political battle thus takes place within (though not solely) the realm of language. This position does not presuppose that everything is discourse and that political struggle can be reduced to linguistic deconstruction. Rather, political and linguistic struggles complement one another while preserving the autonomy of their realms. As already mentioned, Zarathustra, Hamlet, and Giannina exemplify the unity of philosophy, literature, and politics. The novel thus traces the meaning of freedom in these three different domains. Braschi comments on her rejection of metaphors:

> Metaphors are the beginning of the democratic system of envy. They look for what is dissimilar and try to make it similar. Everything that is similar cuts the edge of what is unique. Everything is related to something—and if that cutting edge can be cut shorter or rougher—better. The power of the poet is in his hair. His fertility is counting grains of sand like strands of hair. Pardon my lack of reference when I disjoin metaphors. Instead of making comparisons that work I make comparisons that don't work. Duchamp's bicycle is the modern metaphor because it is a *useless* comparison—it doesn't join—it disjoins—it tries to unite things that can't be united—and nevertheless the stool and the wheel that I can't ride like a bicycle creates music. I can elucidate its thought—shine on its shadows, blow on its horns, whistle the thought, chant the memory, and play the saxophone. (50, emphasis mine)

Braschi's metaphor is thus useless, participating in the creation of a language that refuses the economic logic of exchange. The value of life in the

United States of Banana is determined through its "usefulness," equated to the production of economic value, through its ability to find a job and repay one's debt (echoing chapter 2). In this vein, the Statue of Liberty is described as a laborer and "the slave of usefulness" (99), who must "inform the government of the U. S. of B. about suspicious activities taking place in [her] domain" (99), allegorizing bureaucratic and information machines of the Empire. These are the contradictions of neoliberal freedom: one is free to serve as human capital and enhance his/her value in the free market. Lady Liberty, the protector of freedom, spends her time gathering information to ensure that the "free" do not exceed their freedom. One is free to be competitive, free to work, free to acquire and repay debts. The rest is excess. In opposition to Lady Liberty, Segismundo carries "the stigma of being born into a race of lazy, brutal, happy-go-lucky conquistadores who don't know the meaning of the four-letter word W-O-R-K" (107). The world is divided between the useful and the useless individuals and nations, those who are economically productive and those who are "lazy," those who are deserving of freedom and those who are not. Unlike Lady Liberty, who is employed 24/7, Segismundo comes from a long line of those who supposedly refuse to assume their independence and their responsibility for their poverty, and refuse to pull themselves up by the bootstraps. The language of USofB is the language of the lazy, of those who refuse to be efficient, productive, and useful. This is a useless language that refuses the neoliberal logic of efficiency and rejects plot and easily accessible meaning.

Franco "Bifo" Berardi, in *The Uprising: On Poetry and Finance*, argues that neoliberalism encourages the commodification of all social spheres, subjecting language to the laws of commercial exchange. The crisis of today's global economy is also a crisis of language: the difficulty of extrapolating communication from the realm of finance and profit. Over the past few decades, the accumulation of profit through risky financial speculations, such as futures and derivatives, has become progressively dissociated from the production of goods. Financial markets are increasingly relying on the production of services that are exchanged through communication. Language has thus been incorporated into the work process to an unprecedented level. Braschi's language refuses a concept of usefulness reduced to economic growth and the creation of profit. Its purpose is not to advance plot, recuperating the creative process as that which does not need to be useful. The novel stages a dialogic process, one with no predetermined purpose. The dialogues are long, extend in multiple directions, cover multiple subjects, and do not necessarily end in an agreement. Their objective is the liberation from the logic of usefulness and efficiency.

"Markets," Berardi argues, "are the visible manifestation of the inmost mathematical interfunctionality of algorithms embedded in the techno-linguistic machine: they utter sentences that change the destiny of the living body of society, destroy resources, and swallow the energies of the collective body like a draining pump."[38] Social communication is subsumed by the abstractness of financial algorithms and mathematical calculations that obscure the effects of the markets on living bodies and on nature. For Berardi, "governance is the automation of thought, the automation of social existence."[39] Within this context, a language and a thought that break out of automation are necessary. Poetry can be "an excess of language, a hidden resource which enables us to shift from one paradigm to another."[40] It can allow us to see other modes of being, "exceeding the established meaning of words."[41] USofB gathers the lazy and the useless, whose refusal of usefulness makes them a threat, as they try to liberate freedom from the domains of Lady Liberty, of development, progress, perfectionability, advancement, and elections. May we be useless together, and may we speak a useless language, the characters proclaim.

None of this is, of course, entirely new. Unusual metaphors were beloved by Surrealists and members of the Dada movement, among others. A language that valorizes nothing other than its creative process, ultimately becoming self-referential and extricating itself from productivity, is a common marker of modernism. Braschi, in fact, mentions Marcel Duchamp as a significant influence. However, this is also not quite another example of "art for art's sake." Braschi strives for a useless poetic language, but one that is also highly dialogical. In other words, the characters in USofB spend a lot of time merely talking to each other, philosophizing, and thinking together. The writing thus stages the collective process of collectively rethinking notions like freedom, democracy, and independence. This is a practice that takes time, one that is fairly useless from a neoliberal standpoint. At stake is not simply the outcome of these conversations but the process of coming into relation through dialogue. Braschi's language connects those that seemed to have very little in common.

In *The Return of Ordinary Capitalism*, Sanford Schram argues that "the entire edifice of the liberal, democratic, capitalist order is built on the assumption that there are free consenting individuals who enter into economic, social, and political contracts and other arrangements. Any behaviors that suggest that we are not free or independent, but instead beholden to others, or dependent, undermine the plausibility of this assumed subjectivity and pose a risk to that order that must be resisted."[42] The characters of USofB are useless because they don't act like "human capital," increasing their individual value through competition with others. There are no free, consenting individuals in

USofB; everyone (including language itself) exists in a system of rhyzomatic interconnectedness.

"Declaration of Love" is one of the novel's many parts, focusing on the reinvention of love and a language of love within the context of the under-commons. A very naïve solution, the reader may think. Is there anything more cliché than saying that love will save us all?—a claim that ultimately replaces a collective political solution with a pathway for individual transformation. However, as bell hooks maintains, that love is no longer considered a serious intellectual concept, but only a romantic delusion unworthy of those who engage in academic skepticism, is disconcerting.[43] In the novel, love and mourning are connected, through an ethics of universal mourning. In *Precarious Life*, Butler maintains that the differences in our capacity to mourn "produce and maintain certain exclusionary conceptions of who is normatively human."[44] In response, Butler proposes an ethics of universal mourning, because "without the capacity to mourn, we lose that keener sense of life we need in order to oppose violence."[45] In the aftermath of 9/11, Giannina reflects on the process of mourning: "When I came back to midtown a week after the attack—I mourned—but not in a personal way—it was a cosmic mourning—something that I could not specify because I didn't know any of the dead. I felt grief without knowing its origin. Maybe it was the grief of being an immigrant and of not having roots" (5). This is a mourning not of a specific life but of the precariousness of life in general. The capacity for universal morning comes from the recognition of one's own precariousness and the recognition of that same condition in the other. Braschi suggests that the immigrant condition, the dispossession from one's roots, country, and family, create the conditions of possibility for an ethics of mourning. "Like love, solidarity is not about altruism: it is about the pleasure of sharing the breath and space of the other. Love is the ability to enjoy myself thanks to your presence, to your eyes. This is solidarity," writes Berardi.[46] The characters under Lady Liberty's skirt share their breath and space, as they mourn together.

Comparative Literature in the Age of Neoliberalism

As a teenage girl who had just moved from the Balkans to France, I became an avid reader of immigrant fiction. Azouz Begag's *Le Gone du Chaâba* (1986), Maryse Condé's *Le coeur à rire et à pleurer* (1999), and Gisèle Pineau's *Un papillon dans la cité* (1992) are probably responsible both for the fact that I speak French and that I survived high school. As a college student in the United States, I further discovered Paule Marshall's *Brown Girl, Brownstones* (1959), Julia Alvarez's *How the García Girls Lost Their Accents* (1991), and Cristina García's *Dreaming in Cuban* (1992). Questions of belonging, cultural difference, race, gender, and ethnicity have thus long been at the forefront of my personal and intellectual development. Yet, as I began working on twenty-first-century immigrant fiction, I realized that these questions are insufficient when dealing with immigration in the context of global neoliberalization.

The narratives of *Precarious Crossings* are not coming-of-age stories that helped me transition from adolescence to adulthood. Unlike the urban bildungsroman that I just mentioned, they deal with issues like indebtedness, climate change, and terrorism. They outline "ex-centric" migrations, outside of the historical colonizer/colonized relationship, as they explore possible alliances and solidarities within a highly divided world. As such, they challenge the unstated Eurocentric assumption that immigration begins once immigrants have arrived at their destination (and that only the Global North has to "deal" with increasing global immigration). In other words, while discussions around multiculturalism, diversity, and national immigration policies are extremely important (particularly considering the rise of the extreme right in the United States and Europe), they are also not sufficient, because they deal with the consequences, but not necessarily the causes of immigration. Neoliberalism (as a political, economic, and ideological system) should be part of the conversation, because neoliberalism and immigration are intertwined. Immigration from Mexico to the United States has thus increased since the implementation of NAFTA in 1994.[1] A system that perceives human beings as human capital, insists on the privatization of public and communally owned resources, and considers social programs to be "handouts," has created unsustainable economic conditions in many countries, forcing people to leave their places of origin. A call for immigrant justice must include a call for a different ideology in both the Global North and the Global South, one that does not reduce all spheres of life to the logic of the market.

The narratives of *Precarious Crossings* deal with life under neoliberalism. These works are often no longer set within a single national framework, and questions of identity, assimilation, and integration are no longer their sole concern. They address the connections between rising inequality in the country of origin and rising xenophobia in the country of destination, neocolonialism and neoliberalism, national and personal indebtedness. In a system that reduces human life to numbers, percentages, and decimals, these narratives are necessary because they remind us that human life is irreducible. Within the field of literary studies, they also remind us that global questions require globalized forms. And yet, due to the breadth of issues and geographical locations that they cover, these narratives are not easy to classify. The postcolonial framework seems inadequate, given the fact that immigrant trajectories are often no longer oriented toward their former colonial masters. The outlook of contemporary trans-Atlantic narratives requires a more global theoretical approach, inviting the discipline of comparative literature to experiment with new frameworks.

WHAT CAN WE COMPARE?

At the center of comparative and world literature debates is the question of scale. While acknowledging the increased interconnectedness of the world, how far can we extend our corpuses without losing track of historical and cultural specificities? How do we explore new global connections without creating yet another false universal model? We are, at this point, well aware of the incredible devastations caused by colonialism and imperialism, sustained by the Western belief in its own universality. One of the objectives of postcolonialism has been precisely to preserve cultural difference and introduce a plurality of perspectives into the dominant Eurocentric worldview. So how to reconcile the growing interconnectedness of the world and the importance of cultural and historical difference?

Critics have proposed various models for the study of literature on the global scale: French global, world literature in French, the Latin American global novel, distant reading. In the introduction, I also mention Gayatri Chakravorty Spivak, who in *Death of a Discipline* calls for a revival of area studies, one infused with a careful study of local languages and comparative literature's attention to close reading. And then there is, of course, the concept of world literature, though it has been criticized for its Anglophone focus and domination by English departments.[2] My work lies at the interstices of these debates, and I hope that this book will contribute to existing dialogues.

A multilingual approach within the framework of the globalized Atlantic strives to address the contradictions inherent in dealing with Francophone or Latin American globalization. My main point of departure has been Francophone studies, because that is where my primary academic formation lies, though I have also received training in Latin American studies. The concept of Francophonie has recently come under criticism from both literary authors and critics. As mentioned in the introduction, signatories of *Pour une littérature-monde* have underlined its neocolonial aspect. They have criticized a Francophonie that posits France at the center and emphasizes cultural links between France and former colonies. Whereas I believe that the introduction of Francophonie has been vital in decentering French studies, it is possible to push the boundaries of the discipline further, particularly given the fact that several Francophone writers, including Maryse Condé and Edouard Glissant, have recently set their novels in non-Francophone countries. Others, such as Congolese writer Alain Mabanckou, have repeatedly argued against the idea that African and Caribbean authors should primarily engage their local realities, serving only as vehicles for the expression of their communities. Both Condé and Mabanckou also contend that the categories of nation, race, and territory have fallen short of encapsulating today's reality, and that we need new categories to think of the world and to think of literature.[3] In *Precarious Crossings*, I suggest some possible new categories.

In 2003, Mireille Rosello proposed the concept of "unhoming" Francophone studies through transnational and transdisciplinary encounters.[4] The globalized Atlantic as a framework represents precisely an attempt to unhome Francophone studies. Even more broadly, it participates in recent theoretical efforts to unhome literary studies and monolingual approaches to globalization. However, the intention, it should be specified, is not to replace Francophone, Latin American, or postcolonial studies with the notion of the global and globalization. Rather, I believe that a focus on global neoliberalization can take these studies in new directions. Like Francophonie, the introduction of the postcolonial into French studies has been extremely important in decentering the field. On the other hand, the term assumes the legacy of colonial domination out of or against which cultural practices are seen to emerge, defining cultural projects in terms of a common reference to an earlier period of domination. There exists a risk of reproducing a binary opposition between the inside and the outside, between the colony and the metropole, as if this opposition were the only one at play in these societies. Within this framework, new tensions and oppositions caused by the global spread of neoliberalism have not received enough attention (I do not mean to imply that neoliberalism has replaced (neo)colonial dynamics, but it has rendered more complex the economic and political structures of the Atlantic world).

International financial institutions such as the IMF and the World Bank have been at the forefront of global neoliberalization. Promoting structural adjustment programs, austerity measures, and increased privatization, they have created comparable social and economic contexts across the Atlantic. Increasingly, texts from Africa, the Caribbean, and Latin America are addressing similar questions including debt, privatization, social inequality, and environmental degradation. The tension between a regional and a global framework appears as soon as we conceive of a globalized Atlantic or an Atlantic globalization. However, a close reading of texts written in French, English, and Spanish suggests that the regional and the global are not necessarily in opposition but rather supplement one another.

The novels in my corpus preserve the Atlantic framework. Within the Francophone works, the memory of the Atlantic triangle and trade persists. It is, however, interconnected with the question of contemporary migration, circulation of capital and goods. Within the Latin American works, the question of US imperialism has been central both to the regional American framework and the global spread of neoliberalism. These works thus underline the importance of both historicizing the present and constantly updating our theoretical frameworks and concepts. While there are indeed differences between these literary traditions, the implementation of neoliberal reforms across the Atlantic world invites new points of comparison. This, of course, does not mean that neoliberalism has taken the same form everywhere. In each context, neoliberal ideology encounters local histories and cultures. But similarities across the contexts persist.

Globalization and neoliberalism are connected. Globalization cannot be reduced to the global spread of neoliberalism, but that is certainly one of its major components. In fact, the authors in my corpus are responding, reacting, resisting, and reforming many aspects of neoliberal life. Furthermore, I do not believe that thinking about these literary works in relation to neoliberalism is simply reducing literature to an illustration of economic reforms, thus conflating fields that have nothing in common. First, neoliberalism is based on the reduction of different spheres of life to the economy; it strives to destroy the autonomy of politics, ethics, and identity. It is an ideology that, like any other, requires the formation of a subject that will sustain it. Literary works can help us understand the multiple facets of this subject. They help us understand the different political and economic forces that shape this subject. However, they also offer more than a mere explanation. They gesture toward ways in which human experience and human relations exceed the neoliberal model, which can never fully encompass them. Furthermore, to quote Rancière again, they suspend the normal coordinates of sensory experience and imagine new possibilities of what can be seen, said, and thought, consequently leading to a "new landscape of the sensible."[5] By doing so, they imagine potential transnational solidarities in the age of neoliberalism.

The reader must have realized by now that I find neoliberalism to be an incredibly devastating economic and political system, and that we are in desperate need of alternatives. In order to find them, we will need the contribution of every discipline, including comparative literature. Given the fact that neoliberalism has become a global system, I firmly believe that a successful opposition will have to be transnational, which is why learning to identify cross-cultural similarities and work across cultural differences is an incredibly important ethical and political commitment. In my cross-cultural work, I am tremendously influenced by Chandra Talpade Mohanty, who differentiates "feminism without borders" from "border-less feminism." Feminism without borders "acknowledges the fault lines, conflicts, differences, fears, and containment that borders represent. It acknowledges that there is no one sense of the border, that the lines between and through nations, races, classes, sexualities, religions, and disabilities, are real—and that a feminism without borders must envision change and social justice work across these lines of demarcation and division."[6] In each chapter of this study, I have similarly tried to work across certain lines of demarcation and division. The works studied are not uniform in terms of form or genre. They are, however, all trying to remap the Atlantic space. Whether it is South Africa, Spain, Italy, or Puerto Rico, these works complicate the opposition between emigration and immigration countries as they outline new immigrant trajectories. They challenge us to think about the Atlantic as a multilingual and multinodal space.

It is clear that authors who are racialized in Europe, like Bessora or Fatou Diome, are not in the same position as someone like Roberto Bolaño. Yet, I believe that we need to build theoretical methods that allow us to identify points of commonality between ethical and aesthetic questions raised by these authors. At the same time, we must be careful not to erase the differences between the two that are a result of different precolonial and colonial histories. I borrow here again from Moten and Harney, who claim that this system is killing us all, though at very different speeds. We need to both understand why it is killing us all, and why it is killing us at different speeds. This is the (perhaps impossible) task I have tried to pursue in this book.

Precarity can help us think across lines of demarcation and division. I find it to be a useful framework because I see it as inherent to neoliberalism. As austerity, privatization, and deregulation become the global mantra, more people are suffering from failing social and economic networks of support and are becoming differentially exposed to injury, violence, and death. The objection could be made that one term could not possibly explain such a broad textual corpus. And indeed, I do not believe that it does. But, as a framework, it enables us to address the increasing focus of these authors on global political and economic issues. Precarity underlines both the increased shared condition of economic and political vulnerability, and its differential assignation across nationality, gender, race, and sexuality, among others. The texts in my corpus also add new dimensions to the study of global precarity: cosmopolitanism, debt, multinationals, opacity, and the undercommons are brought in relation to the concept of precarity in each chapter.

Has some of the historical and cultural specificity and depth been lost with such an approach? Inevitably. But I do not see a conflict between more transnational methods and more nationally or culturally specific ones. Why would we have to choose between the two? The choice presupposes that a single approach is enough to understand the complexity of the world and contemporary cultural production. Rather, I believe that it is from the dialogue between different studies and approaches that true knowledge emerges. We need historical depth as much as we need to learn how to work across cultures.

A BRIEF NOTE ON COMPARATIVE LITERATURE IN LIGHT OF THE 2016 US ELECTION

Since I began writing this book, Donald Trump has been elected president of the United States. In the aftermath of the election, a media battle ensued between those who interpreted the results in terms of race and those who prioritized class. The former claimed that the result was the expression of the deeply embedded US racism and a "whitelash" against the first black president. The latter interpreted the election as the revenge of the white working class, impoverished by neoliberal policies and forgotten by the Democratic Party.[7] Several critics, like Robin D. G. Kelley, have rightly pointed out that the entire debate is based on a false dichotomy: "It is not a matter of disaffection *versus* racism or sexism *versus* fear. Rather, racism, class anxieties, and prevailing gender ideologies operate together, inseparably, or as Kimberlé Crenshaw would say, intersectionally. White working-class men understand their plight through a racial and gendered lens. For women and people of color to hold positions of privilege or power *over* them is simply unnatural and can only be explained by an act of unfairness—for example, affirmative action."[8] In fact, never in US history have race and class operated independently.

A similar debate occurred earlier on, during the 2016 democratic primaries. In an encounter between the democratic candidate Bernie Sanders and #BlackLivesMatter activists, the latter criticized Sanders (rightly, one might add) for not explicitly dealing with racism and assuming that once class inequality is dealt with, racism will disappear on its own.[9] This critique against white Marxism can of course be traced much further back in history,[10] as can Marxist critiques of identity politics.[11] On the one hand, there is the argument that minority groups cannot simply be subsumed under the "proletariat," given the fact that oppression based on race and one based on class, though intertwined, are not equivalent (add gender and sexuality to the equation and the situation becomes even more complicated). On the other hand, there is a critique of identity politics as essentializing and contributing to the fragmentation of the Left. As these debates intensified in the US media over the past year, often forgotten was the very long history of black Marxism in the United States and across the world.[12] In other words, critics and activists have been building intersectional models for a very long time; I am certainly not the first to offer one. Still, as I followed the postelection debates, reading social media arguments over whether race *or* class were responsible, I became convinced of the importance of comparative work. Comparative literature as a method works precisely to replace this *or* with an *and*. Speaking about the 2016 election, Wendy Brown contends that "these developments are in part effects of neoliberal reason—its expansion of the domain and claim of the private for persons and corporations alike, and its rejection of political and social (as opposed to market) justice." This does not, of course, mean that neoliberalism invented or that it explicitly encourages racism, xenophobia, and white supremacy. Rather, as Brown explains, it has given these sentiments a "legitimate form."[13] In light of the US election, and the rapid spread of right-wing politics across the globe, it is our ethical and political prerogative to both examine neoliberal reason and to learn to work across differences. Literary narratives can perhaps lead us in the right direction.

BEYOND LITERATURE

I would like to end by saying that literary authors are not the only ones who have recently identified new Atlantic connections. Social movements have done the same. In the 1990s and early 2000s, an antiglobalization movement swept across the Atlantic world. While heterogeneous in terms of goals and strategies, the movement's main targets included the legal status of corporate personhood, free market fundamentalism, and the economic privatization measures of the World Bank, the IMF, and the WTO.

The movement's mode of organizing has been characterized by mass decentralized campaigns of direct action and civil disobedience, often attempting to stop the proceedings of large corporate summits. One of the most renowned confrontations took place on November 30, 1999, when protesters blocked delegates' entrance to WTO meetings in Seattle, Washington, and forced the cancellation of the opening ceremonies. The Genoa Group of Eight Summit protest followed in July 2001. By the end of it, around 200 people (both civilian and policemen) were wounded and a young Genoese murdered.[14]

That same year, the first World Social Forum, an annual meeting of civil society organizations, took place in Porto Alegre, Brazil, as an alternative to the World Economic forum annually held in Davos, in an effort to promote counterhegemonic globalization. In its charter, the World Social Forum defines itself as "an open meeting place for reflective thinking, democratic debate of ideas, formulation of proposals, free exchange of experiences and interlinking for effective action, by groups and movements of civil society that are opposed to neoliberalism and to domination of the world by capital and any form of imperialism, and are committed to building a planetary society directed towards fruitful relationships among Humankind and between it and the Earth."[15] The World Social Forum has thus been envisioned as a space where social and political alternatives to global neoliberalization can be conceived. Since 2001, the World Social Forum has traveled across the Atlantic world. In 2006, NGO representatives, fair-trade advocates, antiglobalization protestors, and activists united in Bamako, Mali, to discuss the consequences of free trade, social inequality, and debt relief, many of the issues discussed throughout this book. But while the forum persists, protests and direct actions against international organizations have subsided in strength and frequency over the past decade, leading many to wonder what has happened to both globalization and antiglobalization.[16]

This was the case until, perhaps, a new wave of uprisings, known as the "Arab spring," began in late 2010. Since then, many other countries, including Chile, Quebec, the United States, Brazil, and Mexico have experienced popular revolts. Whereas the most recent protests have appeared as more local, since their immediate target is not international organizations, they share many critiques and grievances of the antiglobalization movement, including an emphasis on social inequality, forced privatization, and cuts to public services.

In 2011, as Occupy Wall Street was unfolding, I spent a lot of time in Zuccotti Park. I participated in various workshops led by activists from Tunisia, Chile, Mexico, Venezuela, and Quebec. The questions were always the same: how can we help one another? How can we work across cultural differences? How can we learn from one another without simply transposing practices and theories? How can we focus on our local issues while acknowledging that our problems are interconnected? Those questions expressed a desire to think and act transnationally, in a comparative way. Whereas neither fiction nor literary criticism can nor should be expected to solve political problems, perhaps they can participate in an interdisciplinary dialogue about comparative methods. Perhaps they can help form social subjects that believe that our struggles are indeed interconnected.

As I write, social movements are spreading across the Global South and the Global North. Over the past decade or so, many countries in the Global North have experienced their own version of structural adjustment programs. Spain, France, Portugal, and the US are increasingly dealing with some of the issues discussed in the study: privatization, debt, mortgage crisis, tuition hikes. As a result, new transnational connections have emerged between, for instance, student movements in Chile and in Quebec; or teacher strikes in Oaxaca, Mexico, and Chicago. These solidarities are calling into question the traditional colonizer/colonized divide. They are also, hopefully, offering us even more opportunities for comparative work and for unhoming literary studies.

NOTES

NOTES TO INTRODUCTION

1. It should be noted that Stiglitz's book shares its title with Saskia Sassen's collection of essays *Globalization and Its Discontents: Essays on the New Mobility of People and Money* (1998).
2. For a critical analysis of global neoliberalization in Latin America, including the effects of NAFTA on Mexico, see Robinson, *Latin America and Global Capitalism*.
3. Though he does not refer to capitalism directly, William Boelhower explains, "In effect, the European world-system cannot be explained on the basis of causes originating exclusively from within Europe. Colonization of Africa and the Americas went hand in hand with the progress of European world hegemony" (85). More explicitly, Giovanni Arrighi points out that "the earliest beginnings of the nineteenth-century free trade movement can be traced to the Atlantic slave trade" (244). See Boelhower, "The Rise of the New Atlantic Studies Matrix"; Arrighi, *The Long Twentieth Century*. For an Atlantic-based history of capitalism and resistance, see also Linebaugh and Rediker, *The Many-Headed Hydra*.
4. See Wallerstein, *World-Systems Analysis*.
5. Harvey, *A Brief History of Neoliberalism*, 2.
6. Epstein, "Introduction: Financialization and the World Economy," 3.
7. For an analysis of capitalism's historical cycles of accumulation, see Arrighi, *The Long Twentieth Century*.
8. McClanahan, *Dead Pledges*, 13.
9. Balibar, "Politics of the Debt," section 1.2.
10. One should note that the rise of neoliberalism can be traced back to 1947 and the creation of the Mont Pelerin Society around Austrian political philosopher Friedrich Hayek.
11. For a concise explanation of the 1970s crisis, see Hickel, "A Short History of Neoliberalism."
12. See, for instance, Niskanen, *Reaganomics*.
13. Naomi Klein coined the term *disaster capitalism*, which she defines as "using moments of collective trauma to engage in radical social and economic engineering" (8). The aftermath of a crisis—be it economic, political, or environmental—when the population is disoriented and its reference points obfuscated, is the best time to implement economic reforms that may otherwise provoke massive public discontent. She summarizes the set of reforms encouraged by neoliberalism in three words: privatization, deregulation, and austerity. Klein analyzes Chile in the aftermath of the coup as one of the first neoliberal experiments. See Klein, *The Shock Doctrine*.
14. Harvey, *A Brief History of Neoliberalism*, 73.
15. Ibid., 75.

16. See Toussaint and Millet, *Debt, the IMF, and the World Bank*; Peet, *Unholy Trinity*.
17. Hickel, "A Short History of Neoliberalism."

In "Women, Reproduction and Globalization," Silvia Federici similarly describes the emergence of a new international division of labor as the primary characteristic of globalization: "My own perspective is that 'globalization' is a strategy seeking to determine a process of global proletarianization and the formation of a global labor market as means to cheapen the cost of labor, reduce workers' entitlements, and intensify exploitation. These, in fact, are the most unmistakable effects of the policies by which globalization is driven" (60).

18. Hickel, "A Short History of Neoliberalism."
19. Arjun Appadurai argues that money, commodities, and people are chasing each other around the world at an unprecedented speed. He also speaks of a growing disjuncture between various domains of global reality: ethnoscapes (moving groups of people, including tourists, immigrants, refugees, and exiles), technoscapes (global advances in technology), finanscapes (movement of capital across global markets), mediascapes (global dissemination of images and information), and ideoscapes (proliferation of political ideas and images). See Appadurai, "Disjuncture and Difference in the Global Cultural Economy."
20. See Jameson, "Notes on Globalization as a Philosophical Issue."
21. I thus agree with William Robinson that the four main components of globalization are:

> 1. A new capital-labor relation based on the deregulation and "flexibilization" of labor.
> 2. A new round of *extensive* and *intensive* expansion. Extensively, the system expanded through the reincorporation of major areas of the former Third and Second worlds into the world capitalist economy, so that by the 1990s no region remained outside the system. Intensively, public and community spheres that formerly lay outside (or buffered from) the logic of market relations (profit making) were commodified and opened up to accumulation through privatization, state deregulation, and reregulation, including the extension of intellectual property rights, and so on.
> 3. The creation of a global legal and regulatory structure to facilitate what were emerging globalized circuits of accumulation, including the creation of the World Trade Organization (WTO).
> 4. The imposition of the neoliberal model on countries throughout the Third World, and also the First and former Second worlds, involving structural adjustment programs that created the conditions for the free operation of capital within and across borders and the harmonization of accumulation conditions worldwide. Through neoliberalism the world has increasingly become a single unified field for global capitalism. See Robinson, *Latin America and Global Capitalism*, 16.

22. Jay, *Global Matters*, 45.
23. Brown, *Undoing the Demos*.
24. While Brown associates these values with a liberal democracy, I believe there is a risk in romanticizing liberal democracy as a form of governance without fully considering its historical connection to capitalism.
25. Brown, *Undoing the Demos*, 30.
26. Ibid., 33.
27. Bourdieu, "The Essence of Neoliberalism," emphasis in the original.
28. Butler, *Frames of War*, 32.
29. Harney, Moten, and Empson, *The Undercommons*, 141.
30. Butler, *Frames of War*, 58.
31. Sociologists like Pierre Bourdieu and Robert Castel theorized precarity in the late 1990s. Bourdieu announced the advent of a state of insecurity—a new type of domination, which

would force workers into submission through short-term contracts and a lack of economic and social protection. Castel similarly characterized the precariat as a class of workers no longer benefitting from social and economic protection. See Bourdieu, "La précarité est aujourd'hui partout"; Castel, *L'insécurité social, qu'est-ce qu'être protégé?*.

32. Standing, *The Precariat*, 6.
33. Ibid., 8.
34. Ibid., 9.
35. Ibid., 12.
36. Lorey, *State of Insecurity*, 1.
37. Ibid., 4.
38. Butler, *Frames of War*, 3.
39. Ibid., 25.
40. Butler, *Precarious Life*.
41. See, for instance, Barnard. "Beirut, Also the Site of Deadly Attacks, Feels Forgotten"; Mali, "Why Do Deaths in Paris Get More Attention Than Deaths in Beirut?"
42. Butler, *Precarious Life*, xiii.
43. Horning, "Precarity and 'Affective Resistance.'"
44. See, for instance, Halstead, "The Real Reason White People Say 'All Lives Matter'"; Victor, "Why 'All Lives Matter' Is Such a Perilous Phrase."
45. Nyong'o, "Situating Precarity between the Body and the Commons."
46. See Horning, "Precarity and 'Affective Resistance.'"
47. See Federici, *Caliban and the Witch*.
48. Sunkara, "Precarious Thoughts." See also Caffentzis, *In Letters of Blood and Fire: Work, Machines, and Value*.
49. Seymour, "We Are All Precarious."
50. The concept of *Francophonie* took shape during decolonization as a government program to preserve ties with former colonies and to maintain the global status of French. In the 1980s and '90s, however, literary scholars (particularly in Canada, the US, and the UK) have given the term a different valence by emphasizing the pluralization and decentralization of "French" culture. In this regard, contemporary Francophone studies run loosely parallel to postcolonialism. There are, however, some significant structural differences between the two paradigms. For example, whereas postcolonialism has emphasized hybridity and the permeability of borders, Francophonie has tended to locate diversity outside of continental France, in Africa and the Caribbean.
51. Miller, *Nationalists and Nomads*; Thomas, *Black France: Colonialism, Immigration, and Transnationalism*.
52. The "beur" novel entered critical discourse as an analytic category particularly after the publication of Michel Laronde's influential analysis of the genre in 1993. See Laronde, *Autour du roman beur*.
53. Cazenave, *Afrique sur Seine*.
54. Miller, "The Slave Trade, *La Françafrique*, and the Globalization of French," 250. The expanding field of Afro-European (or Afropean) literatures has addressed this phenomenon by "tracing diachronic and synchronic connections that reveal new configurations across linguistic and national boundaries" between black Europeans. See Brancato, "Afro-European Literature(s): A New Discursive Category?," 11. For further discussion of the advantages and challenges involved in working within Afro-Europeanism as a category, see, for instance, Thomas, *Afroeuropean Cartographies*; Van Deventer and Thomas, "Afro-European Studies"; Hitchcott and Thomas, *Francophone Afropean Literatures*.
55. Hakim Abderrezak's recent book focuses on clandestine crossings of the Mediterranean Sea and "ex-centric" migrations from Francophone North Africa to European countries other than France. He draws both new Mediterranean connections and reflects on the Mediterranean as a boundary between the Global North and the Global South. Abder-

rezak's work has been a significant theoretical and methodological influence on my own work. See Abderrezak, *Ex-centric Migrations.*

56. In this respect, my work aligns with recent critical efforts to place Francophonie in a comparative context. For instance, a 2011 issue of *Contemporary French & Francophone Studies,* edited by Martin Munro and Alec Hargreaves, has focused on the relation between the Francophone Caribbean and North America, an area of study thus far undertheorized. This work also strives to decentralize the image of Paris as the primary destination for immigrants from the Francophone world. In the same vein, Ignacio Infante's recent book, *After Translation: The Transfer and Circulation of Modern Poetics across the Atlantic,* offers a detailed historical account of the role translation has played in the trans-Atlantic circulation of modern poetics. Whereas I take cue from Infante's attempt to establish a multilingual and multinational Atlantic paradigm, I do not focus on translation and circulation in this study. Rather, I look at the trans-Atlantic circulation of people, capital, and goods in the novels themselves. See Hargreaves and Munro, "The Francophone Caribbean and North America"; Infante, *After Translation.*

57. Whereas Francophone studies is my point of departure, critical works on immigration outside of this linguistic tradition have also significantly influenced my work. For instance, in *Immigrant Fictions: Contemporary Literature in an Age of Globalization,* Rebecca Walkowitz speaks of "comparison literature," "an emerging genre of world literature for which global comparison is a formal as well as a thematic preoccupation" (536). The works in my corpus are similarly preoccupied with global comparisons. I am also strongly indebted to recent works dealing with immigration from Latin America and the Caribbean. See Walkowitz et al., *Immigrant Fictions;* Pérez-Rosario, *Hispanic Caribbean Literature of Migration;* Kanellos, *Hispanic Immigrant Literature;* Martínez-San Miguel, *Caribe Two Ways.*

58. Subha Xavier dedicates a chapter of her recent book, *The Migrant Text,* to the marketing of Francophone literature. In *Packaging Post/coloniality,* Richard Watts analyzes the paratext surrounding works of Francophone literature and the creation of the figure of the postcolonial writer. For an analysis of the same issue within the Anglophone context, see Brouillette, *Postcolonial Writers in the Global Literary Marketplace;* Huggan, *The Postcolonial Exotic.*

59. Clingman, "Other Voices."

60. Gilroy, *The Black Atlantic,* 15.

61. Ibid., 5.

62. Ibid., 29.

63. Ibid., 19.

64. Atlantic studies as a field has developed in conjunction with other transnational sea/ocean paradigms, such as Mediterranean and Indian Ocean studies. In "The Complicating Sea: The Indian Ocean as Method," Isabel Hofmeyr offers a comprehensive survey of Indian Ocean studies. She argues that the field has strived to identify "crosscutting diasporas" and new transnationalisms across the Global South. In an older publication, "The Black Atlantic Meets the Indian Ocean," Hofmeyr, following the work of Gwyn Campbell, also identifies historical differences between Atlantic and Indian Ocean trades: "The Indian Ocean trade was largely female, not male; it involved predominantly household slaves rather than plantation workers; the boundaries between slave and free were much more blurred than in the Atlantic; and, furthermore, the association of race and slavery did not exist in any marked form" (11). See Hofmeyr, "The Complicating Sea"; "The Black Atlantic Meets the Indian Ocean."

For other studies of the Indian Ocean, see, for instance: Vergès, "Writing on Water"; Moorthy and Jamal, *Indian Ocean Studies.* Similarly, since the publication of Fernand Braudel's comprehensive Mediterranean history, Mediterranean studies has developed as a field. See Braudel, *The Mediterranean and the Mediterranean World;* Chambers, *Medi-*

NOTES TO INTRODUCTION · 187

terranean Crossings; Goldwyn and Silverman, *Mediterranean Modernism*; Parati, *Mediterranean Crossroads*.

   I am methodologically indebted to all of this work, particularly Hofmeyr's notion of "crosscutting diasporas." Yet, in this study I also focus on Atlantic particularities, including the memory of the Middle Passage and the strong contemporary influence of the United States on the region.

65. See Miller, *The French Atlantic Triangle*; Marshall, *The French Atlantic*.
66. Pitman and Stafford, "Introduction: Transatlanticism and Tricontinentalism," 200.
67. Gilroy, *The Black Atlantic*, 19.
68. Games, "Atlantic History," 746.
69. Bystrom and Slaughter, *The Global South Atlantic*, 4.
70. Sharpe, *In the Wake*, 14.
71. Ibid., 15.
72. Gikandi, "Afterword: Outside the Black Atlantic," 244.
73. Mohanty, *Feminism without Borders*, 226.
74. Dirlik, "Global South."
75. Bystrom and Slaughter, *The Global South Atlantic*, 19–20.
76. Harvey, "The 'New' Imperialism," 77.
77. Boelhower, "The Rise of the New Atlantic Studies Matrix," 86.
78. Apter, *Against World Literature*, 41–42.
79. Peter Hallward offers a detailed account of the development of postcolonial criticism in *Absolutely Postcolonial: Writing Between the Singular and the Specific*. He cites, for instance, Ania Loomba, who argues that all postcolonial positions must be "embedded in specific histories" as they respond to an "empirical specificity" (22). As Hallward notes, the insistence on local histories has somewhat surprisingly been accompanied by a reproduction of placelessness with the recent emphasis on nomads, hybridity, in-between spaces, contingency, and the deconstruction of nearly every analytic category.
80. Lionnet, *Postcolonial Representations*, 2.
81. See Harvey, *Spaces of Capital*.
82. Lionnet and Shi, *Minor Transnationalism*, 2.
83. Ibid., 7.
84. Moretti, *Distant Reading*, 53, emphasis in the original.
85. Ibid., 53–54, emphasis in the original.
86. Moretti, "Conjectures on World Literature," emphasis in the original.
87. Spivak, *Death of a Discipline*, 104.
88. See "Pour une 'littérature-monde' en français"; Le Bris, Rouaud, and Almassy, *Pour une littérature-monde*.
89. Glissant cited in Leservot, "From *Weltliteratur* to World Literature to *Littérature-monde*," 36.
90. Maalouf, "Contre la Littérature Francophone."
91. Whereas Maalouf uses the term "hispanophone," one should note that the term is not present in critical discourse to the extent of Francophone and Anglophone. Within the Spanish-speaking world, the Latin American regional framework still predominates.
92. See Cavaille, "Francophones, l'écriture est polyglotte."
93. See also Thomas's compelling analysis of the stakes and shortcomings of the manifesto and the edited collection in *Africa and France: Postcolonial Cultures, Migration, and Racism*.
94. I am not suggesting that monolingual approaches to globalization are no longer valuable. For instance, the edited collection *French Global: A New Approach to Literary History* revisits French literary history from a global perspective in a very compelling way. The authors read works written in French "in relation to the globe: as world, as sphere, as a space of encounter with others and with the very idea of otherness" (xvii). They thus produce original analysis while remaining within the category of "literatures in French." Within the

Latin American context, I take cue particularly from Héctor Hoyos's recent study, *Beyond Bolaño: The Global Latin American Novel,* which focuses on post-1989 Latin American novels and their perspectives on globalization. Hoyos considers narratives, which, as he contends, offer paradoxical representations of the world as a whole. He analyzes a variety of phenomena including the relation between the literary and art spheres, counterfactual "Nazi" histories, escapist narratives, and resistance to literary consumerism. Hoyos ultimately suggests "Latin Americanizing world literature," instead of replacing Latin Americanism with world literature. See McDonald and Suleiman, *French Global;* Hoyos, *Beyond Bolaño.*

95. Goyal, "Introduction: Africa and the Black Atlantic," vi.

NOTES TO CHAPTER 1

1. Kandé, *La quête infinie de l'autre rive.* Mansa is a Mandinka word for "sultan, king, emperor."
2. Condé cited in Broichhagen, Lachman, and Simek, *Feasting on Words,* 25.
3. Goyal, "Introduction: Africa and the Black Atlantic," vi.
4. See Condé, "Pan-Africanism, Feminism, and Culture."
5. Condé, "Order, Disorder, Freedom, and the West Indian Writer," 130.
6. Gulick, "Africa, Pan-Africanism, and the Global Caribbean," 50.
7. Clifford, *Routes,* 268, emphasis in the original.
8. Whereas in this chapter I focus in-depth on three Atlantic authors, new Atlantic geographies are at the center of the work of many other contemporary writers. For instance, after Togolese writer Sami Tchak earned his PhD at the Sorbonne University in 1993, he spent several months in Cuba researching prostitution on the island. His familiarity with Cuban, as well as Mexican and Colombian histories and cultures, has significantly influenced his work. Since the novel *Hermina,* published by Gallimard in 2003, his works take place in an imaginary Latin American setting, outlining later connections between the African and Latin American contexts. See Tchak, *Hermina; Filles de Mexico.*
9. Gulick, "Africa, Pan-Africanism, and the Global Caribbean," 70.
10. Miller, *The French Atlantic Triangle,* 4.
11. Glissant cited in *The French Atlantic Triangle,* 341.
12. Miller, *The French Atlantic Triangle,* 362.
13. Simek, *Feasting on Words,* 11.
14. Condé, *The Story of the Cannibal Woman.*
15. Selasi, "Bye-Bye Babar."
16. Ibid.
17. Mbembe, "Afropolitanism."
18. Ibid., 29.
19. Ibid.
20. Santana, "Exorcizing Afropolitanism."
21. Tveit, "The Afropolitan Must Go."
22. Okwunodu, "'Afropolitanism': Africa without Africans (II)."
23. Wawrzinek and Makokha, *Negotiating Afropolitanism.*
24. Ibid., 10.
25. Spivak, *Death of a Discipline,* 16.
26. Huyssen, *Present Pasts,* 23.
27. Ibid., 24.
28. Lachman, "Le Cannibalisme au Féminin: A Case of Radical Indigestion," 80.
29. Rosello, "Post-cannibalism in Maryse Condé's *Histoire de la femme cannibale,*" 37.
30. Phillips, *A New World Order,* 308.

31. Okazaki, "Dis/location and 'Connectedness' in Caryl Phillips," 89.
32. Ropero, "Travel Writing and Postcoloniality."
33. Clingman, "Other Voices," 122.
34. Phillips, *A New World Order*, 5.
35. Meriwether, "'Walking into the Face of History,'" 80.
36. Naoki, *Translation and Subjectivity*, 13.
37. Clifford, "Diasporas," 322.
38. Clingman, "Other Voices," 120.
39. Meriwether, "'Walking into the Face of History,'" 80.
40. Phillips, *Color Me English*, 16.
41. Glissant, *Poétique de la Relation*, 18. Translation taken from Glissant, *Poetics of Relation*, trans. Wing, 6.
42. Dash, *Edouard Glissant*.
43. Glissant, *Poétique de la relation*, 18; *Poetics of relation*, 6.
44. Translation by Sarah-Louise Raillard.
45. Ibid.
46. Sitchet, "Sylvie Kandé dans les remous d'une quête infinie de l'autre rive," section "À quelle occasion avez-vous commencé à rêver de raconter, et faire se rencontrer, ces deux quêtes?"
47. Translation by Sarah-Louise Raillard.
48. Mongo-Mboussa, "Sylvie Kandé entre deux rives."
49. Translation by Sarah-Louise Raillard.
50. Kesteloot, "The African Epic."
51. Translation by Alexander Dickow. Dickow's award-winning translation of an excerpt from Kandé's poem has been published in *Asymptote* magazine. I use this translation whenever possible. https://www.asymptotejournal.com/special-feature/sylvie-kande-the-neverending-quest-for-the-other-shore/.
52. Ndiaye, "Afrique En Quête D'ailleurs," 245.
53. Translation by Alexander Dickow.
54. Glissant, *Discours Antillais*, 132. Translation taken from Glissant, *Caribbean Discourse*, trans. Dash, 64.
55. Glissant, *Discours Antillais*, 134; *Caribbean Discourse*, 66.
56. Translation by Alexander Dickow.
57. Translation by Sarah-Louise Raillard.
58. Ibid.
59. A video of the event is available online at https://www.youtube.com/watch?v=c9gIT8QcUrA.
60. Ibid.
61. Condé, "Order, Disorder, Freedom," 124.
62. Best, "On Failing to Make the Past Present," 453.
63. Pratt, *Imperial Eyes*, 4.
64. Edwards and Graulund, *Postcolonial Travel Writing*, 2.
65. Loingsigh, *Postcolonial Eyes*, 2
66. Ibid., 12.
67. Ndiaye, "Afrique En Quête D'ailleurs," 244.
68. Translation by Alexander Dickow.
69. Ibid.
70. Translation by Sarah-Louise Raillard. These verses mention Barzakh, generally interpreted in Islamic eschatology as a transitional stage, connecting this world to eternal afterlife. "Barça ou barzakh!" ["Barcelona or die!"] is also the growing motto of clandestine immigrants, who would rather die than not attempt to reach the other shore. See Maher, *Barça Ou Barzakh*.
71. "The List: The 34,361 Men, Women and Children Who Perished Trying to Reach Europe."

NOTES TO CHAPTER 2

1. Sankara, *Thomas Sankara Speaks*, 375.
2. Diome, *Le ventre de l'Atlantique*; *Celles qui attendent*.
3. Hartman, *Scenes of Subjection*, 130.
4. Publisher's cover copy, McClanahan, *Dead Pledges*.
5. Andrew Ross, in his book *Creditocracy: And the Case for Debt Refusal*, describes the emergence of a "full-blown creditocracy." According to Ross, "financialization had to creep into every corner of the household economy before the authority of the creditor class took on a sovereign, unassailable character" (11). Ross further develops an argument in favor of collective debt refusal.
6. See, for instance, Trenz, Ruzza, and Guiraudon, *Europe's Prolonged Crisis*; or "Thomas Piketty: Rise of Anti-Austerity Parties Good News for Europe."
7. See "Greece's Debt Crisis Timeline."
8. See, for instance, Roos, "Greek Referendum"; Krugman, "Europe's Moment of Truth."
9. See, for instance, Jochnick and Preston, *Sovereign Debt at the Crossroads*.
10. Césaire and Kelley, *Discourse on Colonialism*.
11. See "How Puerto Rico's Debt Created a Perfect Storm before the Storm."
12. Lomnitz-Adler, "The Depreciation of Life," cited in Harvey, *A Brief History of Neoliberalism*, 100.
13. Harvey, *A Brief History of Neoliberalism*, 75.
14. Nkrumah, *Neo-Colonialism: The Last Stage of Imperialism*.
15. Žižek, "This Is a Chance for Europe to Awaken," section 1
16. Balibar, "Politics of the Debt," section "From sovereign debts to the sovereignty of debt?"
17. Coleman, "Greek Bailout Talks: Are Stereotypes of Lazy Greeks True?"
18. McClanahan, *Dead Pledges*, 57.
19. Graeber, *Debt: The First 5000 Years*, 8.
20. Brown, *Undoing the Demos*, 65.
21. Ibid., 10.
22. Lazzarato and Jordan, *The Making of the Indebted Man*, 45–46.
23. Ibid., 49.
24. See Lazzarato and Jordan, *Governing by Debt*.
25. Mabanckou, *Black bazar*, 64.
26. Mabanckou, *Black Bazaar*, 62.
27. Mabanckou, *Black bazar*, 69.
28. Mabanckou, *Black Bazaar*, 68.
29. Fanon, *Peau noire, masques blancs*.
30. A lot of compelling work exists on the topic of sexual debt. See, for instance, Bergner, "Who Is That Masked Woman?"; Little, *Between Totem and Taboo*.
31. Diome, *The Belly of the Atlantic*.
32. Dubois, *Soccer Empire*, 25.
33. For a more in-depth discussion of structural adjustment programs and economic neoliberalization, see, for example, Diouf, *L'Afrique dans la mondialisation*; Harvey, *Spaces of Capital*.
34. See Toussaint and Millet, *Debt, the IMF, and the World Bank*; Peet, *Unholy Trinity*.
35. See Ndiaye, "Food for Thought," 85–87.
36. Thomas, *Black France*, 198.
37. Lazzarato and Jordan, *The Making of the Indebted Man*, 30.
38. Hartman, *Scenes of Subjection*, 130.
39. Ibid., 131.
40. McClanahan, *Dead Pledges*, 80.
41. Ibid., 83.
42. Lachman, "The Transatlantic Poetics of Fatou Diome," 54.

43. A few studies, like Abdelmalek Sayad's inspiring sociological analysis of emigration in Algeria, have focused on how the stories of those who return encourage their compatriots to embark on a similar voyage. The term *brain drain* is also sporadically used, mainly to refer to the departure of educated classes from the countries of the Global South. See Sayad, *La double absence.*
44. Nnaemeka, *Female Circumcision and the Politics of Knowledge,* 13.
45. See, for instance, Lionnet, "Feminisms and Universalisms."
46. Thomas, *Black France,* 133–34.
47. Mohanty, *Feminism without Borders,* 9.
48. See Chauhan and Patel, *Empowering Women through Microfinance;* Daley-Harris, *Pathways out of Poverty;* Robinson, *The Microfinance Revolution.*
49. Ledwith, "Muhammad Yunus," introduction.
50. Vishmidt, "Permanent Reproductive Crisis," section "The Tyrannies of Microfinance."
51. Spivak, *A Critique of Postcolonial Reason,* 237.
52. Nnaemeka, *Female Circumcision and the Politics of Knowledge,* 37.
53. Sarah-Louise Raillard translated all the quotes from *Celles qui attendent.*
54. Lachman, "The Transatlantic Poetics of Fatou Diome," 38.
55. Hakim Abderrezak notes a similar dynamic in *L'Enfant endormi,* a movie by Moroccan-Belgium director Yasmine Kassari, which recounts the story of two cousins, raising their children and taking care of their blind grandmother in light of their husbands' departure to Spain. In fact, there are striking similarities between *L'Enfant endormi* and *Celles qui attendent.* As Abderrezak writes: "Mothers are left behind and as a result they have to make difficult compromises, such as giving up a regular pregnancy and a traditional livelihood." Abderrezak, *Ex-centric Migrations,* 179.
56. For Graeber, human economies "refer to those where the primary focus of economic life is on reconfiguring relations between people, rather than the allocation of commodities." Graeber, "On Social Currencies and Human Economies," 411.
57. Graeber, *Debt: The First 5000 Years,* 412.
58. Balibar, "Politics of the Debt," section "Debt economy and the hegemony of finance capital," emphasis in the original.
59. A proliferation of critical studies have analyzed the role of gender in the construction of colonial ideologies. Frantz Fanon has famously written about the public unveilings of women in French Algeria as a symbol of the colonizer's victory over the colonized mind. The colonizer believed, Fanon argues, that by winning over women, he would also win over the men. Western focus on cultural issues like polygamy and cliterodectomy has also been analyzed in illuminating ways. These issues are frequently mobilized to sustain the image of Africa as a backward continent and to avoid talking about European (and US) economic imperialism on the continent. To avoid this binary opposition between traditional Africa and progressive Europe, we need to underline the gendered aspect of contemporary economic imperialism, its focus is on local women as the primary figure of "development." See Fanon, *Sociologie d'une revolution;* Lionnet, "Feminisms and Universalisms."
60. Juventudes Libertarias de Bolivia, "With Dynamite and Molotovs."
61. Pachico, "'No Pago' Confronts Microfinance in Nicaragua."
62. Vishmidt, "Permanent Reproductive Crisis," section "The Tyrannies of Microfinance."
63. Graeber, *Debt: The First 5000 Years,* 380. See also Karim, *Microfinance and Its Discontents.*

NOTES TO CHAPTER 3

1. Carmody, "How to Get Away with Murder."
2. See the 2007 World Investment Report. See also Ghemawat and Pisani, "Are Multinationals Becoming Less Global?"

3. See "Reining in Corporations."

4. Baran and Sweezy, "Notes on the Theory of Imperialism," 25.

5. Berardi, *The Soul at Work*, 88.

6. Arrighi, *The Long Twentieth Century*, 74, emphasis in the original.

7. Ibid., 75.

8. See Friedrich-Ebert-Stiftung Foundation, "Tax Havens and the Taxation of Transnational Corporations."

9. Daly and Goodland, "An Ecological-Economic Assessment," 494.

10. "In Praise of the Stateless Multinational."

11. See the 2007 World Investment Report. See also Greer and Singh, "A Brief History of Transnational Corporations."

12. Suwandi and Foster, "Multinational Corporations and the Globalization of Monopoly Capital," section "Globalized Monopoly-Finance Capital and the New Imperialism."

13. Emmott, "Everybody's Favourite Monsters."

14. Badiou, *Our Wound Is Not So Recent*, 9.

15. The company dropped the adjective "française" after Gabonese independence, becoming the *Société des pétroles d'Afrique-Équatoriale* [SPAE] in 1960, then Elf SPAFE in 1968, and Elf-Gabon in 1973. In 2000, Elf and TotalFina merged into TotalFinaElf. Finally, the company shortened its name to Total in 2003.

16. Gaspar de Alba, "Poor Brown Female," 63.

17. Badiou, *Our Wound Is Not So Recent*, 8.

18. Ireland, "Bessora's Literary Ludics," 7.

19. Koutonin, "Why Are White People Expats When the Rest of Us Are Immigrants?"

20. Dewolf, "In Hong Kong, Just Who Is an Expat, Anyway?"

21. See "Romania and Bulgaria EU Migration Restrictions Lifted"; Bechev, "Britain's Bulgaria-Romania Phobia"; "What Britain Forgets."

22. Koutonin's claim echoes Étienne Balibar's argument that *immigration* has become the term used to talk about race in a postcolonial context. Furthermore, sociologists like Saskia Sassen have argued that whereas the economic immigrant has become the representative figure of the past few decades, globalization has in fact been characterized primarily by the rise of short-term, business-related travel. Yet, just as the cosmopolitan and the immigrant rarely interact, the expat and the immigrant are two figures that more often than not do not cross paths. See Balibar, *Race, Nation, Class*; Sassen, *Globalization and Its Discontents*.

23. Gilroy, *The Black Atlantic*, 4.

24. Sarah-Louise Raillard translated all the quotes from *Petroleum*.

25. Mitchell, *Carbon Democracy*, 29.

26. Ibid., 140.

27. See, for instance, Blyth, *Austerity*.

28. Mitchell, *Carbon Democracy*, 205.

29. Astier, "Elf was Secret Arm of 'French Policy.'"

30. Heise, *Sense of Place and Sense of Planet*, 142.

31. Schwartz, "The Green Guide to Obama's State of the Union Address."

32. Huggan, *Postcolonial Eco-criticism*, 80.

33. Ireland, "Bessora's Literary Ludics," 9.

34. Spivak, "Three Women's Texts."

35. Pollack, "Latin America Translated (Again)." Similarly, the Salvadoran novelist and journalist Horacio Castellanos Moya, building on Pollack's work, suggests that the image of Bolaño created by the publication houses feeds into an exotic myth of a Latin America reduced to road trips and rebellious adventures. See Moya, "Sobre el mito Bolaño," 8

36. Bolaño and Wimmer, *2666*.

37. Baudrillard, *The Agony of Power*, 52.

38. Farred, "The Impossible Closing," 699.

39. Macaya, "Estética, política y el *possible* territorio," 137.
40. Braithwaite, *Bolaño por si mismo*, 69.
41. Federici, "Feminism and the Politics of the Commons," section "Feminist Reconstructions."
42. Higginson, "Mayhem at the Crossroads," 165.
43. Ibid., 175.
44. Echevarría and Pupo-Walker, *The Cambridge History of Latin American Literature.*
45. Close, *Contemporary Hispanic Crime Fiction*, 19.
46. Badiou, *Our Wound Is Not So Recent*, 10.
47. Tani, *The Doomed Detective*, 40.
48. Carrière, "Petroleum de Bessora."
49. Soldàn, "Roberto Bolaño," 226.
50. Cobos, "Entrevista a Roberto Bolaño," section "¿Te parece que la narrativa chilena actual no tiene peso?"
51. Baudelaire, *The Flowers of Evil*, 181.
52. See Macaya, "Estética, política y el *possible* territorio."
53. Velasco and Schmidt, "Mapping a Geography of Hell," 111.

NOTES TO CHAPTER 4

1. Glissant, *Poétique de la Relation*, 209; *Poetics of Relation*, 194.
2. Glissant, *Poétique de la Relation*, 204; *Poetics of Relation*, 190.
3. See Condé, *Histoire de la femme cannibale*; Sebbar, *Shérazade, 17 ans, brune, frisée, les yeux verts*. I have previously written about the concept of opacity in relation to the work of Leila Sebbar. See Perisic, "Beure je suis, opaque je resterai."
4. Throughout this chapter, I use myself as the figure of "the reader." By doing so, I do not mean to suggest that there exists a homogenous category of the reader or a single act of reading. In fact, one's social positioning, nationality, race, and gender inevitably influence one's reading process. Thus, it is undoubtful that a multiplicity of readers have read and will read these texts in a multiplicity of ways. A thoughtful and complex analysis of the production and circulation of these novels would be required to describe those readers; an analysis that is outside the scope of my chapter. I am using my own reading process as a way to reflect on the narrative strategies used to construct opaque protagonists.
5. Glissant, *Poétique de la Relation*, 204; *Poetics of Relation*, 190.
6. Sarraute, "Ce que je cherche à faire," 39.
7. See Robbe-Grillet, *Pour un nouveau roman.*
8. Harney and Moten, *The Undercommons*, 20.
9. Ibid., 9.
10. The question of refusal has been central to a current in contemporary theory and social activism. Autonomous Marxist intellectual, Franco "Bifo" Berardi, has argued that the upcoming "insurrection will not be an insurrection of energy, but an insurrection of slowness, withdrawal, and exhaustion." Similarly, David Graeber has proposed the global cancellation of debts and a significant reduction of work as a way out of the current economic crisis. See Berardi, *The Uprising*, 68; Graeber, "A Practical Utopian's Guide to the Coming Collapse."
11. Xavier, *The Migrant Text*, 69.
12. Huggan, *The Postcolonial Exotic*, 28. In this study of the marketing and circulation of Anglophone postcolonial works, Huggan defines the postcolonial exotic in the following manner: "These three aspects of commodity fetishism—mystification (or leveling-out) of historical experience; imagined access to the cultural other through the process of consumption; reification of people and places into exchangeable aesthetic objects—help these

books and their authors acquire an almost talismanic status" (19). Given that the writer is aware of the reader's exoticizing tendencies, she incorporates their critique into the text.

Sarah Brouillette modifies Huggan's account by arguing that the reader, who is searching for the contemporary exotic, is in fact an imagined figure. This figure enables an opposition between a general readership that reads "badly" and a more sophisticated academic reader. Every reader, however, Brouillette argues, believes that they belong to the latter category. For Brouillette, "strategic exoticism is not something a writer deploys to teach a reader about the errors in her conceptions about other cultures, much though it depends upon a construction of a figure in need of such instruction. Instead it indicates a set of textual strategies that communicates at all because the author and the *actual* reader likely share assumptions about the way culture operates, and concur in their desire to exempt themselves from certain undesirable practices" (43). An implicit solidarity is established between the writer and the reader, neither of which wants to participate in the contemporary exotic.

Within the Francophone context, Suba Xavier uses five case studies (Naïm Kattan, Dany Laferrière, Azouz Begag, Dai Sijie, and Mehdi Charef) to show how immigrant authors negotiate being "called upon as spokespeople, lauded as model citizens and simultaneously accused of betrayal and treachery" (69).

None of the authors studied in this chapter fall neatly into the category of postcolonial writer. However, I believe that questions of otherness and the contemporary exotic are present in all three novels. I see opacity as one of the formal modes of "strategic exoticism" as defined by Huggan and Brouillette. By opting for opacity, contemporary authors refuse to serve as spokespeople, a process that Xavier explains in detail. At the same time, as I show in the rest of the chapter, I do not think that opacity can be entirely reduced to strategic exoticism. See Brouillette, *Postcolonial Writers in the Global Literary Marketplace*; Xavier, *The Migrant Text*.

13. Bhabha, *The Location of Culture*, 95.

14. Ibid., 101.

15. Britton, *Edouard Glissant and Postcolonial Theory*, 24.

16. Pinto, *Difficult Diasporas*, 2.

17. Ibid., 7.

18. A parallel with Abderrezak's work on the Mediterranean can be drawn here as well. Abderrezak similarly notes the increasing presence of "unsound vessels" in narratives dealing with clandestine immigration. He also identifies "leavism"—"the insatiable desire to cross the sea, which precedes an actual instance of clandestine migration" (9) as an important trope in contemporary Maghrebi immigrant narratives. See Abderrezak, *Ex-centric Migrations*.

19. Diógenes Céspedes reads Kapuc as a metaphor for Puerto Rico, similarly dispossessed of its own discourse and of a father figure. Céspedes connects the disappearance of Kapuc's father to the failure of Puerto Rico's independence. Cf. Céspedes, *Migrantes Dominicanos*.

20. Citations from *Los documentados* were translated by Sarah-Louise Raillard.

21. Rancière and Corcoran, *Dissensus*, 37.

22. Ibid., 69.

23. Poniatowska, "Trabajos del reino, libro del escritor Yuri Herrera," Introduction.

24. Erlan, "El lenguaje como frontera, entrevista con Yuri Herrera," section "En 'Señales que precederán al fin del mundo,' el trabajo sobre el territorio de la frontera y sus problemáticas es central y a la vez subterráneo."

25. Herrera and Dillman, *Signs Preceding the End of the World*.

26. Harney and Moten, *The Undercommons*, 51.

27. The name Cora refers to an indigenous Mexican ethnic group and is the second name of the Greek goddess Persephone, who according to Greek mythology ruled the underground

world. The names thus embody the ability of Herrera's characters to connect different worlds.

28. Carini, "Identidades fronterizas."

29. Erlan, "El lenguaje como frontera, entrevista con Yuri Herrera," section "¿Y en relación al lenguaje?"

30. Many critics have compared *Signs Preceding the End of the World* to Juan Rulfo's *Pedro Páramo*. Maya Jaggi thus writes in the *Guardian* that *Signs* "bows to Juan Rulfo's Pedro Páramo." Jaggi, "Signs Preceding the End of the World by Yuri Herrera review—a lyrical Mexican migrants' tale."

Herrera himself has tried to nuance the parallel: "It's not something that I was conscious of when I was writing it. I mean, I love Juan Rulfo, I have read each of his books several times. But he's not one of my intimate, personal authors. I don't mind being compared to Rulfo, because he is probably the best novelist we have ever had—but it's not something I set out to do. Rulfo is, in Mexican culture, a monument. And monuments are in the middle of the square. Whether you know who he is or not, whether you stand in front of the monument and reflect on it, you organize your life around this monument." Bady, "Border Characters," section "Was Rulfo a particular influence?"

31. Bady, "Underneath the Darkness," section 2.

32. Erlan, "El lenguaje como frontera, entrevista con Yuri Herrera," section "Siendo originario de Valle del Mezquital, una zona semidesértica del Estado de Hidalgo, en algún momento dijo que siempre intentó escribir sobre la belleza de lo árido. ¿Podría definir esa belleza?"

33. See Kim, "Yuri Herrera: Interview," section "Can you explain what you mean by 'I like to say that style isn't surface; style is a form of knowledge.'"

34. See Glissant, *Poetics of Relation*.

35. Herrera cited in Bady, "Underneath the Darkness," section 2.

36. Jaggi, "Three Strong Women by Marie NDiaye."

37. Cottille-Foley, "Postmodernité," 81.

According to Cottille-Foley, it is the discontinuity of memory that is responsible for the characters' wandering and loss of identity: "Revenant incessamment, pathologiquement, sur le lieu ultime de leur maison natale, les personnages constatent la discontinuité de leur propre mémoire. Soumis à la démythification de leurs souvenirs, ils se désagrègent peu à peu, perdant par là même leur propre identité" [Relentlessly, even pathologically returning to the ultimate place of their birth house, these characters observe the discontinuity of their own memory. Subject to the demystification of their memories, they slowly come apart, losing their own identity in the process]. Characters become "victimes du leurre d'un lieu de mémoire dont la validité est sans cesse remise en question" [victims of the illusion of a place of memory, whose validity is constantly called into question]. Many critics share the viewpoint that *Rosie Carpe* is a psychological novel. This kind of reading assumes that identity exists as a stable and definable category. There exists an originary identity that at a certain moment characters possessed and that they are now losing. The wandering and the instability of characters are perceived as an existential crisis, a state that needs to be overcome, in order to regain the unity of the self and the continuity of memory.

38. Moudileno, "Marie Ndiaye's Discombobulated Subject," 84.

39. All the translations are taken from NDiaye and Black, *Rosie Carpe*.

40. "Marie Ndiaye: 'Se définir, c'est se réduire.'"

41. Britton, *Edouard Glissant and Postcolonial Theory*, 13.

42. See Glissant, *Poetics of Relation*, 153–55.

43. Argand, "Marie Ndiaye," section "En plus de la cruauté, avez-vous d'autres obsessions?"

44. "Yuri Herrera entre la prosa poética y criminal."

45. Rancière, "The Cause of the Other," 28.

46. Ibid., 29.

47. Ibid.

48. Muñoz, *Disidentifications,* 200.
49. For Peter Hallward, "the specific is the space of interests in relation to other interests, the space of the historical as such, forever ongoing, forever incomplete" (5). On the other hand, "the specified can only define the realm of the essence or essentialist, where the demarcation of an individual (subject, object or culture) follows from its accordance with recognised classifications" (40). See Hallward, *Absolutely Postcolonial.*
50. Rancière and Corcoran, *Dissensus,* 33.
51. In *The Global Commonwealth of Citizens,* Daniele Archibugi develops the concept of cosmopolitan responsibility: "Political action has so far been grounded on responsibilities restricted to certain territories and groups of persons; the raison d'état favors duty toward the interior and mortifies duty toward the exterior. However, previous certainties are beginning to evaporate: as borders become increasingly uncertain, the consequences of political action are expanding. The responsibility of the public sphere must consequently be enlarged, to the point that political action can be taken in the interest of all those who are directly or indirectly involved" (286). I believe that we should be careful when talking about global responsibility, given that in the past it has produced violent outcomes such as the civilizing mission and the white man's burden. At the same time, I think that these novels do raise the question of cosmopolitan responsibility. The acts of disidentification occur in relation to institutions and entities that traditionally define rights and responsibilities. It leaves us with the question of what does cosmopolitan (though I prefer, for instance, the term transnational) responsibility look like?

NOTES TO CHAPTER 5

1. Wallerstein, *The Decline of American Power,* 45–46.
2. Harney, Moten, and Empson, *The Undercommons,* 5.
3. Following Foucault, Butler defines sovereignty as "providing legitimacy for the rule of law and offering a guarantor for the representational claims of state power." Governmentality, on the other hand, "is broadly understood as a mode of power concerned with the maintenance and control of bodies and persons, the production and regulation of persons and populations, and the circulation of goods insofar as they maintain and restrict the life of the population. Governmentality operates through policies and departments, through managerial and bureaucratic institutions, through the law, when the law is understood as 'a set of tactics,' and through forms of state power, although not exclusively" (*Precarious Life,* 52).
4. See Foucault, *Discipline and Punish.*
5. Butler, *Precarious Life,* 55.
6. "Que vise vraiment la mise en place d'un état d'urgence permanent?" section "Des restrictions liberticides."
7. Braschi and O'Dwyer, *Empire of Dreams,* viii.
8. Arnaldo Manuel Cruz-Malavé explains that Braschi might be "rewriting here the famous image of the 1977 takeover of the Statue of Liberty by New York Puerto Rican activists in protest of the incarceration of Puerto Rican nationalist political prisoners and Puerto Rico's continued status as a colony of the United States. In this image, which has been referenced by poets since then, the Puerto Rican flag, which is draped around the statue's crown, may be seen as occupying or taking over Lady Liberty's privileged panoptic gaze." Cruz-Malavé, "'Under the Skirt of Liberty,'" 818.
9. Rivera, "El poder de la palabra," 186.
10. In 2012, the *Economist* included the following lines in its book of business quotations: "Banks are the temples of America. This is a holy war. Our economy is our religion." Somewhat ironically, Braschi's quote follows that of Lloyd Blankfein, a former CEO of Goldman Sachs. See Ridgers, *Book of Business Quotations,* 16.

11. Cruz-Malavé, "'Under the Skirt of Liberty,'" 813.
12. Madelena Gonzalez similarly contends that postcolonialism is not an adequate lens for reading *United States of Banana*. She reads the novel in conjunction with similarly "globalized" works like J. M. Coetzee's *Elizabeth Costello* and Salman Rushdie's *Fury*. See Gonzalez, "*United States of Banana* (2011), *Elizabeth Costello* (2003) and *Fury* (2001)."
13. Nietzsche and Kaufmann, *Thus Spoke Zarathustra*.
14. Cruz-Malavé, "'Under the Skirt of Liberty,'" 806.
15. Multiple studies, including Franco Moretti's *Modern Epic: The World-system from Goethe to García Màrquez* (1996), Stefano Ercolino's *The Maximalist Novel* (2014), as well as Nick Levey's *Maximalism in Contemporary American Literature* (2016) have recently theorized the genre.
16. Moretti, *Modern Epic*, 50.
17. Ibid., 2.
18. While Moretti's readings are highly sophisticated, his corpus encompasses mostly Western works with a brief intrusion of magical realism at the very end of his literary history. The world text thus paradoxically remains mostly Western.
19. Moretti, *Modern Epic*, 143, 238.
20. Balibar, "Politics of the Debt," section "Debt economy and the hegemony of finance capital," emphasis in the original.
21. Berardi, *The Uprising*, 143.
22. Ibid., 74.
23. Kristeva, *Powers of Horror*, 2.
24. Garrigós, "Chicken with the Head Cut Off," 151.
25. Carl Schmidtt has famously defined the sovereign as the person who decides the state of exception. Building on his work, Agamben has written a history of the state of exception in Western Europe and the United States, arguing that in the twentieth century the state of exception has become the norm rather than an anomaly. See Schmidtt, *Political Theology*; Agamben, *State of Exception*.
26. Hardt and Negri, *Empire*, xii.
27. Žižek, "Have Michael Hardt and Antonio Negri Rewritten the *Communist Manifesto* for The Twenty-First Century?" 192.
28. Harvey, "Consolidating Power," section "In the last forty years, the mode of capital accumulation has changed globally. What do these changes mean for the struggle against capitalism?"
29. Cruz-Malavé, "'Under the Skirt of Liberty,'" 815.
30. "52 Weeks / 52 Interviews," section "Philosophy, literature, and politics collide through the monologues and dialogues that make up the book. Can you talk about the confluence of these three in your work. Does one inform the others, or are they, like the characters, in a constant dialogue?"
31. Harney, Moten, and Empson, *The Undercommons*, 125.
32. Ibid., 8.
33. Ibid., 96.
34. In his article, Cruz-Malavé already introduces the concept of the undercommons in relation to *USofB*.
35. Junot Díaz and Ana Lydia Vega have both distinguished themselves through their literary usage of Spanglish. See Díaz, *The Brief Wondrous Life of Oscar Wao*; Vega, "Pollito Chicken."
36. Foster, "Review of Yo-Yo Boing!," 202.
37. Loustau, "Nomadismos Lingüísticos y Culturales en *Yo-Yo Boing!*, 437. It is interesting that Braschi's language(s) is/are still interpreted mostly in terms of identity, even though she has explicitly said: "Originalidad quiere decir volver al origen. Originalidad nace siempre del origen y Puerto Rico es una nación que no ha tenido nacimiento. La identidad no es mi problema. Siempre he estado identificada conmigo misma. No creo que los puertorriqueños tengan ningún problema con la identidad. Los puertorriqueños saben quiénes son

a todos los niveles. Es un problema de origen" [Originality means returning to the origin. Originality is always born from a point of origin and Puerto Rico is a nation that was never born. Identity is not my problem. I've always identified with myself. I don't think that Puerto Ricans have any problems with identity. Puerto Ricans know who they are at all levels. It's a problem of origin]. There is a difference between a search for identity (even a nomadic one) and a desire to express an origin in different languages, to place that origin in relation with other origins. See Betances, "El Yo-Yo en los Estados Unidos de Banana," section "Hay gente que dice que ya no es necesario discutir la identidad."

38. Berardi, *The Uprising*, 32.
39. Ibid., 41.
40. Ibid., 140.
41. Ibid., 158.
42. Schram, *The Return of Ordinary Capitalism*, 91.
43. hooks, *All About Love*.
44. Butler, *Precarious Life*, xiv–xv.
45. Ibid., xviii–xix.
46. Berardi, *The Uprising*, 54–55.

NOTES TO CONCLUSION

1. See, for instance, Hing, *Ethical Borders*.
2. See, for instance, Dorothy Figueira's article on comparative and world literature, "Comparative Literature versus World Literature."
3. In "Chercher nos vérités," her contribution to the edited volume *Penser la créolité*, Maryse Condé contends that the opposition French/Creole has been the focus of Francophone Caribbean criticism, and that Spanish and English influences have not received enough attention. See Condé and Cottenet-Hage, *Penser la créolité*. See also Alain Mabanckou's contribution to *Pour une littérature-monde*.
4. Rosello, "Unhoming Francophone Studies."
5. Rancière and Corcoran, *Dissensus*, 149.
6. Mohanty, *Feminism without Borders*, 2.
7. See Cohn, "Why Trump Won"; Green, "It Was Cultural Anxiety"; McElwee and McDaniel, "Economic Anxiety"; Hasan, "Top Democrats Are Wrong."
8. Kelley, "After Trump, " introduction.
9. Lind, "Black Lives Matter vs. Bernie Sanders, Explained."
10. Outside of the US context, one can of course think of Aimé Césaire's now well-known letter to Maurice Thorez, explaining his reasons for leaving the French communist party. See Césaire, "Letter to Maurice Thorez."
11. See, for instance, Sears, "A Marxist Critiques Identity Politics." In "Who's Afraid of Identity Politics," Linda Alcoff offers a comprehensive history of this debate. See Moya and Hames-Garcia, *Reclaiming Identity*.
12. One of the more recent examples is Keeanga-Yamahtta Taylor's excellent book *From #BlackLivesMatter to Black Liberation* where she calls for a revival of the black socialist tradition.
13. Brown, "Neoliberalism's Frankenstein," 67.
14. See Maeckelbergh, *The Will of the Many*; Smith, "The Dark Side of Globalization."
15. "The World Social Forum Charter of Principles," section 1.
16. Dwyer, "Where Did the Anti-Globalization Movement Go?"

BIBLIOGRAPHY

2007 World Investment Report. United Nations Conference on Trade and Development: "Transnational Corporations, Extractive Industries and Development." Repost available online at https://unctad.org/en/Docs/wir2007_en.pdf. Accessed 14 Oct. 2018.

"52 Weeks/52 Interviews: Week 34: Giannina Braschi." *MonkeyBicycle*. 23 Aug. 2013. http://monkeybicycle.net/52-weeks-52-interviews-week-34-giannina-braschi/. Accessed 19 Jan. 2017.

Abderrezak, Hakim. *Ex-centric Migrations: Europe and the Maghreb in Mediterranean Cinema, Literature, and Music*. Bloomington: Indiana University Press, 2016.

Agamben, Giorgio. *State of Exception*. Chicago: University of Chicago Press, 2005.

Appadurai, Arjun. "Disjuncture and Difference in the Global Cultural Economy." *Theory, Culture & Society*, vol. 7, no. 2–3 (1990): 295–310.

Apter, Emily. *Against World Literature: On the Politics of Untranslatability*. London: Verso, 2013.

Archibugi, Daniele. *The Global Commonwealth of Citizens: Toward Cosmopolitan Democracy*. Princeton, NJ: Princeton University Press, 2008.

Argand, Catherine. "Marie Ndiaye." *L'Express*. 1 Apr. 2001. http://www.lexpress.fr/culture/livre/marie-ndiaye_804357.html. Accessed 8 May 2017.

Arrighi, Giovanni. *The Long Twentieth Century: Money, Power, and the Origins of Our Times*. London: Verso, 1994.

Astier, Henri. "Elf Was Secret Arm of 'French Policy.'" *BBC*. 19 Mar. 2003. http://news.bbc.co.uk/2/hi/europe/2862257.stm. Accessed 15 Jun. 2018.

Badiou, Alain. *Our Wound Is Not So Recent: Thinking the Paris Killings of 13 November*. Cambridge: Polity Press, 2016.

Bady, Aaron. "Border Character." *Nation*. 2 Dec. 2015. https://www.thenation.com/article/border-characters/. Accessed 13 March 2019.

———. "Underneath the Darkness." *Boston Review*. 13 Sep. 2016. http://bostonreview.net/books-ideas/aaron-bady-yuri-herrera-signs-preceding-end-world-transmigration-bodies. Accessed 23 Sep. 2018.

Balibar, Étienne. "Politics of the Debt." *Postmodern Culture*, vol. 23, no. 3 (2013). https://muse.jhu.edu/. Accessed 4 March 2019.

———. *Race, Nation, Class: Ambiguous Identities*. London; New York: Verso, 1991.

Baran, Paul A., and Paul M. Sweezy. "Notes on the Theory of Imperialism." *Monthly Review*, vol. 17, no. 10 (March 1966). https://doi.org/10.14452/MR-017-10-1966-03_3. Accessed 4 March, 2019.

Barnard, Anne. "Beirut, Also the Site of Deadly Attacks, Feels Forgotten." *New York Times*. 15 Nov. 2015. https://www.nytimes.com/2015/11/16/world/middleeast/beirut-lebanon-attacks-paris.html. Accessed 19 Sep. 2018.

Baudelaire, Charles. *The Flowers of Evil*. Trans. Keith Waldrop. Middletown, CT: Wesleyan University Press, 2006.

Bechev, Dimitar. "Britain's Bulgaria-Romania Phobia." *openDemocracy*. 23 Dec. 2013. https://www.opendemocracy.net/can-europe-make-it/dimitar-bechev/britains-bulgaria-romania-phobia. Accessed 10 Jan. 2017.

Berardi, Franco. *The Soul at Work: From Alienation to Autonomy*. Los Angeles: Semiotext(e), 2009.

———. *The Uprising: On Poetry and Finance*. Los Angeles: Semiotext(e), 2012.

Bergner, Gwen. "Who Is That Masked Woman? or, The Role of Gender in Fanon's *Black Skin, White Masks*." *PMLA*, vol. 110, no. 1 (January 1995): 75–88.

Bessora. *Cueillez-moi jolis messieurs—: roman*. Paris: Gallimard, 2006.

———. *Les taches d'encre: roman*. Paris: Serpent à plumes, 2000.

———. *Petroleum: roman*. Paris: Denoël, 2004.

Best, Stephen. "On Failing to Make the Past Present." *Modern Language Quarterly*, vol. 73, no. 3 (Sep. 2012): 453–74.

Betances, Beatriz Ramírez. "El Yo-Yo en los Estados Unidos de Banana." *Cruce: Crítica Socio-Cultural Contemporánea*. n.d. http://revistacruce.com/letras/item/1454-el-yo-yo-en-los-estados-unidos-de-banana. Accessed 9 Jan. 2017.

Bhabha, Homi K. *The Location of Culture*. London: Routledge, 2004.

Blyth, Mark. *Austerity: The History of a Dangerous Idea*. Oxford: Oxford University Press, 2013.

Boelhower, William Q. "The Rise of the New Atlantic Studies Matrix." *American Literary History*, vol. 20, no. 1–2 (Mar. 2008): 83–101.

Bolaño, Roberto. *2666*. Barcelona: Editorial Anagrama, 2004.

Bolaño, Roberto, and Natasha Wimmer. *2666*. New York: Farrar, Straus and Giroux, 2008.

Bourdieu, Pierre. "The Essence of Neoliberalism." *Le Monde Diplomatique*. Dec. 1998. https://mondediplo.com/1998/12/08bourdieu. Accessed 25 Jul. 2018.

———. "La précarité est aujourd'hui partout." In *Contre-feux: Propos pour servir à la résistance contre l'invasion néoliberale*. 95–101. Paris: Liber-Raison d'Agir, 1998.

Braithwaite, Andres. *Bolaño por si mismo: entrevistas escogidas*. Santiago: Ediciones Universidad Diego Portales, 2006.

Brancato, Sabrina. "Afro-European Literature(s): A New Discursive Category?," *Research in African Literatures*, vol. 39, no. 3 (2008): 1–13

Braschi, Giannina. *United States of Banana*. Las Vegas, NV: AmazonCrossing, 2011.

Braschi, Giannina, and Tess O'Dwyer. *Empire of Dreams*. New Haven, CT: Yale University Press, 1994.

———. *Yo-Yo Boing!* Pittsburgh, PA: Latin American Literary Review Press, 1998.

Braudel, Fernand. *The Mediterranean and the Mediterranean World in the Age of Philip II.* New York: Harper & Row, 1972.

Britton, Celia. *Edouard Glissant and Postcolonial Theory: Strategies of Language and Resistance.* Charlottesville: University of Virginia Press, 1999.

Brouillette, Sarah. *Postcolonial Writers in the Global Literary Marketplace.* Basingstoke, UK: Palgrave Macmillan, 2007.

Brown, Wendy. "Neoliberalism's Frankenstein: Authoritarian Freedom in Twenty-First Century 'Democracies.'" *Critical Times,* vol. 1, no. 1 (2018). https://ctjournal.org/index.php/criticaltimes/article/view/12. Accessed 4 March 2019.

———. *Undoing the Demos: Neoliberalism's Stealth Revolution.* New York: Zone Books, 2015.

Butler, Judith. *Frames of War: When Is Life Grievable?* London: Verso, 2009.

———. *Precarious Life: The Powers of Mourning and Violence.* London: Verso, 2004.

Bystrom, Kerry, and Joseph R. Slaughter. *The Global South Atlantic.* New York: Fordham University Press, 2018.

Caffentzis, Constantine George. *In Letters of Blood and Fire: Work, Machines, and the Crisis of Capitalism.* Oakland, Calif: PM Press, 2013.

Carini, Sara. "Identidades fronterizas a través del lenguaje en Trabajos del reino y Señales que precederán el fin del mundo de Yuri Herrera." *Revista Liberia. Hispanic Journal of Cultural Criticism,* vol. 2 (2014): 1–24.

Carmody, Lauren. "How to Get Away with Murder: Transnational Corporations and Human Rights." *Just Cogens.* 31 Jul. 2016. https://justcogens.org/2016/07/31/how-to-get-away-with-murder-transnational-corporations-and-human-rights/. Accessed 25 Aug. 2018.

Castel, Robert. *L'insécurité social, qu'est-ce qu'être protégé?* Paris: Seuil, 2003.

Cavaille, Jean-Pierre. "Francophones, l'écriture est polyglotte." *Libération.* 30 Mar. 2007. http://www.liberation.fr/tribune/010198018-francophones-l-ecriture-est-polyglotte. Accessed 22 Sep. 2018.

Cazenave, Odile M. *Afrique Sur Seine: A New Generation of African Writers in Paris.* Lanham, MD: Lexington Books, 2005.

Césaire, Aimé. "Letter to Maurice Thorez." *Social Text,* vol. 28, no. 2 (103) (2010): 145–52.

Césaire, Aimé, and Robin D. G. Kelley. *Discourse on Colonialism.* New York: Monthly Review Press, 2000.

Céspedes, Diógenes. *Migrantes dominicanos: ideología y figuras independentistas en la literatura feminista puertorriqueña, 1980–2010.* Santo Domingo, República Dominicana: Editora Universitaria-UASD, 2014.

Chambers, Iain. *Mediterranean Crossings: The Politics of an Interrupted Modernity.* Durham, NC: Duke University Press, 2008.

Chauhan, Rameshsingh M., and Hina M. Patel. *Empowering Women through Microfinance.* Jaipur, India: Prism Books, 2014.

Clifford, James. "Diasporas." *Cultural Anthropology,* vol. 9, no. 3 (1994): 302–38 .

———. *Routes: Travel and Translation in the Late Twentieth Century.* Cambridge, MA: Harvard University Press, 1997.

Clingman, Stephen. "Other Voices: An Interview with Caryl Phillips." *Salmagundi*, vol. 143 (2004): 112–40.

Close, Glen S. *Contemporary Hispanic Crime Fiction: A Transatlantic Discourse on Urban Violence.* New York: Palgrave Macmillan, 2008.

Cobos, Eduardo. "Entrevista a Roberto Bolaño: Hay que mantener la ficción en favor de la conjetura." *Crítica.cl.* 18 Sep. 2013. http://critica.cl/entrevistas/entrevista-a-roberto-bolano-hay -que-mantener-la-ficcion-en-favor-de-la-conjetura. Accessed 2 Oct. 2018.

Cohn, Nate. "Why Trump Won: Working-Class Whites." *New York Times.* 9 Nov 2016. https:// www.nytimes.com/2016/11/10/upshot/why-trump-won-working-class-whites.html?mcubz= 0>. Accessed 15 Jul. 2017.

Coleman, Jasmine. "Greek Bailout Talks: Are Stereotypes of Lazy Greeks True?" *BBC News.* 10 Mar. 2015. https://www.bbc.com/news/world-europe-31803814. Accessed 23 Sep. 2018.

Condé, Maryse. *Célanire cou-coupé: roman fantastique.* Paris: R. Laffont, 2000.

———. *Hérémakhonon.* Paris: Union générale d'éditions, 1976.

———. *Histoire de la femme cannibale: roman.* Paris: Mercure de France, 2003.

———. *Moi, Tituba, sorcière—: noire de Salem: roman.* Paris: Mercure de France, 1986.

———. "Order, Disorder, Freedom, and the West Indian Writer." *Yale French Studies,* no. 97 (2000): 121–35.

———. "Pan-Africanism, Feminism, and Culture." In *Imagining Home: Class, Culture, and Nationalism in the African Diaspora,* edited by Sidney J. Lemelle and Robin D. G. Kelley, 55–65. New York: Verso, 1994.

Condé, Maryse, and Madeleine Cottenet-Hage. *Penser la créolité.* Paris: Karthala, 1995.

Condé, Maryse, and Richard Philcox. *The Story of the Cannibal Woman: A Novel.* New York: Atria Books, 2007.

Cottille-Foley, Nora. "Postmodernité, non-lieux et mirages de l'anamnèse dans l'oeuvre de Marie Ndiaye." *French Forum,* vol. 31, no. 2 (Spring 2006): 81–94.

Crumly Van Deventer, Alison, and Dominic Thomas. "Afro-European Studies: Emerging Fields and New Directions." In *A Companion to Comparative Literature,* edited by Ali Behdad and Dominic Thomas, 335–57. Oxford: Blackwell-Wiley Publishers, 2011.

Cruz-Malavé, Arnaldo Manuel. "'Under the Skirt of Liberty': Giannina Braschi Rewrites Empire." *American Quarterly,* vol. 66, no. 3 (Sep. 2014): 801–18.

Daley-Harris, Sam. *Pathways out of Poverty: Innovations in Microfinance for the Poorest Families.* Bloomfield, CT: Kumarian Press, 2002.

Daly, Herman, and Robert Goodland. "An Ecological-Economic Assessment of Deregulation of International Commerce under GATT. Part II." *Population and Environment,* vol. 15, no. 6 (1994):477–503.

Dash, Michael. *Edouard Glissant.* Cambridge: Cambridge University Press, 1995.

De la Barca, Pedro Calderón, and William E. Colford. *Life Is a Dream: La vida es sueño.* Drama. 1958.

Dewolf, Christopher. "In Hong Kong, Just Who Is an Expat, Anyway?" *Wall Street Journal.* 29 Dec. 2014. Web. 10 Jan. 2017. http://blogs.wsj.com/expat/2014/12/29/in-hong-kong-just-who -is-an-expat-anyway/. Accessed 10 Jan. 2017.

Diaz, Junot. *The Brief Wondrous Life of Oscar Wao.* New York: Riverhead Books, 2008.

Diome, Fatou. *Celles qui attendent: roman*. Paris: Flammarion, 2010.

———. *Le Ventre de l'Atlantique*. Paris: Éditions Anne Carrière, 2003.

Diome, Fatou, Lulu Norman, and Ros Schwartz. *The Belly of the Atlantic*. London: Serpent's Tail, 2006.

Diouf, Makhtar. *L'Afrique dans la mondialisation*. Paris: Harmattan, 2002.

Dirlik, Arif. "Global South: Predicament and Promise." *Global South*, vol. 1, no. 1 (2007): 12–23.

Dubois, Laurent. *Soccer Empire: The World Cup and the Future of France*. Berkeley: University of California Press, 2010.

Dwyer, Mimi. "Where Did the Anti-Globalization Movement Go?" *New Republic*. 25 Oct. 2013. http://www.newrepublic.com/article/115360/wto-protests-why-have-they-gotten-smaller. Accessed 27 Sep. 2018.

Echevarría, Roberto González, and Enrique Pupo-Walker. *The Cambridge History of Latin American Literature*. Cambridge: Cambridge University Press, 1996.

Edwards, Justin D., and Rune Graulund. *Postcolonial Travel Writing: Critical Explorations*. Houndmills; Basingstoke; Hampshire, UK: Palgrave Macmillan, 2011.

Emmott, Bill. "Everybody's Favourite Monsters: A Survey of Multinationals." *Economist*, 27 Mar. 1993.

Epstein, Gerald. "Introduction: Financialization and the World Economy." In *Financialization and the World Economy*, edited by Gerald Epstein, 3–17. Cheltenham and Northampton: Edward Elgar, 2005.

Ercolino, Stefano. *The Maximalist Novel: From Thomas Pynchon's* Gravity's Rainbow *to Roberto Bolaño's* 2666. London: Bloomsbury Publishing, 2014.

Erlan, Diego. "El lenguaje como frontera, entrevista con Yuri Herrera." *Clarín, Revista Ñ*. 9 Sep. 2011. https://www.clarin.com/rn/literatura/Entrevista_Yuri_Herrera_0_BJKMGU6nDXx.html. Accessed 12 Sep. 2017.

Fanon, Frantz. *Peau noire, masques blancs*. Paris: Editions du Seuil, 1965.

———. *Sociologie d'une révolution (l'An V de la révolution algérienne)*. Paris: F. Maspero, 1968.

Farred, Grant. "The Impossible Closing: Death, Neoliberalism, and the Postcolonial in Bolaño's *2666*." *MFS Modern Fiction Studies*, vol. 56, no. 4 (2010): 689–708.

Federici, Silvia. *Caliban and the Witch*. New York: Autonomedia, 2004.

———. "Feminism and the Politics of the Commons." *Commoner*, no. 14 (Winter 2010). http://www.commoner.org.uk/?p=113>. Accessed 2 Oct. 2018.

———. "Women, Reproduction and Globalization." In *Économie mondialisée et identités de genre*, edited by Fenneke Reysoo, 57–78. Geneva: Graduate Institute Publications, 2002.

Figueira, Dorothy. "Comparative Literature versus World Literature." *Comparatist*, vol. 34, no. 1, 2010, 29–36.

Foster, David William. "Review of Yo-Yo Biong! by Giannina Braschi." *Review of Contemporary Fiction*, vol. 19, no. 1 (1999): 202–3.

Foucault, Michel. *Discipline and Punish: The Birth of the Prison*. New York: Vintage Books, 1979.

Friedrich-Ebert-Stiftung Foundation. "Tax Havens and the Taxation of Transnational Corporations." *Global Policy Forum*. 21 Jun. 2013. https://www.globalpolicy.org/component/content/article/216-global-taxes/52426-tax-havens-and-the-taxation-of-transnational-corporations.html. Accessed 25 Aug. 2018.

Games, Alison. "Atlantic History: Definitions, Challenges, and Opportunities." *American Historical Review,* vol. 111, no. 3 (2006): 741–57.

Garrigós, Christina. "Chicken with the Head Cut Off: Una conversación con Giannina Braschi." *Voces de América/American Voices: Entrevistas a escritores americanos/Interviews with American Writers.* Cádiz, Spain: Aduana Vieja, 2004.

Gaspar de Alba, Alicia. "Poor Brown Female: The Miller's Compensation for 'Free' Trade." In *Making a Killing: Femicide, Free Trade, and La Frontera,* edited by Alicia Gaspar de Alba and Georgina Guzmán, 63–95. Austin: University of Texas Press, 2010.

Ghemawat, Pankaj, and Niccolò Pisani. "Are Multinationals Becoming Less Global?" *Harvard Business Review.* 28 Oct. 2013. https://hbr.org/2013/10/are-multinationals-becoming-less -global. Accessed 14 Oct. 2018.

Gikandi, Simon. "Afterword: Outside the Black Atlantic." *Research in African Literatures,* vol. 45, no. 3 (2014): 241–44.

Gilroy, Paul. *The Black Atlantic: Modernity and Double Consciousness.* Cambridge, MA: Harvard University Press, 1993.

Glissant, Édouard. *Discours Antillais.* Éditions du Seuil, 1981.

———. *Poetics of Relation.* Trans. Betsy Wing. Ann Arbor: University of Michigan Press, 1997.

———. *Poétique de la Relation.* Paris: Éditions Gallimard, 1990.

Glissant, Édouard, and J. Michael Dash. *Caribbean Discourse: Selected Essays.* Charlottesville: University of Virginia Press, 1989.

Goldwyn, Adam J., and Renée M. Silverman. *Mediterranean Modernism: Intercultural Exchange and Aesthetic Development.* New York: Palgrave Macmillan, 2016.

Gonzalez, Madelena. "*United States of Banana* (2011), *Elizabeth Costello* (2003) and *Fury* (2001): Portrait of the Writer as the 'Bad Subject' of Globalisation," *Études britanniques contemporaines,* vol. 46 (2014). https://journals.openedition.org/ebc/1279. Accessed 4 March 2019.

Goyal, Yogita. "Introduction: Africa and the Black Atlantic." *Research in African Literatures,* vol. 45, no. 3 (2014): v–xxv.

Graeber, David. *Debt: The First 5000 Years.* New York: Melville Publishing Co., 2011.

———. "On Social Currencies and Human Economies: Some Notes on the Violence of Equivalence." *Social Anthropology,* vol. 20, no. 4 (Nov. 2012): 411–28 .

———. "A Practical Utopian's Guide to the Coming Collapse." *The Baffler,* no. 22 (2013). https:// thebaffler.com/salvos/a-practical-utopians-guide-to-the-coming-collapse. Accessed 26 Sep. 2018.

"Greece's Debt Crisis Timeline." *Council on Foreign Relations.* n.d. https://www.cfr.org/timeline/ greeces-debt-crisis-timeline. Accessed 12 Oct. 2018.

Green, Emma. "It Was Cultural Anxiety That Drove White, Working-Class Voters to Trump." *Atlantic.* 9 May 2017. https://www.theatlantic.com/politics/archive/2017/05/white-working -class-trump-cultural-anxiety/525771/. Accessed 17 Jul. 2017.

Greer, Jed, and Kavaljit Singh. "A Brief History of Transnational Corporations." *Global Policy Forum,* 2000. https://www.globalpolicy.org/empire/47068-a-brief-history-of-transnational -corporations.html#ft16. Accessed 14 Oct. 2018.

Gulick, Anne W. "Africa, Pan-Africanism, and the Global Caribbean in Maryse Condé's *The Story of the Cannibal Woman.*" *Global South,* vol. 4, no. 2 (2010): 49–75.

Guttenberg, Karl-Theodor, and Pierpaolo Barbieri. "Trans-Atlantic Trade and Its Discontents." *New York Times.* 19 Jun. 2013. http://www.nytimes.com/2013/06/20/opinion/global/trans -atlantic-trade-and-its-discontents.html?_r=0. Accessed 28 Sep. 2018.

Hallward, Peter. *Absolutely Postcolonial: Writing between the Singular and the Specific.* Manchester, UK: Manchester University Press, 2001.

Halstead, John. "The Real Reason White People Say 'All Lives Matter.'" *Huffington Post.* 25 Jul. 2016. https://www.huffingtonpost.com/john-halstead/dear-fellow-white-people-_b_11109842 .html. Accessed 21 Sep. 2018.

Hardt, Michael, and Antonio Negri. *Empire.* Cambridge, MA: Harvard University Press, 2000.

———. *Multitude: War and Democracy in the Age of Empire.* New York: Penguin Press, 2004.

Hargreaves, Alec G., and Martin Munro, eds. "The Francophone Caribbean and North America." *Contemporary French & Francophone Studies: Sites,* vol. 15, no. 1 (2011).

Harney, Stefano, Fred Moten, and Erik Empson. *The Undercommons: Fugitive Planning & Black Study.* Wivenhoe, UK: Minor Compositions, 2013.

Hartman, Saidiya V. *Scenes of Subjection: Terror, Slavery, and Self-Making in Nineteenth-Century America.* New York: Oxford University Press, 1997.

Harvey, David. *A Brief History of Neoliberalism.* Oxford: Oxford University Press, 2005.

———. "Consolidating Power." *Roar.* N. A. https://roarmag.org/magazine/david-harvey -consolidating-power/. Accessed 26 Sep. 2018.

———. "The 'New' Imperialism: Accumulation by Dispossession." *Socialist Register,* vol. 40 (2004): 63–87.

———. *Spaces of Capital: Towards a Critical Geography.* New York: Routledge, 2001.

Hasan, Mehdi. "Top Democrats Are Wrong: Trump Supporters Were More Motivated by Racism Than Economic Issues." *Intercept.* 6 Apr. 2017. https://theintercept.com/2017/04/06/top -democrats-are-wrong-trump-supporters-were-more-motivated-by-racism-than-economic -issues/. 15 Jul. 2017.

Heise, Ursula K. *Sense of Place and Sense of Planet: The Environmental Imagination of the Global.* Oxford: Oxford University Press, 2008.

Herrera, Yuri. *Señales que precederán al fin del mundo.* Cáceres, Spain: Editorial Periférica, 2009.

———. *Trabajos del reino.* México, D. F.: Consejo Nacional para la Cultura y las Artes, CONACULTA, 2004.

Herrera, Yuri, and Lisa Dillman. *Signs Preceding the End of the World.* London; New York: And Other Stories, 2015.

Hickel, Jason. "A Short History of Neoliberalism (And How We Can Fix It)." *The New Left Project.* 9 Apr. 2012. http://www.newleftproject.org/index.php/site/article_comments/a_short _history_of_neoliberalism_and_how_we_can_fix_it. Accessed 26 Jul. 2018.

Higginson, Pim. "Mayhem at the Crossroads: Francophone African Fiction and the Rise of the Crime Novel." *Yale French Studies,* no. 108 (2005): 160–76.

Hing, Bill Ong. *Ethical Borders: NAFTA, Globalization, and Mexican Migration.* Philadelphia: Temple University Press, 2010.

Hitchcott, Nicki, and Dominic Richard David Thomas, eds. *Francophone Afropean Literatures.* Liverpool: Liverpool University Press, 2014.

Hofmeyr, Isabel. "The Black Atlantic Meets the Indian Ocean: Forging New Paradigms of Trans-nationalism for the Global South—Literary and Cultural Perspectives." *Social Dynamics*, vol. 33, no. 2 (2007): 3–32.

Hofmeyr, Isabel. "The Complicating Sea: The Indian Ocean as Method." *Comparative Studies of South Asia, Africa and the Middle East*, vol. 32, no. 3 (2012): 584–90.

hooks, bell. *All About Love: New Visions*. New York: William Morrow, 2000.

Horning, Rob. "Precarity and 'Affective Resistance.'" *New Inquiry*. 14 Feb. 2012. https://thenewinquiry.com/blogs/marginal-utility/precarity-and-affective-resistance/. Accessed 15 Aug. 2018.

"How Puerto Rico's Debt Created a Perfect Storm before the Storm." *NPR*. 2 May 2018. https://www.npr.org/2018/05/02/607032585/how-puerto-ricos-debt-created-a-perfect-storm-before-the-storm. Accessed 12 Oct. 2018.

Hoyos, Héctor. *Beyond Bolaño: The Global Latin American Novel*. New York: Columbia University Press, 2015.

Huggan, Graham. *Postcolonial Eco-criticism: Literature, Animals, Environment*. New York: Routledge, 2015.

———. *The Postcolonial Exotic: Marketing the Margins*. London: Routledge, 2001.

Huyssen, Andreas. *Present Pasts: Urban Palimpsests and the Politics of Memory*. Stanford, CA: Stanford University Press, 2003.

"In Praise of the Stateless Multinational." *Economist*. 18 Sep. 2008. https://www.economist.com/leaders/2008/09/18/in-praise-of-the-stateless-multinational. Accessed 1 Sep. 2018.

Infante, Ignacio. *After Translation: The Transfer and Circulation of Modern Poetics across the Atlantic*. New York: Fordham University Press, 2013.

Ireland, Susan. "Bessora's Literary Ludics." *Dalhousie French Studies*, vol. 68 (2004): 7–16.

Jaggi, Maya. "Three Strong Women by Marie NDiaye—review." *Guardian*. 6 Jul. 2012. https://www.theguardian.com/books/2012/jul/06/three-strong-women-ndiaye-review. Accessed 26 Sep. 2018.

———. "Signs Preceding the End of the World by Yuri Herrera review—a lyrical Mexican migrants' tale." *Guardian*. 22 Apr. 2015. https://www.theguardian.com/books/2015/apr/22/signs-preceding-the-end-of-the-world-yuri-herrera-review-mexican-migrants. Accessed 13 March 2019.

Jameson, Fredric. "Notes on Globalization as a Philosophical Issue." In *The Cultures of Globalization*, edited by Fredric Jameson and Masao Miyoshi, 54–77 Durham: Duke University Press, 1998.

Jay, Paul. *Global Matters: The Transnational Turn in Literary Studies*. Ithaca, NY: Cornell University Press, 2010.

Jochnick, Chris, and Fraser A. Preston. *Sovereign Debt at the Crossroads: Challenges and Proposals for Resolving the Third World Debt Crisis*. Oxford: Oxford University Press, 2006.

Juventudes Libertarias de Bolivia. "With Dynamite and Molotovs, Anarchists Occupy Government Buildings." Translated by Robby Barnes and Sylvie Kashdan. *A-Infos*. 2 Jul. 2001. http://www.ainfos.ca/01/jul/ainfos00049.html. Accessed 20 Jun. 2017.

Kandé, Sylvie. *La quête infinie de l'autre rive: épopée en trois chants*. Paris: Gallimard, 2011.

Kanellos, Nicolás. *Hispanic Immigrant Literature: El Sueño Del Retorno*. Austin: University of Texas Press, 2011.

Karim, Lamia. *Microfinance and Its Discontents: Women in Debt in Bangladesh.* Minneapolis: University of Minnesota Press, 2011.

Kelley, Robin D. G. "After Trump." *Boston Review.* 5 Nov. 2016. http://bostonreview.net/forum/ after-trump/robin-d-g-kelley-trump-says-go-back-we-say-fight-back. 18 Jul. 2017.

Kesteloot, Lilyan. "The African Epic." *African Languages and Cultures,* vol. 2 (1989): 203–14.

Kim, Elizabeth Sulis. "Yuri Herrera: Interview." *New Orleans Review.* n.d. http://www .neworleansreview.org/yuri-herrera/ Accessed 19 Oct. 2018.

Klein, Naomi. *The Shock Doctrine: The Rise of Disaster Capitalism.* New York: Metropolitan Books/Henry Holt, 2007.

Koutonin, Mawuna Remarque. "Why Are White People Expats When the Rest of Us Are Immigrants?" *Guardian.* 13 Mar. 2015. http://www.theguardian.com/global-development -professionals-network/2015/mar/13/white-people-expats-immigrants-migration. Accessed 2 Oct. 2018.

Kristeva, Julia. *Powers of Horror: An Essay on Abjection.* Trans. Leon S. Roudiez. New York: Columbia University Press, 1982.

Krugman, Paul. "Europe's Moment of Truth." *New York Times.* 27 Jun. 2015. https://krugman .blogs.nytimes.com/2015/06/27/europes-moment-of-truth/?mtrref=www.google.com&gwh= 2EBA8D58806BBD00E2468E4322D91694&gwt=pay&assetType=opinion. Accessed 26 Jun. 2018.

Lachman, Kathryn. "Le Cannibalisme au Féminin: A Case of Radical Indigestion." In *Feasting on Words: Maryse Condé, Cannibalism, & the Caribbean Text,* edited by Vera Broichhagen, Kathryn Lachman, and Nicole Simek, 71–85. PLAS cuadernos, no. 8. Princeton, NJ: Program in Latin American Studies, Princeton University, 2006.

———. "The Transatlantic Poetics of Fatou Diome." In *Francophone Afropean Literatures,* edited by Nicki Hitchcott and Dominic Richard David Thomas, 32–48. Liverpool: Liverpool University Press, 2014.

Laronde, Michel. *Autour du roman beur: Immigration et identité.* Paris: Éd. l'Harmattan, 1993.

Lazzarato, Maurizio, and Joshua David Jordan. *Governing by Debt.* Los Angeles: Semiotext(e), 2015.

———. *The Making of the Indebted Man: An Essay on the Neoliberal Condition.* Los Angeles: Semiotext(e), 2012.

Le Bris, Michel, Jean Rouaud, and Eva Almassy. *Pour une littérature-monde.* Paris: Gallimard, 2007.

Ledwith, Tim. "Muhammad Yunus, Microcredit Pioneer and UNICEF Partner, Awarded Nobel Peace Prize." *Unicef.org.* 13 October, 2006. http://www.unicef.org/infobycountry/bangladesh _36162.html. Accessed 24 Sep. 2018.

Leservot, Typhaine. "From *Weltliteratur* to World Literature to *Littérature-monde*: The History of a Controversial Concept." In *Transnational French Studies: Postcolonialism and Littérature-monde,* edited by Alec G. Hargreaves, Charles Forsdick, and David Murphy, 36–48. Liverpool: Liverpool University Press, 2010.

Levey, Nick. *Maximalism in Contemporary American Literature.* London: Routledge, 2016.

Lind, Dara. "Black Lives Matter vs. Bernie Sanders, Explained." *Vox.* 11 Aug. 2015. https://www .vox.com/2015/8/11/9127653/bernie-sanders-black-lives-matter. Accessed 18 Jul. 2017.

Linebaugh, Peter, and Marcus Rediker. *The Many-Headed Hydra: Sailors, Slaves, Commoners, and the Hidden History of the Revolutionary Atlantic.* Boston: Beacon Press, 2000.

"The List: The 34,361 Men, Women and Children Who Perished Trying to Reach Europe." *Guardian.* 20 Jun. 2018. https://www.theguardian.com/world/2018/jun/20/the-list-34361-men -women-and-children-who-perished-trying-to-reach-europe-world-refugee-day. Accessed 2 Oct. 2018.

Lionnet, Françoise. "Feminisms and Universalisms: 'Universal Rights' and The Legal Debate around the Practice of Female Excision in France." *Inscriptions,* vol. 6 (1992): 97–113. https:// culturalstudies.ucsc.edu/inscriptions/volume-6/francoise-lionnet/. Accessed 2 Oct. 2018.

———. *Postcolonial Representations.* Ithaca, NY: Cornell University Press, 1995.

Lionnet, Françoise, and Shumei Shi. *Minor Transnationalism.* Durham, NC: Duke University Press, 2005.

Little, Roger. *Between Totem and Taboo: Black Man, White Woman in Francographic Literature.* Exeter, UK: University of Exeter Press, 2001.

Loingsigh, Aedín Ní. *Postcolonial Eyes: Intercontinental Travel in Francophone African Literature.* Liverpool: Liverpool University Press, 2009.

Lomnitz-Adler, Claudio. "The Depreciation of Life during Mexico City's Transition into 'The Crisis.'" In *Wounded Cities: Destruction and Reconstruction in a Globalized World,* edited by Jane Schneider and Ida Susser, 47–69. Oxford: Berg, 2003.

Lorey, Isabell. *State of Insecurity: Government of the Precarious.* London: Verso, 2015.

Loustau, Laura. "Nomadismos Lingüísticos y Culturales en *Yo-Yo Boing!* de Giannina Braschi." *Revista Iberoamericana,* vol. 71, no. 211 (Apr.–Jun. 2005): 437–48.

Maalouf, Amin. "Contre la Littérature Francophone." *Le Monde des Livres.* 10 Mar. 2006. http:// medias.lemonde.fr/mmpub/edt/doc/20060309/748928_sup_livres_060309.pdf. Accessed 22 Sep. 2018.

Mabanckou, Alain. *Black Bazaar.* London: Serpent's Tail, 2012.

———. *Black Bazar: roman.* Paris: Seuil, 2009.

Macaya, Ángeles Donoso. "Estética, política y el *posible* territorio de la ficción en *2666* de Roberto Bolaño." *Revista Hispánica Moderna,* vol. 62, no. 2 (Dec. 2009): 125–42.

Maeckelbergh, Marianne. *The Will of the Many: How the Alterglobalisation Movement Is Changing the Face of Democracy.* London: Pluto Press, 2009.

Maher, Stephanie C. *Barça Ou Barzakh: The Social Elsewhere of Failed Clandestine Migration out of Senegal.* Diss. U of Washington, 2016.

Mali, Nesrine. "Why Do Deaths in Paris Get More Attention Than Deaths in Beirut?" *Guardian.* 18 Nov. 2015. https://www.theguardian.com/commentisfree/2015/nov/18/deaths-paris-beirut -media. Accessed 20 Sep. 2018.

"Marie Ndiaye: 'Se définir, c'est se réduire.'" *Le Nouvel Observateur.* 3 Nov. 2009. http://bibliobs .nouvelobs.com/romans/20091103.BIB4345/marie-ndiaye-se-definir-c-039-est-se-reduire .html. Accessed 26 Apr. 2017.

Marshall, Bill. *The French Atlantic: Travels in Culture and History.* Liverpool: Liverpool University Press, 2009.

Martínez-San Miguel, Yolanda. *Caribe Two Ways: Cultura de la migración en el Caribe insular hispánico.* San Juan: Ediciones Callejón, 2003.

Mbembe, Achille. "Afropolitanism." *Africa Remix: Contemporary Art of a Continent,* edited by Simon Njami and Lucy Durán, 26–31. Ostfildern-Ruit: Hatje Cantz, 2005.

McClanahan, Annie. *Dead Pledges: Debt, Crisis, and Twenty-First-Century Culture.* Stanford, CA: Stanford University Press, 2016.

McDonald, Christie, and Susan Rubin Suleiman, eds. *French Global: A New Approach to Literary History.* New York: Columbia University Press, 2010.

McElwee, Sean, and Jason McDaniel. "Economic Anxiety Didn't Make People Vote Trump, Racism Did." *Nation.* 8 May 2017. https://www.thenation.com/article/economic-anxiety-didnt -make-people-vote-trump-racism-did/. 15 Jul. 2017.

Meriwether, Rae Ann. "'Walking into the Face of History': Historical Difference and Diasporic Community in 'The Atlantic Sound.'" *Obsidian,* vol. 12, no. 1 (2011): 79–93.

Miller, Christopher L. *The French Atlantic Triangle: Literature and Culture of the Slave Trade.* Durham, NC: Duke University Press, 2008.

———. *Nationalists and Nomads: Essays on Francophone African Literature and Culture.* Chicago: University of Chicago Press, 1998.

———. "The Slave Trade, *La Françafrique,* and the Globalization of French." In McDonald and Suleiman, *French Global,* 240–57.

Mitchell, Timothy. *Carbon Democracy: Political Power in the Age of Oil.* London: Verso, 2011.

Mohanty, Chandra T. *Feminism without Borders: Decolonizing Theory, Practicing Solidarity.* Durham, NC: Duke University Press, 2003.

Mongo-Mboussa, Boniface. "Sylvie Kandé entre deux rives. " *Africultures.* 17 Mar. 2011. http:// www.africultures.com/php/index.php?nav=article&no=9997. Accessed 5 Jan. 2018.

Moorthy, Shanti, and Ashraf Jamal. *Indian Ocean Studies: Cultural, Social, and Political Perspectives.* New York: Routledge, 2010.

Moretti, Franco. "Conjectures on World Literature." *New Left Review,* vol. 1 (Jan.–Feb. 2000): 54–68. http://geertvdm.wordpress.com/2008/03/05/conjectures-on-world-literature-franco -moretti/. Accessed 22 Sep. 2018.

———. *Distant Reading.* London: Verso, 2013.

———. *Modern Epic: The World-System from Goethe to García Márquez.* London: Verso, 1996.

———. "Marie Ndiaye's Discombobulated Subject." *SubStance,* vol. 35, no. 3 (2006): 83–94.

Moya, Horacio Castellanos. "Sobre el mito Bolaño." *La Nación.* 19 Sep. 2009. http://www.lanacion .com.ar/1176451-sobre-el-mito-bolano. Accessed 2 Oct. 2018.

Moya, Paula M. L., and Michael R. Hames-García, eds. *Reclaiming Identity: Realist Theory and the Predicament of Postmodernism.* Berkeley: University of California Press, 2000.

Muñoz, José Esteban. *Disidentifications: Queers of Color and the Performance of Politics.* Minneapolis: University of Minnesota Press, 1999.

Naoki, Sakai. *Translation and Subjectivity: On "Japan" and Cultural Nationalism.* Minneapolis: University of Minnesota Press, 1997.

Naro, Nancy P., Roger Sansi-Roca, and Dave Treece. *Cultures of the Lusophone Black Atlantic.* New York: Palgrave Macmillan, 2007.

Ndiaye, Abdoulaye. "Food for Thought: Senegal's Struggle with Structural Adjustment." In *50 Years Is Enough: The Case against the World Bank and the International Monetary Fund,* edited by Kevin Danaher, 85–86. Boston: South End Press, 1994.

Ndiaye, El Hadji Malick. "Afrique en quête d'ailleurs." *Nouvelles Études Francophones*, vol. 27, no. 2, (2012): 243–46.

Ndiaye, Marie. *Rosie Carpe*. Paris: Minuit, 2001.

———. *Trois Femmes Puissantes: roman*. Paris: Gallimard, 2009.

Ndiaye, Marie, and Tamsin Black. *Rosie Carpe*. Lincoln: University of Nebraska Press, 2004.

Nietzsche, Friedrich Wilhelm, and Walter Kaufmann. *Thus Spoke Zarathustra: A Book for All and None*. New York: Modern Library, 1995.

Niskanen, William A. *Reaganomics: An Insider's Account of the Policies and the People*. Oxford: Oxford University Press, 1988.

Nkrumah, Kwame. *Neo-Colonialism: The Last Stage of Imperialism*. New York: International Publishers, 1965.

Nnaemeka, Obioma. *Female Circumcision and the Politics of Knowledge: African Women in Imperialist Discourses*. Westport, CT: Praeger, 2005.

Nyong'o, Tavia. "Situating Precarity between the Body and the Commons." *Women & Performance: A Journal of Feminist Theory*, vol. 23, no. 2 (Jul. 2013): 157–61.

Okazaki, Hank. "Dis/location and 'Connectedness' in Caryl Phillips." *Journal of West Indian Literature*, vol. 6, no. 2 (May 1994): 88–96.

Okwunodu, Ogbechie. "'Afropolitanism': Africa without Africans (II)," *AACHRONYM*. 4 Apr. 2008. http://aachronym.blogspot.co.uk/2008/04/afropolitanism-more-africa-without.html. Accessed 15 Jun. 2018.

Pachico, Elyssa. "'No Pago' Confronts Microfinance in Nicaragua." *NACLA*. 28 Oct. 2009. https://nacla.org/news/no-pago-confronts-microfinance-nicaragua. Accessed 15 Jun. 2017.

Parati, Graziella. *Mediterranean Crossroads: Migration Literature in Italy*. Madison, NJ: Fairleigh Dickinson University Press, 1999.

Peet, Richard. *Unholy Trinity: The IMF, World Bank and WTO*. New York: Zed Books, 2003.

Pérez-Rosario, Vanessa. *Hispanic Caribbean Literature of Migration: Narratives of Displacement*. New York: Palgrave Macmillan, 2010.

Perisic, Alexandra. "Beure je suis, opaque je resterai." *CELAAN*, vol. 23, no. 2 (2016): 95–108.

Phillips, Caryl. *The Atlantic Sound*. New York: Alfred Knopf, 2000.

———. *Color Me English: Migration and Belonging before and after 9/11*. New York: New Press, 2011.

———. *The European Tribe*. New York: Farrar, Straus, Giroux, 1987.

———. *A New World Order: Essays*. New York: Vintage International, 2002.

Pinto, Samantha. *Difficult Diasporas: The Transnational Feminist Aesthetic of the Black Atlantic*. New York: New York University Press, 2013.

Pitman, Thea, and Andy Stafford. "Introduction: Transatlanticism and Tricontinentalism." *Journal of Transatlantic Studies*, vol. 7, no. 3 (2009):197–207.

Pizarro, Yolanda Arroyo. *Los documentados: novela*. San Juan, P.R.: Ediciones Situm, 2005.

Pollack, Sarah. "Latin America Translated (Again): Roberto Bolaño's *The Savage Detectives* in the United States." *Comparative Literature*, vol. 61, no. 3 (2009): 346–65.

Poniatowska, Elena. "Trabajos del reino, libro del escritor Yuri Herrera." *La Jornada*. 5 Dec. 2004. http://www.jornada.unam.mx/2004/12/05/03a1cul.php. Accessed 26 Sep. 2018.

"Pour une 'littérature-monde' en français." *Le Monde.* 15 Mar. 2007. http://www.lemonde.fr/livres/article/2007/03/15/des-ecrivains-plaident-pour-un-roman-en-francais-ouvert-sur-le-monde_883572_3260.html. Accessed 25 Apr. 2017.

Pratt, Mary Louise. *Imperial Eyes: Travel Writing and Transculturation.* London: Routledge, 1992.

"Que vise vraiment la mise en place d'un état d'urgence permanent?" *L'Humanité.* 9 Mar. 2016. http://www.humanite.fr/que-vise-vraiment-la-mise-en-place-dun-etat-durgence-permanent-601499. Accessed 20 Dec. 2017.

Rancière, Jacques. "The Cause of the Other." *Parallax,* vol. 4, no. 2 (1998): 25–33.

Rancière, Jacques, and Steve Corcoran. *Dissensus: On Politics and Aesthetics.* London: Continuum, 2010.

"Reining in Corporations." *Global Justice Now,* n.d. http://www.globaljustice.org.uk/reining-corporations. Accessed 1 Sep. 2018.

Ridgers, Bill. *Book of Business Quotations.* Hoboken, NJ: John Wiley & Sons, 2012.

Rivera, Carmen Haydée. "El poder de la palabra y la experiencia transnacional: una entrevista con Giannina Braschi." *Revista del Centro de Investigaciones Historicas,* vol. 20 (2011): 181–201.

Robbe-Grillet, Alain. *Pour un nouveau roman.* Paris: Editions de Mínuit, 1963.

Robinson, Marguerite S. *The Microfinance Revolution.* Washington, DC: World Bank, 2001.

Robinson, William I. *Latin America and Global Capitalism: A Critical Globalization Perspective.* Baltimore: Johns Hopkins University Press, 2008.

"Romania and Bulgaria EU migration restrictions lifted." *BBC News.* 1 Jan. 2014. http://www.bbc.com/news/world-europe-25565302. Accessed 10 Jan. 2017.

Roos, Jerome. "Greek Referendum: Euro Crisis Explodes into Dramatic Climax." *Roar Magazine.* 29 Jun. 2015. https://roarmag.org/essays/greece-referendum-euro-crisis/. Accessed 26 Jun. 2018.

Ropero, María Lourdes López. "Travel Writing and Postcoloniality: Caryl Phillips's *The Atlantic Sound.*" *Atlantis,* vol. 25, no. 1 (June 2003): 51–62.

Rosello, Mireille. "Unhoming Francophone Studies: A House in the Middle of the Current." *Yale French Studies,* vol. 103 (2003): 123–32.

———. "Post-cannibalism in Maryse Condé's Histoire de la femme cannibale." In *Feasting on Words: Maryse Condé, Cannibalism, & the Caribbean Text,* edited by Vera Broichhagen, Kathryn Lachman, and Nicole Simek, 35–51. PLAS cuadernos, no. 8. Princeton, NJ: Program in Latin American Studies, Princeton University, 2006.

Ross, Andrew. *Creditocracy: And the Case for Debt Refusal.* New York; London: OR Books, 2013.

Sankara, Thomas. *Thomas Sankara Speaks: The Burkina Faso Revolution, 1983–87.* New York: Pathfinder Press, 1988.

Santana, Stephanie. "Exorcizing Afropolitanism: Binyavanga Wainaina Explains Why 'I Am a Pan-Africanist, Not an Afropolitan' at ASAUK 2012." *Africa in Words.* 8 Feb. 2013. http://africainwords.com/2013/02/08/exorcizing-afropolitanism-binyavanga-wainaina-explains-why-i-am-a-pan-africanist-not-an-afropolitan-at-asauk-2012/. Accessed 23 Sep. 2018.

Sarraute, Nathalie. "Ce que je cherche à faire." *Nouveau roman: hier aujourd'hui,* edited by Jean Ricardou and Françoise van Rossum-Guyon, 25–40. Paris: Union générale d'éditions, 1972.

Sassen, Saskia. *Globalization and Its Discontents: Essays on the New Mobility of People and Money.* New York: New Press, 1998.

Sayad, Abdelmalek. *La double absence. Des illusions de l'émigré aux souffrances de l'immigré.* Paris, Seuil, 1999.

Schmidtt, Carl. *Political Theology: Four Chapters on the Concept of Sovereignty* (1922). Trans. G. Schwab. Chicago: University of Chicago Press, 2005.

Schram, Sanfrod. *The Return of Ordinary Capitalism: Neoliberalism, Precarity, Occupy.* Oxford; New York: Oxford University Press, 2015.

Schwartz, Ariel. "The Green Guide to Obama's State of the Union Address." *Fast Company.* 26 Jan. 2011. https://www.fastcompany.com/1721057/green-guide-obamas-state-union-address. Accessed 15 Feb. 2017.

Sears, Kelton. "A Marxist Critiques Identity Politics." *Seattle Weekly.* 25 Apr. 2017. http://www.seattleweekly.com/news/a-marxist-critiques-identity-politics/. 15 Jul. 2017.

Sebbar, Leïla. *Shérazade, 17 ans, brune, frisée, les yeux verts.* Paris: Editions Stock, 1982.

Selasi, Taiye. "Bye-Bye Babar." *LIP.* 3 Mar. 2005. http://thelip.robertsharp.co.uk/?p=76. Accessed 23 Sep. 2018.

Seymour, Richard. "We Are All Precarious—On the Concept of the 'Precariat' and Its Misuses." *New Left Project.* 10 Feb. 2012. http://www.newleftproject.org/index.php/site/article_comments/we_are_all_precarious_on_the_concept_of_the_precariat_and_its_misuses. Accessed 21 Sep. 2018.

Sharpe, Christina E. *In the Wake: On Blackness and Being.* Durham, NC: Duke University Press, 2016.

Sitchet, Christine. "Sylvie Kandé dans les remous d'une quête infinie de l'autre rive." *Afrik.com.* 30 May 2011. http://www.afrik.com/article22970.html. Accessed 15 Dec. 2017.

Smith, Noah. "The Dark Side of Globalization: Why Seattle's 1999 Protesters Were Right." *Atlantic,* 6 Jan. 2014. http://www.theatlantic.com/business/archive/2014/01/the-dark-side-of-globalization-why-seattles-1999-protesters-were-right/282831/. 27 Sep. 2018.

Soldàn, Edmundo Paz. "Roberto Bolaño: Literatura y apocalipsis." *Entre lo local y lo global: La narrativa latinoamericana en el cambio de siglo (1990–2006),* edited by Jesús Montoya Juárez and Angel Esteban. Madrid: Iberoamericana, 2008.

Spivak, Gayatri Chakravorty. *A Critique of Postcolonial Reason: Toward a History of the Vanishing Present.* Cambridge, MA: Harvard University Press, 1999.

———. *Death of a Discipline.* New York: Columbia University Press, 2003.

———. "Three Women's Texts and a Critique of Imperialism." *Critical Inquiry,* vol. 12, no. 1 (1985): 243–61.

Standing, Guy. *The Precariat: The New Dangerous Class.* London: Bloomsbury Academic, 2011.

Sunkara, Bhaskar. "Precarious Thoughts." *Jacobin.* 13 Jan. 2012. https://www.jacobinmag.com/2012/01/precarious-thought/. Accessed 15 Jun. 2018.

Suwandi, Intan, and John Bellamy Foster. "Multinational Corporations and the Globalization of Monopoly Capital." *Monthly Review.* 1 Jul. 2016. https://monthlyreview.org/2016/07/01/multinational-corporations-and-the-globalization-of-monopoly-capital-from-the-1960s-to-the-present/#en8. Accessed 25 Aug. 2018.

Tani, Stefano. *The Doomed Detective: The Contribution of the Detective Novel to Postmodern American and Italian Fiction.* Carbondale: Southern Illinois University Press, 1984.

Taylor, Keeanga-Yamahtta. *From #BlackLivesMatter to Black Liberation.* Chicago: Haymarket Books, 2016.

Tchak, Sami. *Filles de Mexico*. Paris: Mercure de France, 2008.

———. *Hermina*. Paris: Gallimard, 2003.

Thomas, Dominic Richard David. *Africa and France: Postcolonial Cultures, Migration, and Racism*. Bloomington: Indiana University Press, 2013.

———. *Afroeuropean Cartographies*. Newcastle upon Tyne: Cambridge Scholars Publishing, 2013.

———. *Black France Colonialism, Immigration, and Transnationalism*. Bloomington: Indiana University Press, 2007.

"Thomas Piketty: Rise of Anti-Austerity Parties Good News for Europe." *Guardian*. 12 Jan. 2015. https://www.theguardian.com/business/2015/jan/12/thomas-piketty-austerity-europe-greece -spain Accessed 2 Sep. 2018.

Toussaint, Eric, and Damien Millet. *Debt, the IMF, and the World Bank Sixty Questions, Sixty Answers*. New York: Monthly Review Press, 2010.

Trenz, Hans-Jörg, Carlo Ruzza, and Virginie Guiraudon. *Europe's Prolonged Crisis: The Making or the Unmaking of a Political Union*. Houndmills, Basingstoke: Palgrave Macmillan, 2015.

Tveit, Marta. "The Afropolitan Must Go." *Africa Is a Country*. 28 Nov. 2013. http://africasacountry .com/2013/11/the-afropolitan-must-go/. Accessed 15 Jun. 2018.

Vega, Ana Lydia. "Pollito Chicken." In *Virgenes y martires: (cuentos),* edited by Carmen Lugo Filippi and Ana Lydia Vega, 73–80. Rio Piedras, PR: Antillana, 1981.

Velasco, Juan, and Tanya Schmidt. "Mapping a Geography of Hell: Evil, Neoliberalism, and the Femicides in Roberto Bolaño's *2666*." *Latin American Literary Review,* vol. 42, no. 83 (Jan.–Jun. 2014): 97–116.

Vergès, Françoise. "Writing on Water: Peripheries, Flows, Capital, and Struggles in the Indian Ocean." *Positions: East Asia Cultures Critique,* vol. 11, no. 1 (2003): 241–57.

Victor, Daniel. "Why 'All Lives Matter' Is Such a Perilous Phrase." *New York Times*. 15 Jul. 2016. https://www.nytimes.com/2016/07/16/us/all-lives-matter-black-lives-matter.html. Accessed 20 Sep. 2018.

Vishmidt, Marina. "Permanent Reproductive Crisis: An Interview with Silvia Federici." *Mute*. 7 Mar. 2013 http://www.metamute.org/editorial/articles/permanent-reproductive-crisis -interview-silvia-federici. Accessed 24 Sep. 2018.

Waberi, Abdourahman. *Aux Etats-Unis d'Afrique*. Paris: Éditions Jean-Claude Lattès, 2006.

Walkowitz, Rebecca L., Matthew Hart, Wen Jin, Eric Hayot, Věra Eliášová, J. Dillon Brown, and Alistair Cormack. *Immigrant Fictions: Contemporary Literature in an Age of Globalization*. Madison: University of Wisconsin Press, 2006.

Wallerstein, Immanuel Maurice. *The Decline of American Power: The US in a Chaotic World*. New York: New Press, 2003.

———. *World-Systems Analysis: An Introduction*. Durham, NC: Duke University Press, 2004.

Watts, Richard. *Packaging Post/coloniality: The Manufacture of Literary Identity in the Francophone World*. Lanham, MD: Lexington Books, 2005.

Wawrzinek, Jennifer, and J. K. S. Makokha. *Negotiating Afropolitanism: Essays on Borders and Spaces in Contemporary African Literature and Folklore*. Amsterdam: Rodopi, 2011.

"What Britain Forgets: Romania Is Booming." *Economist*. 17 Dec. 2013. http://www.economist .com/blogs/blighty/2013/12/what-britain-forgets. Accessed 10 Jan. 2017.

"The World Social Forum Charter of Principles." 5 Jul. 2017. https://wsf2018.org/carta-de
-principios-do-forum-social/. Accessed 27 Sep. 2018.

Xavier, Subha. *The Migrant Text: Making and Marketing a Global French Literature.* Montreal:
McGill-Queen's University Press, 2016.

"Yuri Herrera entre la prosa poética y criminal." *La Hoje de Arena.* n.d. http://www.lahojadearena
.com/yuri-herrera-entre-la-prosa-poetica-y-criminal/. Accessed 27 Jan. 2017.

Žižek, Slavoj. "Have Michael Hardt and Antonio Negri Rewritten the Communist Manifesto for
the Twenty-First Century?" *Rethinking Marxism,* vol. 3, no. 4 (2001): 190–98.

———. "This Is a Chance for Europe to Awaken." *New Statesman.* 6 Jul. 2015. https://www
.newstatesman.com/politics/2015/07/Slavoj-Zizek-greece-chance-europe-awaken. Accessed
23 Jun. 2018.

INDEX